To my good friend and
colleague of Riverside Church, New York,

Frank Somerby

David Andrew Weaver

BUILDERS OF AMERICAN UNIVERSITIES

VOLUME I

(I)

Builders of American Universities

Inaugural Addresses

PRIVATELY CONTROLLED INSTITUTIONS

VOLUME I

DAVID ANDREW WEAVER, Editor
President of Shurtleff College

1950
SHURTLEFF COLLEGE PRESS
ALTON, ILLINOIS

Printed in Alton, Illinois, U.S.A.
On the Palisades of the Majestic Mississippi

(IV)

TO

ROBERT LEE MOORE

Inspiring Teacher

Builder of Character

Leader of Men

Christian Gentleman

Devoted Friend

(V)

ACKNOWLEDGMENTS

Acknowledgment of appreciation is herein expressed to the following publishers: The Appleton-Century-Croft Company, Charles Scribner's Sons, and Phipps Samson & Company.

Acknowledgment of appreciation is also expressed to the following colleges and universities: Yale University, Princeton University, University of Pennsylvania, Dartmouth College, Williams College, New York University, Baylor University, University of Rochester, Birmingham-Southern College, Vassar College, Cornell University, Smith College, Vanderbilt University, Stanford University, and Clark University.

Appreciation is expressed for the suggestions by Dr. Ernest V. Hollis, a former colleague, now specialist in higher education in the United States Office of Education; to Dr. A. Gordon Melvin, of the College of the City of New York, and also to the late President Nicholas Murray Butler, who offered encouragement for the compilation of this valuable reference material. To my efficient assistant, Mrs. Margaret Kohlhepp, I am grateful for her painstaking effort in the completion of the manuscript.

FOREWORD

The president of a college or a university is the executive head of a complex enterprise. To be successful he must not only be a good business man, an advisory architect for new college buildings, a landscape architect and road builder, a custodian of investments and able to raise additional funds, but also a scholar, teacher, writer, speaker, and above all a leader of men.

It is a sobering thought to any college or university president when he realizes that he is to a degree, more or less responsible for the destiny of the Republic. The colleges and universities educate the vast majority of leaders in church and state, in the professions and in industry, in civic and social activities. Our peculiar form of higher education is the bulwark of our American way of life—a way recently challenged by a most powerful combination of nations demanding universally a totalitarian form of government.

When we consider the large sums of money invested in the buildings, campuses and equipment as well as in the endowments, and the monies received and spent annually from tuition fees, gifts and other sources, there is a better realization of the size and importance of the business side of higher education. About two per cent of the total population are in college and university life each year. Counting the persons who have had some college connections of one sort and another, probably twenty per cent or more of the people in the country can be included. With the relatives and friends interested, it is safe to assume that a great majority of Americans do have a serious interest in and sympathy with the colleges and universities.

College trustees do not always realize the importance of their trust when they are choosing a new president. The records indicate that there is an unusually high turnover in the college presidential office. Although the responsibilities and hazards are great, a president should stay in office longer than six years, which seems to be the present average.

In the choice of presidential addresses included in this volume, care was taken to include those from men who held office for an average of twenty years or more.

Quite correctly the Colonial colleges are included. The others are chosen from universities and colleges founded during the one hundred and ten years elapsing since the American Revolution. They represent institutions of various types and sizes, located in different sections of the country.

The addresses indicate their authors to be men of vision. Some have wielded considerable influence locally, others great influence nationally.

It would be interesting to discover if many or most of the proposals made in the inaugural addresses have been realized.

Newly elected presidents might receive inspiration and some valuable information if they could refer to a volume of this sort. They might visualize better their own problems after familiarizing themselves with the plans, hopes and ambitions of others who have trod the thorny presidential path before them.

Dr. David Andrew Weaver, who has compiled these addresses, has peculiar training, experience and background for the task. He has written numerous articles in the field of higher education. He is the founder and editor of the UNIVERSITY ADMINISTRATION QUARTERLY.

—Guy E. Snavely

Washington, D. C.

TABLE OF CONTENTS

INTRODUCTION

This book is the first in a series of three volumes of inaugural addresses of college and university presidents. While we have a very excellent compilation in WHAT COLLEGE PRESIDENTS SAY by Dr. Knight, we do not have the complete addresses compiled in reference form of the presidents who have so profoundly influenced higher education in America.

The purpose of this series is to make available the significant guide posts of the past, for students in higher education, for presidents assuming office, and for the Boards of Trustees.

This volume contains the addresses of the presidents of privately controlled institutions. This period is what has been termed in America, "The Golden Age of Higher Education." While Mark Hopkins in 1836 demonstrated not only good administration but artistic teaching, he also left with us the idea which more recently we have explored rather widely; namely, general education. Woodrow Wilson referred to this challenge a number of times in his inaugural address in 1902. Recently a number of books have appeared on General Education. There are many fundamental principles enumerated by these earlier educators who so profoundly increased the emphasis on higher education in the United States. Many of these principles remain as challenges for the present and the future.

The influence of highly trained faculty which was emphasized by Eliot of Harvard, Jordan of Stanford, Harper of Chicago and Butler of Columbia remain as an area which no administrator of any age can ignore. Scholarship was encouraged by all of our leaders, either directly or indirectly, but special emphasis was given to it by Butler of Columbia, Kirkland of Vanderbilt, and Gilman of Hopkins. White of Cornell introduced the era of practical arts which to him was on a par with academic subjects. Likewise the saving of time in the educational process was emphasized by such thinkers as Eliot of Harvard and Snavely of Birmingham-Southern.

The trend away from the purely secular college was ushered in by the founding of Johns Hopkins, Cornell, Clark and Stanford.

Perhaps at no period in our history has the idea of service been more appropriate than at present. We have in the addresses of Butler and Wilson the idea of service eloquently discussed and appropriately illustrated in their own lives.

This series of addresses is designed to illustrate the trend in higher education in America both through what was said and what was accomplished by distinguished leaders in administration.*

Building a faculty of a university is one of the prime responsibilities of any president. This was acknowledged long before modern research revealed some of our limitations in college and university administrations. Among the men who distinguished themselves as being keen judges of human nature were: Presidents Eliot of Harvard, Jordan of Stanford, Harper of Chicago, Gilman of Johns Hopkins, Butler of Columbia and Wilson of Princeton.

For much of the mechanical routine an administrator may call in assistants to perform the various functions, but he can only consult his colleagues concerning the ability of a prospective faculty member. His ability to discover talent is perhaps the one characteristic that makes him most valuable as an educational leader. Before William Rainey Harper left Yale for the presidency of the University of Chicago he discovered such talent in Braeasted and encouraged this young student to pursue his education further by taking graduate work in Europe. The world will be reminded of that discovery for generations to come.

The other great men mentioned in this category made similar discoveries and likewise distinguished themselves as possessing unusual insight into talents necessary for the compliment of their faculties. Nicholas Murray Butler at an early age demonstrated this rare quality. Woodrow Wilson with his revolutionary tutorial plan brought 50 tutors to Princeton University, most of whom proved to be men of rare distinction. These leaders possessed not only ability to recognize talent, but capacity to develop it after it had been discovered.

---

*Presidents Harper of Chicago and Wayland of Brown did not deliver inaugural addresses. However they influenced the age in which they lived so profoundly that no effort to trace the trend of higher education in America would be complete without reference to these outstanding leaders.

Inaugural Address

Educational Reform

by

CHARLES WILLIAM ELIOT

President of Harvard University

October 19, 1869

CHARLES WILLIAM ELIOT (*March 20, 1834 — August 22, 1926*) was President of Harvard for forty years and one of the most influential educational leaders of his time.

Charles William Eliot was born in Boston of prominent New England parents who were identified with cultural and civic movements in that city. He attended Boston Latin School, Harvard University, and the University of Berlin. He taught at Harvard and at the Massachusetts Institute of Technology before accepting the presidency of Harvard University. His administration marked a new era in which he enhanced the elective system, emphasized the significance of extreme care in faculty selection and advocated increased salary scales and greater use of sabbatical leaves for teachers.

The endless controversies whether language, philosophy, mathematics, or science supplies the best mental training, whether general education should be chiefly literary or chiefly scientific, have no practical lesson for us to-day. This University recognizes no real antagonism between literature and science, and consents to no such narrow alternatives as mathematics or classics, science or metaphysics. We would have them all, and at their best. To observe keenly, to reason soundly, and to imagine vividly are operations as essential as that of clear and forcible expression; and to develop one of these faculties, it is not necessary to repress and dwarf the others. A university is not closely concerned with the applications of knowledge, until its general education branches into professional. Poetry and philosophy and science do indeed conspire to promote the material welfare of mankind; but science no more than poetry finds its best warrant in its utility. Truth and right are above utility in all realms of thought and action.

It were a bitter mockery to suggest that any subject whatever should be taught less than it now is in American colleges. The only conceivable aim of a college government in our day is to broaden, deepen, and invigorate American teaching in all branches of learning. It will be generations before the best of American institutions of education will get growth enough to bear pruning. The descendants of the Pilgrim Fathers are still very thankful for the parched corn of learning.

Recent discussions have added pitifully little to the world's stock of wisdom about the staple of education. Who blows to-day such a ringing trumpet-call to the study of language as Luther blew? Hardly a significant word has been added in two centuries to Milton's description of the unprofitable way to study languages. Would any young American learn how to profit by travel, that foolish beginning but excellent sequel to education, he can find no apter advice than Bacon's. The practice of England and America is literally centuries behind the precept of the best thinkers upon education. A striking illus-

15

tration may be found in the prevailing neglect of the systematic study of the English language. How lamentably true today are these words of Locke: "If any one among us have a facility or purity more than ordinary in his mother-tongue, it is owing to chance, or his genius, or anything rather than to his education or any care of his teacher."

The best result of the discussion which has raged so long about the relative educational value of the main branches of learning is the conviction that there is room for them all in a sound scheme, provided that right methods of teaching be employed. It is not because of the limitation of their faculties that boys of eighteen come to college, having mastered nothing but a few score pages of Latin and Greek, and the bare elements of mathematics. Not nature, but an unintelligent system of instruction from the primary school through the college, is responsible for the fact that many college graduates have so inadequate a conception of what is meant by scientific observation, reasoning, and proof. It is possible for the young to get actual experience of all the principal methods of thought. There is a method of thought in language, and a method in mathematics, and another of natural and physical science, and another of faith. With wise direction, even a child would drink at all these springs. The actual problem to be solved is not what to teach, but how to teach. The revolutions accomplished in other fields of labor have a lesson for teachers. New England could not cut her hay with scythes, or the West her wheat with sickles. When millions are to be fed where formerly there were but scores, the single fish-line must be replaced by seines and trawls, the human shoulders by steam-elevators, and the wooden-axled ox-cart on a corduroy road by the smooth-running freight train. In education, there is a great hungry multitude to be fed. The great well at Orvieto, up whose spiral paths files of donkeys painfully brought the sweet water in kegs, was an admirable construction in its day; but now we tap Fresh Pond in our chambers. The Orvieto well might remind

16

some persons of educational methods not yet extinct. With good methods, we may confidently hope to give young men of twenty to twenty-five an accurate general knowledge of all the main subjects of human interest, besides a minute and thorough knowledge of the one subject which each may select as his principal occupation in life. To think this impossible is to despair of mankind; for unless a general acquaintance with many branches of knowledge, good so far as it goes, be attainable by great numbers of men, there can be no such thing as an intelligent public opinion; and in the modern world the intelligence of public opinion is the one indispensable condition of social progress.

What has been said of needed reformation in methods of teaching the subjects which have already been nominally admitted to the American curriculum applies not only to the university, but to the preparatory schools of every grade down to the primary. The American college is obliged to supplement the American school. Whatever elementary instruction the schools fail to give, the college must supply. The improvement of the schools has of late years permitted the college to advance the grade of its teaching, and adapt the methods of its later years to men instead of boys. The improvement of the college reacts upon the schools to their advantage; and this action and reaction will be continuous. A university is not built in the air, but on social and literary foundations which preceding generations have bequeathed. If the whole structure needs rebuilding, it must be rebuilt from the foundation. Hence, sudden reconstruction is impossible in our high places of education. Such inducements as the College can offer for enriching and enlarging the course of study pursued in preparatory schools, the Faculty has recently decided to give. The requirements in Latin and Greek grammar are to be set at a thorough knowledge of forms and general principles; the lists of classical authors accepted as equivalents for the regular standards are to be enlarged; an acquaintance with physical geography is to be required; the study of elementary mechanics is to be recommended, and prizes are to be offered for reading aloud, and for the critical analysis of passages from English authors. At the same time the University will take to heart the counsel which it gives to others.

In every department of learning the University would search out by trial and reflection the best methods of instruction. The University believes in the thorough study of language. It contends for all languages—Oriental, Greek, Latin, Romance, German, and especially for the mother-tongue; seeing in them all one institution, one history, one means of discipline, one department of learning. In teaching languages, it is for this American generation to invent, or to accept from abroad, better tools than the old; to devise, or to transplant from Europe, prompter and more comprehensive methods than the prevailing; and to command more intelligent labor, in order to gather rapidly and surely the best fruit of that culture and have time for other harvests.

The University recognizes the natural and physical sciences as indispensable branches of education, and has long acted upon this opinion; but it would have science taught in a rational way, objects and instruments in hand—not from books merely, not through the memory chiefly, but by the seeing eye and the informing fingers. Some of the scientific scoffers at gerund grinding and nonsense verses might well look at home; the prevailing methods of teaching science, the world over, are on the whole, less intelligent than the methods of teaching language. The University would have scientific studies in school and college and professional school develop and discipline those powers of the mind by which science has been created and is daily nourished—the powers of observation, the inductive faculty, the sober imagination, the sincere and proportionate judgment. A student in the elements gets no such training by studying even a good text-book, though he really masters it, nor yet by sitting at the feet of the most admirable lecturer.

If there be any subject which seems fixed and settled in its educational aspects, it is the mathematics; yet there is no department of the University which has been, during the last fifteen years, in such a state of vigorous experiment upon methods and appliances of teaching as the mathematical department. It would be well if the primary schools had as much faith in the possiblity of improving their way of teaching multiplication.

The important place which history, and mental, moral, and political philosophy, should hold in any broad scheme of education is recognized of all; but none know so well how crude are the prevailing methods of teaching these subjects as those who teach them best. They cannot be taught from books alone, but must be vivified and illustrated by teachers of active, comprehensive, and judicial mind. To learn by rote a list of dates is not to study history. Mr. Emerson says that history is biography. In a deep sense this is true. Certainly, the best way to impart the facts of history to the young is through the quick interest they take in the lives of the men and women who fill great historical scenes or epitomize epochs. From the centers so established, their interest may be spread over great areas. For the young especially, it is better to enter with intense sympathy into the great moments of history, than to stretch a thin attention through its weary centuries.

Philosophical subjects should never be taught with authority. They are not established sciences; they are full of disputed matters, open questions, and bottomless speculations. It is not the function of the teacher to settle philosophical and political controversies for the pupil, or even to recommend to him any one set of opinions as better than another. Exposition, not imposition, of opinions is the professor's part. The student should be made acquainted with all sides of these controversies, with the salient points of each system; he should be shown what is still in force of institutions or philosophies mainly outgrown, and what is new in those now in vogue. The very word "education" is a standing protest against dogmatic teaching. The notion that education consists in the authoritative inculcation of what the teacher deems true may be logical and appropriate in a convent, or a seminary for priests, but it is intolerable in universities and public schools, from primary to professional. The worthy fruit of academic culture is an open mind, trained to careful thinking, instructed in the methods of philosophic investigation, acquainted in a general way with the accumulated thought of past generations, and penetrated with humility. It is thus that the university in our day serves Christ and the church.

The increasing weight, range, and thoroughness of the examination for admission to college may strike some observers with dismay. The increase of real requisitions is hardly perceptible from year to year; but on looking back ten or twenty years, the changes are marked, and all in one direction. The dignity and importance of this examination have been steadily rising, and this rise measures the improvement of the preparatory schools. When the gradual improvement of American schools has lifted them to a level with the German gymnasia, we may expect to see the American college bearing a nearer resemblance to the German faculties of philosophy than it now does. The actual admission examination may best be compared with the first examination of the University of France. This examination, which comes at the end of a French boy's school life, is for the degree of Bachelor of Arts or of Sciences. The degree is given to young men who come fresh from school and have never been under university teachers; a large part of the recipients never enter the university. The young men who come to our examination for admission to college are older than the average of French Bachelors of Arts.

The examination tests not only the capacity of the candidates, but also the quality of their school instruction; it is a great event in their lives, though not, as in France, marked by any degree. The examination is conducted by college professors and tutors who have never had any relations whatsoever with those examined. It would be a great gain if all subsequent college examinations could be as impartially conducted by competent examiners brought from without the college and paid for their services. When the teacher examines his class, there is no effective examination of the teacher. If the examinations for the scientific, theological, medical, and dental degrees were conducted by independent boards of examiners, appointed by professional bodies of dignity and influence, the significance of these degrees would be greatly enhanced. The same might be said of the degree of Bachelor of Laws, were it not that this degree is, at present, earned by attendance alone, and not by attendance and examination. The American practice of allowing the teaching body to examine for degrees has been partly dictated by the scarcity of men outside the faculties who are at once throughly acquainted with the subjects of examination, and sufficiently versed in teaching to know what may fairly be expected of both students and instructors. This difficulty could now be overcome. The chief reason, however, for the existence of this practice is that the faculties were the only bodies that could confer degrees intelligently, when degrees were obtained by passing through a prescribed course of study without serious checks, and completing a certain term of residence without disgrace. The change in the manner of earning the University degrees ought, by right, to have brought into being an examining body distinct from the teaching body. So far as the College proper is concerned, the Board of Overseers have, during the past year, taken a step which tends in this direction.

The rigorous examination for admission has one good effect throughout the college course: it prevents a waste of instruction upon incompetent persons. A school with a low standard for admission and a high standard of graduation, like West Point, is obliged to dismiss a large proportion of its students by the way. Hence much individual distress, and a great wastes of resourses, both public and private. But, on the other hand, it must not be supposed that every student who enters Harvard College necessarily graduates. Strict annual examinations are to be passed. More than a fourth of those who enter College fail to take their degree.

Only a few years ago, all students who graduated at this College passed through one uniform curriculum. Every man studied the same subjects in the same proportions, without regard to his natural bent or preference. The individual student had no choice of either subjects or teachers. This system is still the prevailing system among American colleges, and finds vigorous defenders. It has the merit of simplicity. So had the school methods of our grandfathers—one primer, one catechism, one rod for all children. On the whole, a single common course of studies, tolerably well selected to meet the average needs, seems to most Americans a very proper and natural thing, even for grown men.

As a people, we do not apply to mental activities the principle of division of labor; and we have but a halting faith in special training for high professional employments. The vulgar conceit that a Yankee can turn his hand to anything we insensibly carry into high places, where it is preposterous and criminal. We are accustomed to seeing men leap from farm or shop to court-room or pulpit, and we half believe that common men can safely use the seven-league boots of genius. What amount of knowledge and experience do we habitually demand of our lawgivers? What special training do we ordinarily think necessary for our diplomatists?—although in great emergencies the nation has known where to turn. Only after years of bitterest experience did we come to believe the professional train-

22

ing of a soldier to be of value in war. This lack of faith in the prophecy of a natual bent, and in the value of a discipline concentrated upon a single object, amounts to a national danger.

In education, the individual traits of different minds have not been sufficiently attended to. Through all the periods of boyhood the school studies should be representative; all the main fields of knowledge should be entered upon. But the young man of nineteen or twenty ought to know what he likes best and is most fit for. If his previous training has been sufficiently wide, he will know by that time whether he is most apt at language or philosophy or natural science or mathematics. If he feels no loves, he will at least have his hates. At that age the teacher may wisely abandon the school-dame's practice of giving a copy of nothing but zeros to the child who alleges that he cannot make that figure. When the revelation of his peculiar taste and capacity comes to a young man, let him reverently give it welcome, thank God, and take courage. Thereafter he knows his way to happy, enthusiastic work, and, God willing, to usefulness and success. The civilization of a people may be inferred from the variety of its tools. There are thousands of years between the stone hatchet and the machine-shop. As tools multiply, each is more ingeniously adapted to its own exclusive purpose. So with the men that make the State. For the individual, concentration, and the highest development of his own peculiar faculty, is the only prudence. But for the State, it is variety, not uniformity, of intellectual product, which is needful.

These principles are the justification of the system of elective studies which has been gradually developed in this College during the past forty years. At present the Freshman year is the only one in which there is a fixed course prescribed for all. In the other three years, more than half the time allotted to study is filled with subjects chosen by each student from lists which comprise six studies in the Sophomore year, nine in the Junior year, and eleven in the Senior year. The range of elective studies is large, though there are some striking deficiencies. The liberty of choice of subject is wide, but yet has very rigid limits. There is a certain framework which must be filled; and about half the material of the filling is prescribed. The choice offered to the student does not lie between liberal studies and professional or utilitarian studies. All the studies which are open to him are liberal and disciplinary, not narrow or special. Under this system the College does not demand, it is true, one invariable set of studies of every candidate for the first degree in Arts; but its requisitions for this degree are nevertheless high and inflexible, being nothing less than four years devoted to liberal culture.

It has been alleged that the elective system must weaken the bond which unites members of the same class. This is true; but in view of another much more efficient cause of the diminution of class intimacy, the point is not very significant. The increased size of the college classes inevitably works a great change in this respect. One hundred and fifty young men cannot be so intimate with each other as fifty used to be. This increase is progressive. Taken in connection with the rising average age of the students, it would compel the adoption of methods of instruction different from the old, if there were no better motive for such change. The elective system fosters scholarship, because it gives free play to natural preferences and inborn aptitudes, makes possible enthusiasm for a chosen work, relieves the professor and the ardent disciple of the presence of a body of students who are compelled to an unwelcome task, and enlarges instruction by submitting many and various lessons given to small, lively classes, for a few lessons many times repeated to different sections of a numerous class. The College therefore proposes to persevere in its efforts to establish, improve, and extend the elective system. Its administrative difficulties, which seem formidable at first, vanish before a brief experience.

24

There has been much discussion about the comparative merits of lectures and recitations. Both are useful—lectures, for inspiration, guidance, and the comprehensive methodizing which only one who has a view of the whole field can rightly contrive; recitations, for securing and testifying a thorough mastery on the part of the pupil of the treaties or author in hand, for conversational comment and amplification, for emulation and competition. Recitations alone readily degenerate into dusty repetitions, and lectures alone are too often a useless expenditure of force. The lecturer pumps laboriously into sieves. The water may be wholesome, but it runs through. A mind must work to grow. Just as far, however, as the student can be relief on to master and appreciate his author without the aid of frequent questioning and repetitions, so far is it possible to dispense with recitations. Accordingly, the later College years there is a decided tendency to diminish the number of recitations, the faithfulness of the student being tested by periodical examinations. This tendency is in a right direction, if prudently controlled.

The discussion about lectures and recitations has brought out some strong opinions about text-books and their use. Impatience with text-books and manuals is very natural in both teachers and taught. These books are indeed, for the most part, very imperfect, and stand in constant need of correction by the well-informed teacher. Stereotyping, in its present undeveloped condition, is in part to blame for their most exasperating defects. To make the metal plates keep pace with the progress of learning is costly. The manifest deficiencies of textbooks must not, however, drive us into a too sweeping condemnation of their use. It is a rare teacher who is superior to all manuals in his subject. Scientific manuals, are as a rule, much worse than those upon language, literature, or philosophy; yet the main improvement in medical education in this country during the last twenty years has been the addition of systematic recitations from text-books to the lectures which were

25

formerly the principal means of theoretical instruction. The training of a medical student, inadequate as it is, offers the best example we have of the methods and fruits of an education mainly scientific. The transformation which the average student of a good medical school undergoes in three years is strong testimony to the efficiency of the training he receives.

There are certain common misapprehensions about colleges in general, and this College in particular, to which I wish to devote a few moments' attention. And, first, in spite of the familiar picture of the moral dangers which environ the student, there is no place so safe as a good college during the critical passage from boyhood to manhood. The security of the college commonwealth is large due to its exuberant activity. Its public opinion, though easily led astray, is still high in the main. Its scholarly tastes and habits, its eager friendship and quick hatreds, its keen debates, its frank discussions of character and of deep political and religious questions, all are safeguards against sloth, vulgarity, and depravity. Its society and, not less, its solitudes are full of teaching. Shams, conceit, and fictitious distinctions get no mercy. There is nothing but ridicule for bombast and sentimentality. Repression of genuine sentiment and emotion is indeed, in this College, carried too far. Reserve is more respectable than any undiscerning communicativeness; but neither Yankee shamefacedness nor English stolidity is admirable. This point especially touches you, young men, who are still undergraduates. When you feel a true admiration for a teacher, a glow of enthusiasm for work, a thrill of pleasure at some excellent saying, give it expression. Do not be ashamed of these emotions. Cherish the natural sentiment of personal devotion to the teacher who calls out your better powers. It is a great delight to serve an intellectual master. We Americans are but too apt to lose this happiness. German and French students get it. If ever in after years you come to smile at the youthful reverence you paid, believe me, it will be with tears in your eyes.

26

Many excellent persons see great offense in any system of college rank; but why should we expect more of young men than we do of their elders? How many men and women perform their daily tasks from the highest motives alone—for the glory of God and the relief of man's estate? Most people work for bare bread, a few for cake. The college rank-list reinforces higher motives. In the campaign for character, no auxiliaries are to be refused. Next to despising the enemy, it is dangerous to reject allies. To devise a suitable method of estimating the fidelity and attainments of college students is, however, a problem which has long been under discussion, and has not yet received a satisfactory solution. The worst of rank as a stimulus is the self-reference it implies in the aspirants. The less a young man thinks about the cultivation of his mind, about his own mental progress,—about himself, in short,—the better.

The petty discipline of colleges attracts altogether too much attention from both friends and foes. It is to be remembered that the rules concerning decorum, however necessary to maintain the high standard of manners and conduct which characterizes this College, are nevertheless justly described as petty. What is technically called a quiet term cannot be accepted as the acme of university success. This success is not to be measured by the frequency or rarity of college punishments. The criteria of success or failure in a high place of learning are not the boyish escapades of an insignificant minority, nor the exceptional cases of ruinous vice. Each year must be judged by the added opportunities of instruction, by the prevailing enthusiasm in learning, and by the gathered wealth of culture and character. The best way to put boyishness to shame is to foster scholarship and manliness. The manners of a community cannot be improved by main force any more than its morals. The Statutes of the University need some amendment and reduction in the chapters on crimes and misdemeanors. But let us render to our fathers the justice we

27

shall need from our sons. What is too minute or precise for our use was doubtless wise and proper in its day. It was to inculcate a reverent bearing and due consideration for things sacred that the regulations prescribed a black dress on Sunday. Black is not the only decorous wear in these days; but we must not seem, in ceasing from this particular mode of good manners, to think less of the gentle breeding of which only the outward signs, and not the substance, have been changed.

Harvard College has always attracted and still attracts students in all conditions of life. From the city trader or professional man, who may be careless how much his son spends at Cambridge, to the farmer or mechanic, who finds it a hard sacrifice to give his boy his time early enough to enable him to prepare for college, all sorts and condition of men have wished and still wish to send their sons hither. There are always scores of young men in this University who earn or borrow every dollar they spend here. Every year many young men enter this College without any resources whatever. If they prove themselves men of capacity and character, they never go away for lack of money. More than twenty thousand dollars a year is now devoted to aiding students of narrow means to compass their education, besides all the remitted fees and the numerous private benefactions. These latter are unfailing. Taken in connection with the proceeds of the funds applicable to the aid of poor students, they enable the Corporation to say that no good student need ever stay away from Cambridge or leave college simply because he is poor. There is one uniform condition, however, on which help is given: the recipient must be of promising ability and the best character. The community does not owe superior education to all children, but only to the elite—to those who, having the capacity, prove by hard work that they have also the necessary perseverance and endurance. The process of preparing to enter college under the difficulties which poverty entails is just such a test of worthiness as is needed. At this moment there is no college in the

28

country more eligible for a poor student than Harvard on the mere ground of economy. The scholarship funds are mainly the fruit of the last fifteen years. The future will take care of itself; for it is to be expected that the men who in this generation have had the benefit of these funds, and who succeed in after life, will pay manifold to their successors in need the debt which they owe, not to the College, but to benefactors whom they cannot even thank, save in heaven. No wonder that scholarships are founded. What greater privilege than this of giving young men of promise the coveted means of intellectual growth and freedom? The angels of heaven might envy mortals so fine a luxury. The happiness which the winning of a scholarship gives is not the recipient's alone: it flashes back to the home whence he came, and gladdens anxious hearts there. The good which it does is not his alone, but descends, multiplying at every step, through generations. Thanks to the beneficent mysteries of hereditary transmission, no capital earns such interest as personal culture. The poorest and the richest students are equally welcome here, provided that with their poverty or their wealth they bring capacity, ambition, and purity. The poverty of scholars is of inestimable worth in this money-getting nation. It maintains the true standards of virtue and honor. The poor friars, not the bishops, saved the church. The poor scholars and preachers of duty defend the modern community against its own material prosperity. Luxury and learning are ill bedfellows. Nevertheless, this College owes much of its distinctive character to those who, bringing hither from refined homes good breeding, gentle tastes, and a manly delicacy, add to them openness and activity of mind, intellectual interests, and a sense of public duty. It is as high a privilege for a rich man's son as for a poor man's to resort to these academic halls, and so to take his proper place among cultivated and intellectual men. To lose altogether the presence of those who in early life have enjoyed the domestic and social advantages of wealth would be as great

29

a blow to the College as to lose the sons of the poor. The interests of the College and the country are identical in this regard. The country suffers when the rich are ignorant and unrefined. Inherited wealth is an unmitigated curse when divorced from culture. Harvard College is sometimes reproached with being aristocratic. If by aristocracy be meant a stupid and pretentious caste, founded on wealth, and birth, and an affectation of European manners, no charge could be more preposterous: the College is intensely American in affection, and intensely democratic in temper. But there is an aristocracy to which the sons of Harvard have belonged, and, let us hope, will ever aspire to belong—the aristocracy which excels in manly sports, carries off the honors and prizes of the learned professions, and bears itself with distinction in all fields of intellectual labor and combat; the aristocracy which in peace stands firmest for the public honor and renown, and in war rides first into the murderous thickets.

The attitudes of the University in the prevailing discussions touching the education and fit employments of women demands brief explanation. America is the natural arena for these debates; for here the female sex has a better past and a better present than elsewhere. Americans, as a rule, hate disabilities of all sorts, whether religious, political, or social. Equality between the sexes, without privilege or oppression on either side, is the happy custom of American homes. While this great discussion is going on, it is the duty of the University to maintain a cautious and expectant policy. The Corporation will not receive women as students into the College proper, nor into any school whose discipline requires residence near the school. The difficulties involved in a common residence of hundreds of young men and women of immature character and marriageable age are very grave. The necessary police regulations are exceedingly burdensome. The Corporation are not influenced to this decision, however, by any crude notions about the innate capacities of women. The world knows

30

next to nothing about the natural mental capacities of the female sex. Only after generations of civil freedom and social equality will it be possible to obtain the data necessary for an adequate discussion of woman's natural tendencies, tastes, and capabilities. Again, the Corporation do not find it necessary to entertain a confident opinion upon the fitness or unfitness of women for professional pursuits. It is not the business of the University to decide this mooted point. In this country the University does not undertake to protect the community against incompetent lawyers, ministers, or doctors. The community must protect itself by refusing to employ such. Practical, not theoretical, considerations determine the policy of the University. Upon a matter concerning which prejudices are deep, and opinion inflammable, and experience scanty, only one course is prudent or justifiable when such great interests are at stake—that of cautious and well-considered experiment. The practical problem is to devise a safe, promising, and instructive experiment. Such an experiment the Corporation have meant to try in opening the newly established University Courses of Instruction to competent women. In these courses the University offers to young women who have been to good schools as many years as they wish of liberal culture in studies which have no direct professional value, to be sure, but which enrich and enlarge both intellect and character. The University hopes thus to contribute to the intellectual emancipation of women. It hopes to prepare some women better than they would otherwise have been prepared for the profession of teaching, the one learned profession to which women have already acquired a clear title. It hopes that the proffer of this higher instruction will have some reflex influence upon schools for girls—to discourage superficiality, and to promote substantial education.

The governing bodies of the University are the Faculties, the Board of Overseers, and the Corporation. The University as a place of study and instruction is, at any moment, what the

31

Faculties make it. The professors, lecturers, and tutors of the University are the living sources of learning and enthusiasm. They personally represent the possibilities of instruction. They are united in several distinct bodies the academic and professional Faculties, each of which practically determines its own processes and rules. The discussion of methods of instruction is the principal business of these bodies. As a fact, progress comes mainly from Faculties. This has been conspicuously the case with the Academic and Medical Faculties during the last fifteen or twenty years. The undergraduates used to have a notion that the time of the Academic Faculty was mainly devoted to petty discipline. Nothing could be further from the truth. The Academic Faculty is the most active, vigilant, and devoted body connected with the University. It indeed is constantly obliged to discuss minute details, which might appear trivial to an inexperienced observer. But, in education, technical details tell. Whether German be studied by the Juniors once a week as an extra study, or twice a week as an elective, seems, perhaps, an unimportant matter; but twenty years hence, it makes all the difference between a generation of Alumni who know German and a generation who do not. The Faculty renews its youth, through the frequent appointments of tutors and assistant professors, better and oftener than any other organization within the University. Two kinds of men make good teachers—young men and men who never grow old. The incessant discussions of the Academic Faculty have borne much fruit: witness the transformation of the University since the beginning of President Walker's administration. And it never tires. New men take up the old debates, and one year's progress is not less than another's. The divisions within the Faculty are never between the old and the young officers. There are always old radicals and young conservatives.

The Medical Faculty affords another illustration of the same principle—that for real university progress we must look principally to the teaching bodies. The Medical School to-day is almost three times as strong as it was fifteen years ago. Its teaching power is greatly increased, and its methods have been much improved. This gain is the work of the Faculty of the School.

If then the Faculties be so important, it is a vital question how the quality of these bodies can be maintained and improved. It is very hard to find competent professors for the University. Very few Americans of eminent ability are attracted to this profession. The pay has been too low, and there has been no gradual rise out of drudgery, such as may reasonably be expected in other learned callings. The law of supply and demand, or the commercial principle that the quality as well as the price of goods is best regulated by the natural contest between producers and consumers, never has worked well in the province of high education. And in spite of the high standing of some of its advocates, it is well-nigh certain that the so-called law never can work well in such a field. The reason is that the demand for instructors of the highest class on the part of parents and trustees is an ignorant demand, and the supply of highly educated teachers is so limited that the consumer has not sufficient opportunities of informing himself concerning the real qualities of the article he seeks. Originally a bad judge, he remains a bad judge, because the supply is not sufficiently abundant and various to instruct him. Moreover, a need is not necessarily a demand. Everybody knows that the supposed law affords a very imperfect protection against short weight, adulteration, and sham, even in the case of those commodities which are most abundant in the market and most familiar to buyers. The most intelligent community is defenseless enough in buying clothes and groceries. When it comes to hiring learning and inspiration and personal weight, the law of supply and demand breaks down altogether. A university cannot be managed like a railroad or a cottonmill.

There are, however, two practicable improvements in the position of college professors which will be of very good ef-

33

fect. Their regular stipend must and will be increased, and the repetitions which now harass them must be diminished in number. It is a strong point of the elective system that, by reducing the size of classes or divisions, and increasing the variety of subjects, it makes the professors' labors more agreeable.

Experience teaches that the strongest and most devoted professors will contribute something to the patrimony of knowledge; or if they invent little themselves, they will do something toward defending, interpreting, or diffusing the contributions of others. Nevertheless, the prime business of American professors in this generation must be regular and assiduous class teaching. With the exception of the endowments of the Observatory, the University does not hold a single fund primarily intended to secure to men of learning the leisure and means to prosecute original researches.

The organization and functions of the Board of Overseers deserve the serious attention of all men who are interested in the American method of providing the community with high education through the agency of private corporations. Since 1866 the Overseers have been elected by the Alumni. Five men are chosen each year to serve six years. The body has, therefore, a large and very intelligent constituency, and is rapidly renewed. The ingenious method of nominating to the electors twice as many candidates as there are places to be filled in any year is worthy of careful study as a device of possible application in politics. The real function of the Board of Overseers is to stimulate and watch the President and Fellows. Without the Overseers, the President and Fellows would be a board of private trustees, self-perpetuated and self-controlled. Provided as it is with two governing boards, the University enjoys that principal safeguard of all American governments——the natural antagonism between two bodies of different constitution, powers, and privileges. While having with the Corporation a common interest of the deepest kind in the welfare of the University and the advancement of learning,

34

the Overseers should always hold toward the Corporation an attitude of suspicious vigilance. They ought always to be pushing and prying. It would be hard to over-state the importance of the public supervision exercised by the Board of Overseers. Experience proves that our main hope for the permanence and ever-widening usefulness of the University must rest upon this double-headed organization. The English practice of setting up a single body of private trustees to carry on a school or charity according to the personal instructions of some founder or founders has certainly proved a lamentably bad one; and when we count by generations, the institutions thus established have proved short-lived. The same causes which have brought about the decline of English endowed schools would threaten the life of this University were it not for the existence of the Board of Overseers. These schools were generally managed by close corporations, self-elected, self-controlled, without motive for activity, and destitute of external stimulus and aid. Such bodies are too irresponsible for human nature. At the time of life at which men generally come to such places of trust, rest is sweet, and the easiest way is apt to seem the best way; and the responsibility of inaction, though really heavier, seems lighter than the responsibility of action. These corporations were often hampered by founders' wills and statutory provisions which could not be executed, and yet stood in the way of organic improvements. There was no systematic provision for thorough inspections and public reports thereupon. We cannot flatter ourselves that under like circumstances we should always be secure against like dangers. Provoked by crying abuses, some of the best friends of education in England have gone the length of maintaining that all these school endowments ought to be destroyed, and the future creation of such trusts rendered impossible. French law practically prohibits the creation of such trusts by private persons.

Incident to the Overseers' power of inspecting the University publicly reporting upon its condition, is the important function of suggesting and urging improvements. The inertia of a massive University is formidable. A good past is positively dangerous, if it make us content with the present, and so unprepared for the future. The present constitution of our Board of Overseers has already stimulated the Alumni of several other New England colleges to demand a similar control over the property-holding board of trustees which has heretofore been the single source of all authority.

We come now to the heart of the University—the Corporation. This board holds the funds, makes appointments, fixes salaries, and has, by right, the initiative in all changes of the organic law of the University. Such an executive board must be small to be efficient. It must always contain men of sound judgment in finance; and literature and the learned professions should be adequately represented in it. The Corporation should also be but slowly renewed; for it is of the utmost consequence to the University that the Government should have a steady aim, and a prevailing spirit which is independent of individuals and transmissible from generation to generation. And what should this spirit be? First, it should be a catholic spirit. A university must be indigenous; it must be rich; but above all, it must be free. The winnowing breeze of freedom must blow through all its chambers. It takes a hurricane to blow wheat away. An atmosphere of intellectual freedom is the native air of literature and science. This University aspires to serve the nation by training men to intellectual honesty and independence of mind. The Corporation demands of all its teachers that they be grave, reverent, and high-minded; but it leaves them, like their pupils, free. A university is built, not by a sect, but by a nation.

Secondly, the actuating spirit of the Corporation must be a spirit of fidelity—fidelity to the many and various trusts reposed in them by the hundreds of persons who, out of their penury or their abundance, have given money to the President and Fellows of Harvard College in the beautiful hope of

36

doing some perpetual good upon this earth. The Corporation has constantly done its utmost to make this hope a living fact. One hundred and ninety-nine years ago, William Pennoyer gave the rents of certain estates in the county of Norfolk, England, that "two fellows and two scholars forever should be educated, brought up, and maintained" in this College. The income from this bequest has never failed; and to-day one of the four Pennoyer scholarships is held by a lineal descendent of William Pennoyer's brother Robert. So a lineal descendent of Governor Danforth takes this year the income of the property which Danforth bequeathed to the College in 1699. The Corporation have been as faithful in the greater things as in the less. They have been greatly blessed in one respect: in the whole life of the Corporation, seven generations of men, nothing has ever been lost by malfeasance of officers or servants. A reputation for scrupulous fidelity to all trusts is the most precious possession of the Corporation. That safe, the College might lose everything else and yet survive; that lost beyond repair, and the days of the College would be numbered. Testators look first to the trustworthiness and permanence of the body which is to dispense their benefactions. The Corporation thankfully receives all gifts which may advance learning; but they believe that the interests of the University may be most effectually promoted by not restricting too narrowly the use to which a gift may be applied. Whenever the giver desires it, the Corporation will agree to keep any fund separately invested under the name of the giver, and to apply the whole proceeds of such investment to any object the giver may designate. By such special investments, however, the insurance which results from the absorption of a specific gift in the general funds is lost. A fund invested by itself may be impaired or lost by a single error of judgment in investing. The chance of such loss is small in any one generation, but appreciable in centuries. Such general designations as salaries, books, dormitories, public buildings, scholarship graduate or undergraduate, scientific collections, and expenses of experimental laboratories, are of permanent significance and effect; while experience proves that too specific and minute directions concerning the application of funds must often fail of fulfilment, simply in consequence of the changing needs and habits of successive generations.

Again, the Corporation should always be filled with the spirit of enterprise. An institution like this College is getting decrepit when it sits down contentedly on its mortgages. On its invested funds the Corporation should be always seeking how safely to make a quarter of a per cent more. A quarter of one per cent means a new professorship. It should be always pushing after more professorships, better professors, more land and buildings, and better apparatus. It should be eager, sleepless, and untiring, never wasting a moment in counting laurels won, ever prompt to welcome and apply the liberality of the community, and liking no prospect so well as that of difficulties to be overcome and labors to be done in the cause of learning and public virtue.

You recognize, gentlemen, the picture which I have drawn in thus delineating the true spirit of the Corporation of this College. I have described the noble quintessence of the New England character—that character which has made us a free and enlightened people; that character which, please God, shall yet do a great work in the world for the lifting up of humanity.

Apart from the responsibility which rests upon the Corporation, its actual labors are far heavier than the community imagines. The business of the University has greatly increased in volume and complexity during the past twenty years, and the drafts made upon the time and thought of every member of the Corporation are heavy indeed. The high honors of the function are in these days most generously earned.

The President of the University is primarily an executive officer; but, being a member of both governing boards and of all the faculties, he has also the influence in their debates to which his more or less perfect intimacy with the University and greater or less personal weight may happen to entitle him. An administrative officer who undertakes to do everything himself will do but little, and that little ill. The President's first duty is that of supervision. He should know what each officer's and servant's work is, and how it's done. But the days are past in which the President could be called on to decide everything from the purchase of a door-mat to the appointment of a professor. The principle of divided and subordinate responsibilities, which rules in government bureaus, in manufactories, and all great companies, which makes a modern army a possibility, must be applied in the University. The President should be able to discern the practical essence of complicated and long-drawn discussions. He must often pick out that promising part of theory which ought to be tested by experiment, and must decide how many of things desirable are also attainable, and what one of many projects is ripest for execution. He must watch and look before—watch, to seize opportunities to get money, to secure eminent teachers and scholars, and to influence public opinion toward the advancement of learning; and look before, to anticipate the due effect on the University of the fluctuations of public opinion on educational problems; of the progress of the institutions which feed the University; of the changing conditions of the professions which the University supplies; of the rise of new professions; of the gradual alteration of social and religious habits in the community. The University must accomodate itself promptly to significant changes in the character of the people for whom it exists. The institutions of higher education in any nation are always a faithful mirror in which are sharply reflected the national history and character. In this mobile nation the action and reaction between the University and society at large are more sensitive and rapid than in stiffer communities. The President, therefore, must not need to see a house built before he can comprehend the plan of it. He can profit by a wide intercourse with all sorts of men, and by every real discussion on education, legislation, and sociology.

The most important function of the President is that of advising the Corporation concerning appointments, particularly about appointments of young men who have not had time and opportunity to approve themselves to the public. It is in discharging this duty that the President holds the future of the University in his hands. He cannot do it well unless he have insight, unless he be able to recognize, at times beneath some crusts, the real gentleman and the natural teacher. This is one oppressive responsibility of the President: all other cares are light beside it. To see every day the evil fruit of a bad appointment must be the cruelest of official torments. Fortunately, the good effect of a judicious appointment is also inestimable; and here, as everywhere good is more penetrating and diffuse than evil.

It is imperative that the statutes which define the President's duties should be recast, and the customs of the College be somewhat modified, in order that lesser duties may not crowd out the greater. But, however important the functions of the President, it must not be forgotten that he is emphatically a constitutional executive. It is his character and his judgment which are of importance, not his opinions. He is the executive officer of deliberative bodies, in which decisions are reached after discussion by a majority vote. Those decisions bind him. He cannot force his own opinions upon anybody. A university is the last place in the world for a dictator. Learning is always republican. It has idols, but not masters.

What can the community do for the University? It can love, honor, and cherish it. Love it and honor it. The University is upheld by this public affection and respect. In the loyalty of her children she finds strength and courage. The Corporation, the Overseers, and the several faculties need to feel that the leaders of public opinion, and especially the sons of the College, are at their back, always ready to give them a generous and intelligent support. Therefore we welcome the Chief Magistrate of the Commonwealth, the Senators, Judges, and other dignitaries of the State, who by their presence at this ancient ceremonial bear witness to the pride which Massachusetts feels in her eldest university. Therefore we rejoice in the presence of this throng of the Alumni, testifying their devotion to the College which, through all changes, is still their home. Cherish it. This University, though rich among American colleges, is very poor in comparison with the great universities of Europe. The wants of the American community have far outgrown the capacity of the University to supply them. We must try to satisfy the cravings of the select few as well as the needs of the average many. We cannot afford to neglect the Fine Arts. We need groves and meadows as well as barracks; and soon there will be no chances to get them in this expanding city. But, above all, we need professorship, books, and apparatus, that teaching and scholarship may abound.

And what will the University do for the community? First, it will make a rich return of learning, poetry, and piety. Secondly, it will foster the sense of public duty—that great virtue which makes republics possible. The founding of Harvard College was an heroic act of public spirit. For more than a century the breath of life was kept in it by the public spirit of the Province and of its private benefactors. In the last fifty years the public spirit of the friends of the College has quadrupled its endowments. And how have the young men nurtured here in successive generations repaid the founders for their pious care? Have they honored freedom and loved their country? For answer we appeal to the records of the national service; to the lists of the Senate, the cabinet, and the diplomatic service, and to the rolls of the army and navy. Honored men, here present, illustrate before the world the public quality of the graduates of this College. Theirs is no mercenary service.

Other fields of labor attract them more and would reward them better; but they are filled with the noble ambition to deserve well of the republic. There have been doubts, in times yet recent, whether culture were not selfish; whether men of refined tastes and manners could really love Liberty, and be ready to endure hardness for her sake; whether, in short, gentlemen would in this century prove as loyal to noble ideas as in other times, they had been to kings. In yonder old playground, fit spot whereon to commemorate the manliness which there was nurtured, shall soon rise a noble monument which for generations will give convincing answer to such shallow doubts; for over its gates will be written: "In memory of the sons of Harvard who died for their country." The future of the University will not be unworthy of its past.

Inaugural Address

by

ARTHUR TWINING HADLEY

President of Yale University

October 18, 1899

ARTHUR TWINING HADLEY (*April 23, 1856—March 6, 1930*) *was born in New Haven, Connecticut. His father and his grandfather were identified with the teaching profession. His father was professor of Greek at Yale University for a time. After graduating from Yale, Arthur Twining Hadley spent three years in the study of history and political science, two of which were spent at the University of Berlin. Upon his return from Europe in 1879, he became tutor in Yale College. He was a fluent writer and world traveller. During the period of his presidency from 1899-1921, the amount of writing was diminished because of administrative duties. Following his retirement, he embraced increased opportunities for both writing and travel.*

Thirteen years ago my honored predecessor traced in his inaugural address the changes which two centuries had developed in Yale's educational methods and ideals, and showed with clearness what were the corresponding changes in organization which would best fit her to apply these methods and approach these ideals. What has once been done so well we need not undertake to do again. Let us rather proceed to a detailed consideration of the problems which now confront us in the various departments of college and university life. Let us formulate the questions which press for solution. Let us study the good and evil attendant on various methods of dealing with them. Let us see, as far as we may, what lines of policy in these matters of immediate practical moment will enable us best to meet the demands of the oncoming century.

These problems are for the most part not peculiar to Yale. The questions which present themselves to the authorities here are in large measure the same which arise elsewhere. But the conditions governing their solution are different. We may best understand the work which Yale has to do if we study the problems in their general form, as they come before the whole brotherhood of educators as a body; and then try to solve them in the particular form which is fixed by the special circumstances, past and present, which have made Yale University what it is.

Fifty years ago the duties of college administration were relatively simple. There was at that time a certain curriculum of studies, chiefly in classics and in deductive science, which the public accepted as necessary for the development of an educated man. These studies were taught by traditional methods which compelled the pupil to perform a considerable amount of work whether he liked it or not. The student body was a homogeneous one, meeting in the same recitation rooms day by day. The classes readily acquired a spirit of good fellowship and democracy. Outside conditions favored the maintenance of this spirit. Differences in wealth throughout the community were less conspicuous than they are to-day. College education was so cheap that it fell within the reach of all. Most of the students were poor. The few who possessed wealth found comparatively little opportunity for spending it in legitimate ways. Rich and poor stood on a common footing as regarded participation in the social ambitions and privileges of college life. The intellectual education which such a college gave to the majority of its students was but an incidental service as compared with their education in sterling virtue. The institution which could furnish this double training met fully the requirements which public opinion imposed.

The first of the disturbing elements which entered to complicate the problem of college education was found in the development of professional schools. Down to the early part of the present century, professional study was largely done in private, in the office of some successful lawyer, or doctor, or in the study of some experienced minister. Even when schools of theology, of law, or of medicine were established, they at first occupied themselves largely with teaching the same kind of things that might have been learned in the office by the old method. But about the middle of the present century a new and more enlightened view of technical training arose. It was seen that a professional school did its best work when it taught principles rather than practice. Instead of cramming the students with details which they would otherwise learn afterward, it found much better to train them in methods of reasoning which otherwise they would not learn at all. This study of principles, to be thoroughly effective, necessarily occupied several years. There was a strong pressure to introduce the elements of these studies into the curriculum; and a demand that when once they were incorporated in the college course they should be taught, not in a perfunctory way, but with the same standard of excellence which was achieved in our best professional schools.

Meantime, apart from these changes in the method of technical training, the sphere of interest of the cultivated man of the country was constantly widening. The course of college study which satisfied an earlier generation was inadequate for a later one. The man who would have breadth of sympathy with the various departments of human knowledge could not content himself with classics, mathematics and psychology. He must be familiar with modern literature as well as ancient, with physical science as well as deductive.

If we had at once widened the college curriculum enough to correspond to the increased range of human interest, and lengthened the period of professional study enough to give each man the fullest recognized training for his specialty—if, to quote the old educational phrase, we had taught each man something of everything and everything of something—the time of university education would have lengthened itself to ten or fifteen years. Its complete fruition would have been a luxury out of reach of all but the favored few. The difficulty could be met only by the adoption of an elective system; a system which ceased to treat the college course as a fixed curriculum for all, and gave an opportunity for the selection of groups of studies adapted to the varying needs of the several students.

The introduction of these methods of university education, necessary as it was, has been nevertheless attended with serious dangers and evils.

In the first place, there is apt to be a change in the mode of instruction, which while good for the best students, runs the risk of proving bad for the ordinary ones. The old method of handling large classes in a fixed course of study under the recitation system required all the students to do a modicum of work, and enabled the teacher to see whether they were doing it or not. The divisions were adjusted and could be constantly readjusted with that end in view. The time of the instructors was so far economized by the narrow range of subjects taught that their attention could be properly concentrated on this one point of keeping the students up to their work by a daily oral examination. But with the increasing number of things to be taught, the variation in the size of the classes, and the demands which the best students now make for really advanced teaching, this supervision and concentration is no longer possible. The instructor who is teaching small groups of selected men who have a particular interest in his subject, is forced to content himself with what is little more than a lecture in teaching the larger groups or ordinary men to whom the subject has only a general interest. A lecture system of this kind is beset with perils. It is something of which we have to make use, because there are not enought first-rate men in the country to teach all the subjects of study which this generation demands, in classes of size small enough to adapt themselves to the recitation system. The choice in many lines of study lies between having recitations with fourth-rate men or lectures from first-rate ones. I never met a good teacher who really approved of the lecture system, or who did not prefer small classes to large ones. But these really good teachers are just the men that we wish to bring in contact with as many students as possible. If we refuse to let them lecture, we either confine the benefit of their instructions to a few, or increase their hours beyond the possibility of human endurance.

Another evil connected with the elective system is the loss of *esprit de corps*. In a college like West Point or Annapolis, where a homogeneous body of men are pursuing a common scheme of studies, with a common end in view, and with rigorous requirements as to the work which must be done by each individual, this spirit is seen at its strongest. The place sets its character stamp upon every one; sometimes perhaps for evil, but in the vast majority of cases for good. An approximation to this state of things was seen in our early American colleges. In many of them it is still maintained to a considerable degree. But the forces which maintain it are far less potent to-day than they were fifty years ago. The community of interests is less, the community of hard work is very much less. If this college spirit once passes away, the whole group of qualities which we have known by the name of college democracy is in danger of passing also. For the increase of wealth in the outside world is a perpetual menace to old-fashioned democratic equality. If we have within the college life not only differences in things studied, but differences in enjoyment between rich and poor, we are at once in danger of witnessing a development of social distinctions and class interests which shall sweep away the thing which was most characteristic and most valuable in the earlier education of our colleges. Not the intellectual life only, nor the social life only but the whole religious and moral atmosphere suffers deterioration if a place becomes known either as a rich man's college; or, worse yet, as a college where rich and poor meet on different footings. What shall it profit us, if we gain the whole world and lose our own soul; if we develop the intellectual and material side of our education, and lose the traditional spirit of democracy and loyalty and Christianity?

That there will be an advance in thoroughness of preparation for the special lines of work which our students are to undertake, is a thing of which we may safely rest assured. That there shall be a similar advance in the general training for citizenship in the United States, is an obligation for whose fulfilment our universities are responsible. The Yale of the future must count for even more than the Yale of the past in the work of city, state, and nation. It must come into closer touch with our political life, and be a larger part of that life. To this end it is not enough for her to train experts competent to deal with the financial and legal problems which are before us. Side by side with this training, she must evoke in the whole body of her students and alumni that wider sense of their obligation as members of a free commonwealth which the America of the twentieth century requires.

The central problem, which we all have to face, and about which all other problems group themselves, is this: How shall we make our educational system meet the world's demands for progress on the intellectual side, without endangering the growth of that which has proved most valuable on the moral side? And it is the latter part which demands the most immediate attention from a college president, not necessarily because it is more important in itself—for where two things are both absolutely indispensable, a comparison of relative values is meaningless—but because the individual professors can, and under the keen competition between universities must, attend in large measure to the excellence of instruction in their several departments, while the action of the university as a whole, and the intelligent thought of the university administration, is requisite to prevent the sacrifice of the moral interest of the whole commonwealth.

There are four ways in which we may strive to deal with this difficulty.

(1) By relegating the work of character development more and more to the preparatory school. Our acceptance or non-acceptance of this solution determines our attitude toward the problem of entrance requirements.

(2) By striving to limit the occasion for the use of money on the part of the student. The necessity for such limitation constitutes the problem of college expenses.

(3) By endeavoring to create a body of common interests and traditions outside of the college course which shall make up for the diversity of interests within it. The most widely discussed, though possibly not the most important, point under this head is furnished by the problem of college athletics.

50

(4) By so arranging the work of the different departments of study that the variety inherent in the elective system shall not be attended with intellectual dissipation; providing the chance for economy of effort on the part of the instructor and the assurance of systematic cooperation on the part of the pupils. This is the problem of university organization.

The plan of relegating the responsibility for character development to the preparatory schools has at first sight much to commend it. It relieves the college officers of the most disagreeable part of their duty, that which pertains to matters of discipline, and enables them to concentrate their attention on their function as teachers. It meets the demands of many progressive men engaged in secondary education, some of whom long for an extension of their professional functions into new fields of activity, while others, justly proud of their success in the formation of character under existing conditions, desire the additional opportunity which is given them if they can keep their oldest boys a year or two longer under their influence. The larger the university the greater becomes the pressure in this direction.

But with conditions as they exist at Yale, I cannot think it wise to yield to this pressure. If we take a year from the beginning of the college course, that year will be spent by most of the boys either in a high school or a large academy. In the former case we approach the German or French system of education; in the latter the English. A compromise between the two, whereby a boy finishes his high school course and then takes the additional year at an academy, is hardly admissible on any ground; the single year is somewhat too short to give the intellectual influences of the new place to which the boy goes, and far too short to give its character influences. I cannot believe that any one who has watched the workings of the French or German system would desire to see it adopted in this country. The passage at an advanced age from the discipline of the lycee or gymnasium to the freedom of the

51

university, however well it may work in its intellectual results, does not produce the kind of moral ones which we need. The English system has wider possibilities; and for England it does extremely well. But it is essentially a product of English conditions,—that is, of aristocratic ones. It is an education for a privileged class. In America, on the other hand, we wish our higher education to remain democratic. We should not be satisfied with a system which excluded from its benefits the large number of boys who come from institutions, public or private, which are situated near their own home, and prepare only small groups for college. And even to those who are fortunate enough to come from the best preparatory schools, the loss in college life would often outweigh the gain in school life. A system of influences whose operation terminates at nineteen or twenty fixes a boy's moral and social place too soon. For the young man who has grown to the full measure of his moral stature at this age it is good; for the one who matures later it is distinctly bad. In our everyday experience at Yale as we watch the interaction between school estimates and college estimates of character, we can see that what-ever postpones a man's final social rating to as late a day as possible lengthens the period of strenuous moral effort, increases the chance of continued growth, and is of the largest value to the boys and men of the best type.

The abandonment of the responsibility for forming character would have its disadvantage for the university no less than for the students. A boy's loyalty will remain where his moral character has formed itself. The devotion and sentiment of the Englishman play not about Oxford or Cambridge, but about Eton, Harrow, and Rugby. Universities which derive their prestige and their wealth from the past rather than from the present may perhaps endure this deprivation. Not so the American college or university, which looks for its strongest support to the loyalty of its alumni.

With the desire of secondary school teachers to extend their work I have the strongest sympathy. To the idea of co-operation between universities and schools, whereby each shall arrange its teaching with reference to the other's needs, I am fully and absolutely committed, and purpose to do all that I can to further it. A university fulfills its true functions only when it thus seeks and gives aid outside of itself. But I believe that the chance for this extension, this cooperation, and this leadership, is to come through the freer inter-change of thought and interchange of men between school teaching and university teaching, rather than through a transference of subjects from one to the other. I believe that with the conditions as they exist, the true policy for our university with regard to entrance requirements is to find out what our secondary schools can do for their pupils, intellectually and morally, and adapt our requirements to these conditions. Detailed questions as to what specific subjects we shall require must be subordinated to this general principle of requiring those things, and only those things, which the schools can do well. To know whether we can substitute French or German for Greek, we must know whether any considerable number of schools teach French or German in such a way as to make it a real equivalent for Greek in the way of preparation for more advanced studies. Unless we keep our minds on this principle, we shall be in perpetual danger of receiving students who have been crammed for their examinations rather than trained for their work.

The second of our leading problems is the question of college expenses. Though the increase in this respect is less than is popularly supposed, there is no doubt that it is large enough to constitute a serious danger. It is far from easy to see how this danger is to be avoided. It is all very well to talk of returning to the Spartan simplicity of ancient times, but we cannot do it, nor ought we to if we could. We cannot, for the sake of saving the cost of a bathroom, return to the time when people took no baths. Nor can we meet the difficulty by furn-

ishing the comforts of modern civilization and charging no
price for them. If the university could afford to do it for every
one, it might be well; but to do it for some and not for others
works against the spirit of democracy. It may readily become
a form of pauperization. This same danger lurks in the whole
system of beneficiary aid, as at present given in Yale and in
most other colleges. To avoid this danger, and at the same
time give the men the help which they fairly ought to have,
we need not so much an increase of beneficiary funds as an
increase of the opportunities for students to earn their living.
Aid in education, if given without exacting a corresponding
return, becomes demoralizing. If it is earned by the student as
he goes, it has just the opposite effect. This holds good of
graduate scholarships and fellowships no less than of undergraduate ones. There is no doubt that in the somewhat indis-
criminate competition of different universities anxious to increase the size, real or apparent, of their graduate departments,
there has been an abuse of these appliances which, unless
promptly corrected, threatens the future of the teaching profession with an over-abundant influx of inferior men.

The true policy in the matter of expenses and beneficiary
aid would appear to be as follows:

1st. In building new dormitories and other appliances
connected with this daily life of the students, we should strive
to use the kind of intelligent economy which any but the richest man would use in building a house for himself. We should
construct them on the standard set by our homes rather than
by our clubs. In this way we should create a general level of
average expenses in the college life which would attract rather
than repel the boy who has to make his own way. We should
indeed welcome beautiful buildings, given to the university
as memorials of affection; but we should strive to have them
so designed that their beauty may be a means of enjoyment to
the whole community.

2nd. Tuition should be remitted with the utmost freedom to those who maintain a respectable standing. Such tuition should be either earned by service or regarded as a loan——a loan without interest, if you please, or at any rate at a purely nominal interest charge, and payable at the option of the holder, but in its essence a loan——a thing to be paid ultimately, unless disease or death intervene. By establishing a system of such repayment we could give aid far more universally than we now do, could perhaps lower the tuition fees in general, and could avoid a system of fraud which is at present practiced somewhat extensively on our colleges.

3rd. All scholarship aid beyond the tuition fees, whether for undergraduates or for graduates, should be distinctly in the nature of a prize for really distinguished work, or a payment for services rendered. I am aware that there are great practical obstacles which oppose the carrying out of this view, and I do not feel sure how quickly Yale will be in a position to put it into effect; but that it is a desirable ideal and goal there appears to be no doubt whatever. Renumeration rather than pauperization should be the principle underlying such aid.

4th. Above all things——and this is a matter where we need the cooperation of persons outside as well as inside the university——the utmost study should be bestowed on the possibility of utilizing the powers of the students in such a way that they can be of service to the college community and the world at large, and thus earn the aid which is given them. The problem is a most difficult one; too difficult even to be analyzed in the brief time before us to-day. But the amount of progress made already, in the few experiments which have been seriously tried, leads me to believe in an almost unbounded opportunity for ultimate developments of this idea.

Our third group of problems is connected with the development and preservation of common student interests and student life outside of the immediate work of the classroom.

Of all these interests, the most fundamental are those connected with religious observances and religious feeling. Yale is, and has been from the first, a Christian college. All her institutions show this throughout their structure. This was the dominant purpose in Yale's foundation; and the work and thought of the children have conformed to the wish of the fathers. What changes time may bring in the outward observances, or how soon it may bring them, I know not. The question of compulsory attendance on religious exercises is one which is seriously discussed by the faculty, the students, and the graduates; nor can we predict the outcome of such discussion. But this I know: that it is approached by all, young as well as old, in a spirit of wise conservatism and reverence for past usage, and that no change will be made unless it shall surely and clearly appear to those in authority that we are but modifying the letter of a tradition for the sake of preserving its spirit.

Even in matters of far less fundamental importance we may, I think, wisely preserve this same spirit of conservatism. An ancient university has a great advantage in the existence of a body of time-honored usages and traditions. Some of these it inevitably outgrows as time goes on. But a large majority serve a most useful purpose in binding the students together by bonds none the less real because so intangible. Such college customs and traditions we should maintain to the utmost. Even where they seem artificial or meaningless we should be careful how we let them go. It is not inconsistent with the spirit of progress to value them highly. Edmund Burke, was one of the most liberal and progressive men of his century; yet Burke was the man who set the truest value on those forms of the English constitution which, as he himself avowed, were rooted in prejudice. The constitution of Yale to-day, with its strange combination of liberty and privilege, of prescriptive custom and progressive individualism, has not a few points of resemblance to Burke's England. I can avow myself a conservative in the sense that Burke was a conservative; with him, I should hesitate to cast away the coat of prejudice and leave nothing but the naked reason.

Another group of cohesive forces which strengthen the influence of a university upon its members is connected with college athletics. The value of athletic sports when practiced in the right spirit is only equalled by their perniciousness when practiced in the wrong spirit. They deserve cordial and enthusiastic support. The time or thought spent upon them, great as it may seem, is justified by their educational influence. But side by side with this support and part of it, we must have unsparing condemnation of the whole spirit of professionalism. I do not refer to those grosser and more obvious forms of professionalism which college sentiment has already learned to condemn. Nor do I chiefly refer to the betting by which intercollegiate contests are accompanied, though this is a real and great evil, and does much to bring other evils in its train. I refer to something far more widespread, which still remains a menace to American college athletics,—the whole system of regarding the athletic achievement as a sort of advertisment of one's prowess, and of valuing success for its own sake rather than for the sake of the honor which comes in achieving it by honorable methods. I rejoice in Yale's victories, I mourn in her defeats; but I mourn still more whenever I see a Yale man who regards athletics as a sort of competitive means for pushing the university ahead of some rival. This is professionalism of the most subtle and the most dangerous sort. I know that the condition of athletic discipline in a college makes a difference in its attractiveness to a large and desirable class of young men and rightly so. Whether a victory or a series of victories makes such a difference, and increases the numbers that attend the university, I do not know and I do not care to know. The man who allows his mind to dwell on such a question, if he is not tempted to violate the ethics of amateur sport, is at any rate playing with temptation in a dangerous and reprehensible way. I am glad to believe that our colleges, and our nation as a whole, are becoming better able to understand the love of sport for its own sake. The growth of this spirit through three generations has relieved English universities of some of the problems which to-day confront us in America. To the growth of this spirit we must ourselves trust for their solution here. I am ready heartily to cooperate in any attempts that other colleges may make to lay down clear rules for the practice of inter-collegiate athletics, because the absence of such cooperation would be misunderstood and would give cause for suspicion where none ought to exist. But I cannot conceal the fact that the majority of such rules can only touch the surface of the difficulty; and that so far as they distract attention from the moral element in the case which is beyond all reach of rules, they may prove a positive hindrance to progress. If we can enter into athletics for the love of honor, in the broadest sense of the word, unmixed with the love of gain in any sense, we may now and then lose a few students, but we shall grow better year after year in all that makes for sound university life.

Last in order of discussion, though perhaps first in the imminence with which they press upon us for solution, are some of the problems of university organization, on whose proper treatment depends resources which is necessary for the efficient working of the institution as it stands and for its growth in the immediate future. It is hardly neccessary to say to this audience that Yale's organization differs somewhat fundamentally from that of most other American universities. It is a group of colleges, whose property is held in the name of a single corporation, but whose management is, by tradition and in some slight degree by legal authority, located in the hands of separate faculties. In this respect, Yale is not without points of resemblance to Oxford or Cambridge. I shall not try to discuss whether this system is on the whole a good one. It is here, and we cannot for the present change it. Like all other systems, it has its advantages and its disadvantages. The advantages are those which are possessed by local government everywhere,—an independence of initiative; a loyal spirit among the members of the several faculties which is the natural result of such independence; a sort of natural grouping of the students under which a common set of rules can be made for each department, and the evils of too great freedom may be avoided. The independence of initiative has manifested itself in the development of new methods of instruction, like those of the Sheffield Scientific School in the past, or the Department of Music in the present. The loyalty has been exemplified over and over again in the readiness to work for salaries even more conspicuously inadequate than those which have been paid at other universities, by men who seek their reward in the possibilities of future greatness. This history of disinterested effort for future rather than present reward has repeated itself in each department of instruction. The effect of the grouping of the students in separate departments has shown itself in the preservation of that *esprit de corps* which Yale has succeeded in maintaining, I believe, to a greater degree than any other university of the same magnitude.

On the other hand, the system has the disadvantages which everywhere pertains to a scheme of independent local government. There is sometimes a difficulty in carrying the whole university sharply forward into any definite line of policy, however strongly it may be demanded. There is yet more frequently a lack of coordination in courses; the work of each of the separate parts or schools having been originally devised with reference to the needs of members of that school, rather than to those of the university as a whole. And finally, there is a certain amount of duplication of appliances, which involves some actual loss of economy and makes the impression on the public of causing even more loss than really exists. Especially severe does this loss seem to some of the most zealous members of the professional schools, who believe that by combining the work of their opening years with that of the later years of the Academic Department of Sheffield Scientific School, they can serve the University and the cause of learning with far more fullness and freedom than at present.

Reform under these circumstances can only be the result of unconstrained negotiation. The best possibilities lie not in the exercise of authority but of diplomacy. The effort to impose a prearranged policy is likely to prove futile. We cannot insist on an external appearance of harmony without losing more than gain. To say that the Scientific School ought to have a four years' course because the Academic Department has one, or to insist that the Academic Department should withdraw from the teaching of natural science because the Scientific Schol has made such full provision for it, serves only to retard the movement toward cooperation, The president who would succeed in establishing real harmony must occupy himself first with providing the means to lead men to mutual understanding, rather than with predicting the results which should follow.

Foremost among the means which we must use is free and unreserved discussion of principles. Even within the departments, such discussion has been by no means so universal as it might have been. In more than one of them there has been a tendency, both in matters of administration and of educational policy, to rest content with a compromise between conflicting interests, rather than a reconciliation of conflicting views. A typical result of this policy is seen in the present course of study in the Academic Department, where the so-called elective system is really not a system at all, but the haphazard result of competition between the advocates of different lines of instruction——a thing which all unite in desiring to reform. With a reasonable degree of diplomacy and patience, the task of reform in cases like this should not prove a hard one.

Still less adequate has been the interchange of ideas between the different departments. Under the old system the several faculties have had no organized means of discussing subjects of common interest, or even of learning one another's views. The establishment of a university council for such interchange of thought is an imperative necessity. What will ultimately prove the best form and constitution for such a council can only be a matter of conjecture. For the present, at any rate, such a body is likely to be for the most part deliberative in its functions. Whatever else such a body may do or fail to do, it can prevent many of the misunderstandings and cross purposes which arise from imperfect information, and can thus contribute to the successful transaction of all business that is possible by preventing attempts at the impossible.

In the second place, we must so use those funds which are at the disposal of the central administration as to make it an object for men in the different departments to cooperate at those points where the absence of such cooperation does most harm.

As far as elementary teaching is concerned, the waste from having the same subject taught in two or more departments may be more apparent than real. It involves no very great loss to teach elementary chemistry in two independent sets of laboratories if both laboratories are always kept full of students. The waste comes in thus teaching advanced chemistry where there are relatively few students and where there is much need of specialization. Under such circumstances the existence of separate laboratories tends to prevent proper division of labor. Under such circumstances duplication is a waste and coordination a necessity. If the material appliances for higher education are not the property of any one department, but stand in relation to the university as a whole, the instructors of the different departments tend of their own free will to cooperate with one another in the higher instruction in their several branches. Under proper management, institutions like the Peabody Museum or the Winchester Observatory tend thus to systematize instruction at this point where such an effect is most needed. With a very moderate increase of endowment, properly applied, I believe that the same sort of harmony can be attained in many other lines of instruction. Among the achievements of my predecessor in office, there is none so wide-reaching in its effects as the development of a large university fund, which without threatening the independence of the several departments, can be used to provide means for promoting unity of action where such unity is indispensable.

In the English Universities the teaching is in large measure done by the several colleges, while the examinations are, with few exceptions, the affair of the university. It seems probable that the development of Yale in the future may be just the reverse of this; the several colleges taking charge of the examinations and of those more elementary studies whose control naturally connects itself with the control of examinations, while the distinctive teaching appliances come, to a constantly greater extent, into the hands of the university authorities. Under such a system we should have a well-ordered scheme of local government, where each department could make its own rules, prescribe the conditions of entrance and graduation and be subject to the minimum of interference from without; but where at the same time the instruction would be so ordered that students whose course lay under the control of one faculty could yet enjoy to the fullest possible extent the teaching provided by another, and where, as the subject of study became more and more advanced, the distinction of separate faculties or colleges would disappear altogether.

Such are, in brief outline a few of the problems which we have inherited from the past. It would be indeed a large burden had we not also inherited from that past an inspiration yet larger. Yale's seal bears the motto, 'Light and Truth;' Yale's history has been worthy of its signer. Never has there been wanting torch-bearers to take the light from the hands that relinquished it. In this place, hallowed by the deeds of our fathers, all words of formal acceptance of the duties which they have left us are meaningless. It is a God-given trust: may God bless the issue!

Inaugural Address

Princeton for the Nation's Service

by

WOODROW WILSON

President of Princeton University

October 25, 1902

WOODROW WILSON (December 28, 1856—February 3, 1924) was born in Staunton, Virginia. His family background was that of the Middle West, but his youth was spent in the South. He studied at Davidson College, the University of North Carolina, the University of Virginia, Princeton University, and Johns Hopkins University, from which institution he received the doctorate. Woodrow Wilson was elected President of Princeton from the Department of Political Science there. He had also taught at Bryn Mawr and at Wesleyan University. It is conceded by many that Wilson's greatest contribution to education was his emphasis upon scholarship and upon democracy in university administration.

Six years ago I had the honor of standing in this place to speak of the memories with which Princeton men heartened themselves as they looked back a century and a half to the founding of their college. To-day my task is more difficult, more delicate. Standing here in the light of those older days, we must now assess our present purposes and powers and sketch the creed by which we shall be willing to live in the days to come. We are but men of a single generation in the long life of an institution which will still be young when we are dead, but while we live her life is in us. What we conceive she conceives. In planning for Princeton, moreover, we are planning for the country. The service of institutions of learning is not private but public. It is plain what the nation needs as its affairs grow more and more complex and its interests begin to touch the ends of the earth. It needs efficient and enlightened men. The universities of the country must take part in supplying them.

American universities serve a free nation whose progress, whose power, whose prosperity, whose happiness, whose integrity depend upon individual initiative and the sound sense and equipment of the rank and file. Their history, moreover, has set them apart to a character and service of their own. They are not mere seminaries of scholars. They never can be. Most of them, the greatest of them and the most distinguished, were first of all great colleges before they became universities; and their task is two-fold; the production of a great body of informed and thoughtful men and the production of a small body of trained scholars and investigators. It is one of their functions to take large bodies of young men up to the places of outlook whence the world of thought and affairs is to be viewed; it is another of their functions to take some men, a little more mature, a little more studious, men self-selected by aptitude and industry, into the quiet libraries and laboratories where the close contacts of study are learned which yield the world new insight into the processes of nature, of reason, and of the human spirit. These two functions are not to be performed separately, but side by side, and are to be informed with one spirit, the spirit of enlightenment, a spirit of learning which is neither superficial nor pedantic, which values life more than it values the mere acquisitions of the mind.

Universities, we have learned to think, include within their scope, when complete, schools of law, of medicine, of theology, and of those more recondite mechanic arts, such as the use of electricity, upon which the skilled industry of the modern world is built up; and, though in dwelling upon such an association of schools as of the gist of the matter in our definitions of a university, we are relying upon historical accidents rather than upon essential principles for our conceptions, they are accidents which show the happy order and system with which things often come to pass. Though the university may dispense with professional schools, professional schools may not dispense with the university. Professional schools have nowhere their right atmosphere and association except where they are parts of a university and share its spirit and method. They must love learnings as well as professional success in order to have their perfect usefulness. This is not the verdict of the universities merely but of the professional men themselves, spoken out of hard experience of the facts of the business. It was but the other day that the Society for the Promotion of Engineering Education indorsed the opinion of their president, Mr. Eddy, that the crying need of the engineering profession was men whose technical knowledge and proficiency should rest upon a broad basis of general culture which should make them free of the wider worlds of learning and experience, which should give them largeness of views, judgment, and easy knowledge of men. The modern world nowhere shows a closeted profession shut in to a narrow round of technical functions to which no knowledge of the outside world need ever penetrate. Whatever our calling, our thoughts must often be afield among men of many kinds, amidst interests as various as the phases of modern life. The managing minds of the world, even the efficient working minds of the world, must be equipped for a mastery whose chief characteristic is adaptability, play, an initiative which transcends the bounds of mere technical training. Technical schools whose training is not built up on the foundation of a broad and general discipline cannot impart this. The stuff they work upon must be prepared for them by processes which produce fibre and elasticity, and their own methods must be shot through with the impulses of the university.

It is this that makes our age and our task so interesting: this complex inter-dependence and interrelationship of all the processes which prepare the mind for effectual service; this necessity that the merchant and the financier should have traveled minds, the engineer a knowledge of books and men, the lawyer a wide view of affairs, the physician a familiar acquaintance with the abstract data of science, and that the closeted scholar should throw his windows open to the four quarters of the world. Every considerable undertaking has come to be based on knowledge, on thoughtfulness, on the masterful handling of men and facts. The university must stand in the midst, where the roads of thought and knowledge interlace and cross, and, building upon some coign of vantage, command them all.

It has happened that throughout two long generations,—long because filled with industrial and social transformation of the world,—the thought of studious men has been bent upon devising methods by which special aptitudes could be developed, detailed investigations carried forward, inquiry broadened and deepened to meet the scientific needs of the age, knowledge extended and made various and yet exact by the minute and particular researches of men who devoted all the energies of their minds to a single task. And so we have gained much, though we have also lost much which must be recovered. We have gained immensely in knowledge but we have lost system. We have acquired an admirable, sober passion for accuracy. Our pulses have been quickened, moreover, by discovery. The world of learning has been transformed. No study has stood still. Scholars have won their fame, not by erudition, but by exploration, the conquest of new territory, the addition of infinite detail to the map of knowledge. And so we have gained a splendid proficiency in investigation. We know the right methods of advanced study. We have made exhaustive records of the questions waiting to be answered, the doubts waiting to be resolved, in every domain of inquiry; thousands of problems once unsolved, apparently insoluble, we have reduced to their elements and settled, and their answers have been added to the common places of knowledge. But, meanwhile, what of the preliminary training of specialists, what of the general foundations of knowledge, what of the general equipment of mind, which all men must have who are to serve this busy, this sophisticated generation?

Probably no one is to blame for the neglect of the general into which we have been led by our eager pursuit of the particular. Every age has lain under the reproach of doing but one thing at a time, of having some one signal object for the sake of which other things were slighted or ignored. But the plain fact is, that we have so spread and diversified the scheme of knowledge in our day that it has lost coherence. We have dropped the threads of system in our teaching. And system begins at the beginning. We must find the common term for college and university; and those who have great colleges at the heart of the universities they are trying to develop are under a special compulsion to find it. Learning is not divided. Its kingdom and government are centered, unitary, single. The processes of instruction which fit a large body of young men to serve their generation with powers released and fit for great tasks ought also to serve as the initial processes by which scholars and investigators are made. They ought to be but the first parts of the method by which the crude force of untrained men is reduced to the expert uses of civilization. There may come a day when general study will be no part of the function of a university, when it shall have been handed over, as some now talk of handing it over, to the secondary schools, after the German fashion; but that day will not be ours, and I for one, do not wish to see it come. The masters who guide the youngsters engaged in general studies are very useful neighbors for those who prosecute detailed inquiries and devote themselves to special tasks. No investigator can afford to keep his doors shut against the comradeships of the wide world of effort and of thought.

To have a great body of undergraduates crowding our class-rooms and setting the pace of our lives must always be a very wholesome thing. These young fellows, who do not mean to make finished scholars of themselves, but who do mean to learn from their elders, now at the outset of their lives, what the thoughts of the world have been and its processes of progress, in order that they may start with light about them, and not doubt or darkness, learning in the brief span of four years what it would else take them a half a lifetime to discover by mere contact with men, must teach us the real destiny with which knowledge came into the world. Its mission is enlightenment and edification, and these young gentlemen shall keep us in mind of this.

The age has hurried us, has shouldered us out of the old ways, has bidden us be moving and look to the cares of a practical generation; and we have suffered ourselves to be a little disconcerted. No doubt we were pedants. It is a happy thing that the days have gone by when the texts we studied loomed bigger to our view than the human spirit which underlay them. But there are some principles of which we must not let go. We must not lose sight of that fine conception of a general training which led our fathers, in the days when men knew how to build great states, to build great colleges also to sustain them. No man who knows the world has ever supposed that a day would come when every young man would seek a college training. The college is not for the majority who carry forward the common labor of the world, nor even for those who work at the skilled handicrafts which multiply the convenience and the luxuries of the complex modern life. It is for the minority who plan, who conceive, who superintend, who mediate between group and group, and who must see the wide stage as a whole. Democratic nations must be served in this wise no less than those whose leaders are chosen by birth and privilege; and the college is no less democratic because it is for those who play a special part. I know that there are men of genius who play these parts of captaincy and yet have never been in the classrooms of a college, whose only school has been the world itself. The world is an excellent school for those who have vision and self-discipline enough to use it. It works in this wise, in part, upon us all. Raw lads are made men by the mere sweep of their lives through the various school of experience. It is this very sweep of life that we wish to bring to the conciousness of young men by the shorter processes of the college. We have seen the adaptation take place; we have seen crude boys made fit in four years to become men of the world.

Every man who plays a leading or conceiving part in any affair, must somehow get this schooling of his spirit, this quickening and adaptation of his perceptions. He must either spread the process through his lifetime and get it by an extraordinary gift of insight and upon his own initiative, or else he must get it by the alchemy of mind practiced in college halls. We ought distinctly to set forth in our philosophy of this matter the difference between a man's preparation for the specific and definite tasks he is to perform in the world and that general enlargement of spirit and release of powers which he shall need if his task is not to crush and belittle him. When we insist that a certain general education shall precede all special training which is not merely mechanical in its scope and purpose, we mean simply that every mind needs for its highest serviceability a certain preliminary orientation, that it may get its bearings and release its perceptions for a wide and catholic view. We must deal in college with the spirits of men, not with their fortunes. Here, in history and philosophy and literature and science, are the experiences of the world summed up. These are but so many names which we give to the records of what men have done and thought and comprehended. If we be not pedants, if we be able to get at the spirit of the matter, we shall extract from them the edification and enlightenment as of those who have gone the long journey of experience with the race.

There are two ways of preparing a young man for his life work. One is to give him the skill and special knowledge which shall make a good tool, an excellent bread-winning tool, of him; and for thousands of young men that way must be followed. It is a good way. It is honorable. It is indispensable. But it is not for the college, and it never can be. The college should seek to make the men whom it receives something more than excellent servants of a trade or skilled practitioners of a profession. It should give them elasticity of faculty and breadth of vision, so that they shall have a surplus of mind to expend, not upon their profession only, for its liberalization and enlargement, but also upon the broader interests which lie about them, in the spheres in which they are to be, not bread-winners merely, but citizens as well, and in their own hearts, where they are to the stature of real nobility. It is this free capital of mind the world most stands in need of,—this free capital that awaits investment in undertakings, spiritual as well as material, which advance the race and help all men to a better life.

And are we to do this great thing by the old discipline of Greek, Latin, mathematics, and English? The day has gone by when that is possible. The circle of liberal studies is too much enlarged, the area of general learning is too much extended, to make it any longer possible to make these few things stand

71

for all. Science has opened a new world of learning, as great as the old. The influence of science has broadened and transformed old themes of study and created new, and all the boundaries of knowledge are altered. In the days of our grandfathers all learning was literary, was of the book; the phenomena of nature were brought together under the general terms of an encyclopaedic Natural Philosophy. Now the quiet rooms where once a few students sat agaze before a long table at which, with a little apparatus in front of him, a lecturer discoursed of the laws of matter and of force, are replaced by great laboratories, physical, chemical, biological, in which the pupil's own direct observation and experiment take the place of the cunning of mere theory and generalization, and men handle the immediate stuff of which nature is made. Museums of natural history, of geology, of paleontology, stretch themselves amidst our lecture rooms, for demonstration of what we say of the life and structure of the globe. The telescope, the spectroscope, not the text-book merely, are our means of teaching the laws and movements of the sky. An age of science has transmuted speculation into knowledge and doubled the dominion of the mind. Heavens and earth swing together in a new universe of knowledge. And so it is impossible that the old discipline should stand alone, to serve us as an education. With it alone we should get no introduction into the modern world either of thought or affairs. The mind of the modern student must be carried through a wide range of studies in which science shall have a place not less distinguished than that accorded literature, philosophy, or politics.

But we must observe proportion and remember what it is that we seek. We seek in our general education, not universal knowledge, but the opening up of the mind to a catholic appreciation of the best achievements of men and the best processes of thought since days of thought set in. We seek to appraise young men of what has been settled and made sure of, of the thinking that has been carried through and made an end of. We seek to set them securely forward at the point at which the mind of the race has definitely arrived, and save them the trouble of attempting the journey over again, so that they may know from the outset what relation their own thought and effort bear to what the world has already done. We speak of the "disciplinary" studies through which a boy is put in his school days and during the period of his introduction into the full privileges of college work, having in our thought the mathematics of arithmetic, elementary algebra, and geometry, the Greek and Latin texts and grammars, the elements of English and of French or German; but a better, truer name for them were to be desired. They are indeed disciplinary. The mind takes fibre, facility, strength, adaptibility, certainty of touch from handling them, when the teacher knows his art and their power. But they are disciplinary only because of their definiteness and their established method; and they take their determinateness from their age and perfection. It is their age and completeness that render them so serviceable and so suitable for the first processes of education. By their means the boy is informed of the bodies of knowledge which are not experimental but settled, definitive, fundamental. This is the stock upon which time out of mind all the thoughtful world has traded. These have been food of the mind for long generations.

It is in this view of the matter that we get an explanation of the fact that the classical languages of antiquity afford better discipline and are a more indispensable means of culture than any language of our own day except the language, the intimate language, of our own thought, which is for us universal coin of exchange in the intellectual world and must have its values determined to a nicety before we pay it out. No modern language is definitive, classically made up. Modern tongues, moreover, carry the modern babel of voices. The thoughts they utter fluctuate and change; the phrases they speak alter and are dissolved with every change of current in

73

modern thought or impulse. They have had, first or last, the same saturations of thought that our own language has had; they carry the same atmosphere; in traversing their pleasant territory, we see only different phases of our familiar world, the world of our own experience; and, valuable as it is to have this various view of the world we live in and send our minds upon travels up and down the modern age, it is not fundamental, it is not an indispensable first process of training. It can be postponed. The classical literatures give us, in tones and with an authentic accent we can nowhere else hear, the thoughts of an age we cannot visit. They contain airs of a time not our own, unlike our own, and yet its foster parent. To these things was the modern thinking world first bred. In them speaks a time naive, pagan, an early morning day when men looked upon the earth while it was fresh, untrodden by crowding thought, an age when the mind moved, as it were, without prepossessions and with an unsophisticated, childlike curiosity, a season apart during which those seats upon the Mediterranean seem the first seats of thoughtful men. We shall not anywhere else get a substitute for it. The modern mind has been built upon that culture and there is no authentic equivalent.

Drill in the mathematics stands in the same category with familiar knowledge of the thought and speech of classical antiquity, because in them also we get the lifelong accepted discipline of the race, the processes of pure reasoning which lie at once at the basis of science and at the basis of philosophy, grounded upon observation and physical fact and yet abstract and of the very stuff of the essential processes of the mind, a bridge between reason and nature. Here, too, as in the classics, a definitive body of knowledge and of reason, a discipline which has been made tests of through long generations, a method of thought which has in all ages steadied, perfected, enlarged, strengthened, and given precision to the powers of the mind. Mathematical drill is an introduction of the boy's mind to the most definitely settled rational experiences of the world.

I shall attempt no proof that English also is of the fundamental group of studies. You will not require me to argue that no man has been made free of the world of thought who does not know the literature, the idiomatic flavor, the discriminative and masterful use of his own tongue.

But, if we cannot doubt that these great studies are fundamental, neither can we doubt that the circle of fundamental studies has widened in our day and that education, even general education, has been extended to new boundaries. And that chiefly because science has had its credentials accepted as of the true patriciate of learning. It is as necessary that the lad should be inducted into the thinking of the modern time as it is that he should be carefully grounded in the old, accepted thought which has stood test from age to age; and the thought of the modern time is based upon science. It is only a question of choice in a vast field. Special developments of science, the parts which lie in controversy, the parts which are as yet but half built up by experiment and hypothesis, do not constitute the proper subject matter of general education. For that you need, in the field of science as in every other field, the bodies of knowledge which are most definitely determined and which are most fundamental. Undoubtedly the fundamental sciences are physics, chemistry, and biology. Physics and chemistry afford a systematic body of knowledge as abundant for instruction, as definitive almost, as mathematics itself; and biology, young as it is, has already supplied us with a scheme of physical life which lifts its study to the place of a distinctive discipline. These great bodies of knowledge claim their place at the foundation of liberal training not merely for our information, but because they afford us direct introduction into the most essential analytical and rational processes of scientific study, impart penetration, precision, candor, openness of mind, and afford the close contacts of concrete thinking. And there stand alongside of these geology and astronomy, whose part in general culture, aside from their connection with physics, mechanics, and chemistry, is to apply to the mind the stimulation which comes from being brought into the presence and in some sort into the comprehension of stupendous, systematized physical fact,—from seeing nature in the mass and system of her might and structure. These, too, are essential parts of the wide scheme which the college must plot out. And when we have added to these the manifold discipline of philosophy, the indispensable instructions of history, and the enlightenments of economic and political study, and to these the modern languages which are the tools of scholarship, we stand confused. How are we to marshal this host of studies within a common plan which shall not put the pupil out of breath?

No doubt we must make choice among them, and suffer the pupil himself to make choice. But the choice that we make must be the chief choice, the choice the pupil makes the subordinate choice. Since he cannot in the time at his disposal go the grand tour of accepted modern knowledge, we who have studied the geography of learning and who have observed several generation of men attempt the journey, must instruct him how in a brief space he may see most of the world, and he must choose only which one of several tours that we may map out he will take. Else there is no difference between young men and old, between the novice and the man of experience, in fundamental matters of choice. We must supply the synthesis and must see to it that, whatever group of studies the student selects, it shall at least represent the round whole, contain all the elements of modern knowledge, and be itself a complete circle of general subjects. Princeton can never have any uncertainty of view on that point.

And that not only because we conceive it to be our business to give a general, liberalizing, enlightening training to men who do not mean to go to any special work by which

76

they may make men of science or scholars of themselves or skilled practitioners of a learned profession, but also because we would create a right atmosphere for special study. Critics of education have recently given themselves great concern about over-specialization. The only specialists about whom, I think, the thoughtful critic need give himself serious anxiety are the specialists who have never had any general education in which to give their special studies wide rootage and nourishment. The true American university seems to me to get its best characteristics, its surest guarantee of sane and catholic learning, from the presence at its very heart of a college of liberal arts. Its vital union with the college gives it, it seems to me, the true university atmosphere, a pervading sense of the unity and unbroken circle of learning,—not so much because of the presence of a great body of undergraduates in search of general training (because until these youngsters get what they seek they create ideals more by their lack than by their achievement), as because of the presence of a great body of teachers whose life-work it is to find the general outlooks of knowledge and give vision of them every day from quiet rooms which, while they talk, shall seem to command all the prospects of the wide world.

I should dread to see those who guide special study and research altogether excused from undergraduate instruction, should dread to see them withdraw themselves altogether from the broad and general survey of the subjects of which they have sought to make themselves masters. I should equally despair of seeing any student made a truly serviceable specialist who had not turned to his specialty in the spirit of a broad and catholic learning,—unless, indeed, he were one of those rare spirits who once and again appear amongst us, whose peculiar, individual privilege it is to have safe vision of but a little segment of truth, and yet keep his poise and reason. It is not the education that concentrates that is to be dreaded, but the education that narrows,—that is narrow from the first. I should wish to see every student made, not a man of his task, but a man of the world, whatever his world may be. If it be the world of learning, then he should be a conscious and a broad-minded citizen of it. If it be the world of letters, his thought should run free upon the whole field of it. If it be the world of affairs, he should move amidst affairs like a man of thought. What we seek in education is full liberation of the faculties, and the man who has not some surplus of thought and energy to expend outside the narrow circle of his own task and interest is a dwarfed, uneducated man. We judge the range and excellence of every man's abilities by their play outside the task by which he earns his livelihood. Does he merely work, or does he also look abroad and plan? Does he, at the least, enlarge the things he handles? No task, rightly done, is truly private. It is part of the world's work. The subtle and yet universal connections of things are what the truly educated man, be he man of science, man of letters, or statesman, must keep always in his thought, if he would fit his work to the work of the world. His adjustment is as important as his energy.

We mean, so soon as our generous friends have arranged their private finances in such a way as to enable them to release for our use enough money for the purpose, to build a notable graduate college. I say "build" because it will be not only a college of teachers and students but also a college of residence, where men shall live together in the close and wholesome comradeships of learning. We shall build it, not apart, but as nearly as may be at the very heart, the geographical heart, of the university; and its comradeships shall be for young men and old, for the novice as well as for the graduate. It will constitute but a single term in the scheme of coordination which is our ideal. The windows of the graduate college must open straight upon the walks and quadrangles and lecture halls of the *studium generale*.

In our attempt to escape the pedantry and narrowness of

the old fixed curriculum we have, no doubt, gone so far as to be in danger of losing the old ideals. Our ultilitarianism has carried us so far afield that we are in a fair way to forget the real utilities of the mind. No doubt the old, purely literary training made too much of the development of mere taste, mere delicacy of perception, but our modern training makes too little. We pity the young child who, ere its physical life has come to maturity, is put to some task which will dwarf and narrow it into a mere mechanical tool. We know that it needs first its free years in the sunlight and fresh air, its irresponsible youth. And yet we do not hesitate to deny to the young mind its irresponsible years of mere development in the free air of general studies. We have too ignorantly served the spirit of the age,—have made no bold and sanguine attempt to instruct and lead it. Its call is for efficiency, but not for narrow, purblind efficiency. Surely no other age ever had tasks which made so shrewdly for the testing of the general powers of the mind. No sort of knowledge, no sort of training of the perceptions and the facility of the mind could come amiss to the modern man of affairs, or the modern student. A general awakening of the faculties, and then a close and careful adaptation to some special task is the programme of mere prudence for every man who would succeed.

And there are other things besides material success with which we must supply our generation. It must be supplied with men who care more for principles than for money, for the right adjustments of life than for the gross accumulations of profit. The problems that call for sober thoughtfulness and mere devotion are as pressing as those which call for practical efficiency. We are here not merely to release the faculties of men for their own use, but also to quicken their social understanding, instruct their consciences, and give them the catholic vision of those who know their just relations to their fellow men. Here in America, for every man touched with nobility, for every man touched with the spirit of our institutions, social service is the high law of duty, and every American university must square its standards by that law or lack its national title. It is serving the nation to give men the enlightments of a general training; it is serving the nation to equip fit men for thorough scientific investigation and for the tasks of exact scholarship, for science and scholarship carry the truth forward from generation to generation and give the certain touch of knowledge to the processes of life. But the whole service demanded is not rendered until something is added to the mere training of the undergraduate and the mere equipment of the investigator, something ideal and of the very spirit of all action. The final synthesis of learning is in philosophy. You shall most clearly judge the spirit of a university if you judge it by the philosophy it teaches; and the philosophy of conduct is what every wise man should wish to derive from his knowledge of the thoughts and the affairs of the generations that have gone before him. We are not put into this world to sit still and know; we are put into it to act.

It is true that in order to learn men must for a little while withdraw from action, must seek some quiet place or remove from the bustle of affairs, where their thoughts may run clear and tranquil, and the heats of business be for the time put off; but that cloistered refuge is no place to dream in. It is a place for the first conspectus of the mind, for a thoughtful poring upon the map of life; and the boundaries which should emerge to the mind's eye are not more the intellectual than the moral boundaries of thought and action. I do not see how any university can afford such an outlook if its teachings be not informed with the spirit of religion, and that the religion of Christ, with the energy of a positive faith. The argument for efficiency in education can have no permanent validity if the efficiency sought be not moral as well as intellectual. The ages of strong and definite moral impulse have been the ages of achievement; and the moral impulses which have lifted highest have come from Christian peoples,—the moving history of our nation were proof enough of that. Moral efficiency is, in the last analysis, the fundamental argument for liberal culture. A merely literary education, got out of books and old literatures, is a poor thing enough if the teacher stick at grammatical and syntactical drill; but if it be indeed an introduction into the thoughtful labors of men of all generations it may be made a prologue to the mind's emancipation; its emancipation from narrowness,—from narrowness of sympathy, of perception, of motive, of purpose, and of hope. And the deep fountains of Christian teaching are its most refreshing springs.

I have said already, let me say again, that in such a place as this we have charge, not of men's fortunes, but of their spirits. This is not the place in which to teach men their specific tasks, except their tasks be those of scholarship and investigation; it is the place in which to teach them the relations which all tasks bear to the work of the world. Some men there are who are condemned to learn only the technical skill by which they are to live; but these are not the men whose privilege it is to come to a university. University men ought to hold themselves bound to walk the upper roads of usefulness which run along the ridges and command views of the general fields of life. This is why I believe general training, with no particular occupation in view, to be the very heart and essence of university training, and the indispensible foundation of every special development of knowledge or of aptitude that is to lift a man to his profession or a scholar to his function of investigation.

I have studied the history of America; I have seen her grow great in the paths of liberty and of progress by following after great ideals. Every concrete thing that she has done has seemed to rise out of some abstract principle, some vision of the mind. Her greatest victories have been the victories of peace and of humanity. And in days quiet and troubled alike Princeton has stood for the nation's service, to produce men and patriots. Her national tradition began with John Witherspoon, the master, and James Madison, the pupil, and has not been broken until this day. I do not know what the friends of this sound and tested foundation may have in store to build upon it; but whatever they add shall be added in that spirit and with that conception of duty. There is no better way to build up learning and increase power. A new age is before us, in which it would seem, we must lead the world. No doubt we shall set it an example unprecedented not only in the magnitude and telling perfection of our industries and arts, but also in the splendid scale and studied detail of our university establishments; the spirit of the age will lift us to every great enterprise. But the ancient spirit of sound learning will also rule us; we shall demonstrate in our lecture rooms again and again, with increasing volume of proof, the old principles that have made us free and great; reading men shall read here the chastened thoughts that have kept us young and shall make us pure; the school of learning shall be the school of memory and of ideal hopes; and the men who spring from our loins shall take their lineage from the founders of the republic.

Inaugural Address

Scholarship and Service

by

NICHOLAS MURRAY BUTLER

President of Columbia University

April 19, 1902

NICHOLAS MURRAY BUTLER (1862 —1947) *was born in Elizabeth, New Jersey. He graduated from Columbia University from which institution he also received the doctorate. He studied in Berlin and Paris and was the recipient of honorary degrees from leading universities throughout the world. He was an active member in educational, political and civic affairs and held memberships in the leading organizations contributing to the improvement of these areas of culture. A man of rare charm, a distinguished scholar, world traveler, an executive of exceptional ability. A champion of world peace. In 1902, he became President of Columbia University, from which he retired in October, 1945.*

For these kindly and generous greetings I am profoundly grateful. To make adequate response to them is beyond my power. The words that have been spoken humble as well as inspire. They express a confidence and a hopefulness which it will tax human capacity to the utmost to justify, while they picture a possible future for this university which fires the imagination and stirs the soul. We may truthfully say of Columbia, as Daniel Webster said of Massachusetts, that her past, at least, is secure; and we look into the future with high hope and happy augury.

Today it would be pleasant to dwell upon the labors and the service of the splendid body of men and women, the university's teaching scholars, in whose keeping the honor and the glory of Columbia rest. Their learning, their devotion, and their skill call gratitude to the heart and words of praise to the lips. It would be pleasant, too, to think aloud of the procession of men which has gone out from Columbia's doors for well nigh a century and a half to serve God and the state; and of those younger ones who are even now lighting the lamps of their lives at the altar-fires of eternal truth. Equally pleasant would be to pause to tell those who labor with us—north, south, east, and west—and our nation's schools, higher and lower alike, how much they have taught us and by what bonds of affection and fellow service we are linked to them.

All these themes crowd the mind as we reflect upon the significance of the ideals which we are gathered to celebrate; for this is no personal function. The passing of position or power from one servant of the university to another is but an incident; the university itself is lasting, let us hope eternal. Its spirit and its life, its usefulness and its service, are the proper subject for our contemplation today.

The shifting panorama of the centuries reveals three separate and underlying forces which shape and direct the higher civilization. Two of these have a spiritual character, and one appears to be, in part, at least, economic, although clearer vision may one day show that they all spring from a common source. These three forces are the church, the state, and science, or better, scholarship. Many have been their interdependences and manifold their inter-twinings. Now one, now another seems uppermost. Charlemagne, Hildebrand, Darwin are central figures, each for his time. At one epoch these forces are in alliance, at another in opposition. Socrates died in prison, Bruno at the stake. Marcus Aurelius sat on an emperor's throne, and Thomas Aquinas ruled the mind of a universal church. All else is tributary to these three, and we grow in civilization as mankind comes to recognize the existence and the importance of each.

It is commonplace that in the earliest family community church and state were one. The patriarch was both ruler and priest. There was neither division of labor nor separation of function. When development took place, church and state, while substantially one, had distinct organs of expression. These often clashed, and the separation of the two principles was thereby hastened. As yet scholarship had hardly any representatives. When they did begin to appear, when science and philosophy took their rise, they were often prophets without honor either within or without their own country, and were either misunderstood or persecuted by church and state alike. But the time came when scholarship, truth-seeking for its own sake, had so far justified itself that both church and state united to give it permanent organization and a visible body. This organization and body was the university. For nearly ten centuries—a period longer than the history of parliamentary government or of Protestantism—the university has existed to embody the spirit of scholarship. Its arms have been extended to every science and to all letters. It has known periods of doubt, of weakness, and of obscurantism; but the spirit which gave it life has persisted and has overcome every obstacle. Today, in the opening century, the university proudly asserts itself in every civilized land, not least in our own, as the bearer of a tradition and the servant of an ideal without which life would be barren, and the two remaining principles which underlie civilization robbed of half their power. To destroy the university would be to turn back the hands upon the dial of history for centuries; to cripple it is to put shackles upon every forward movement that we prize—research, industry, commerce, the liberal and practical arts and sciences. To support and enhance it is to set free new and vitalizing energy in every field of human endeavor. Scholarship has shown the world that knowledge is convertible into comfort, prosperity, and success, as well as into new and higher types of social order and of spirituality. "Take fast hold of instruction," said the Wise Man; "let her not go: keep her; for she is thy life."

Man's conception of what is most worthy knowing and reflecting upon, of what may best compel his scholarly energies, has changed greatly with the years. His earliest impressions were of his own insignificance and of the stupendous powers and forces by which he was surrounded and ruled. The heavenly fires, the storm-cloud and the thunderbolt, the rush of waters and the change of seasons, all filled him with an awe which straightway saw in them manifestations of the superhuman and the divine. Man was absorbed in nature, a mythical and legendary nature to be sure, but still the nature out of which science was one day to arise. Then, at the call of Socrates, he turned his back on nature and sought to know himself; to learn the secrets of those mysterious and hidden processes by which he felt and thought and acted. The intellectual centre of gravity had passed from nature to man. From that day to this the goal of scholarship has been the understanding of both nature and man, the uniting of them in one scheme or plan of knowledge, and the explaining of them as the offspring of the omnipotent activity of a Creative Spirit, the Christian God. Slow and painful have been the steps toward the goal which to St. Augustine seemed so near at hand, but which has receded through the intervening centuries as the problems grew more complex and as the processes of inquiry became so refined that whole worlds of new and unsuspected facts revealed themselves. Scholars divided into two camps. The one would have ultimate and complete explanations at any cost; the other, overcome by the greatness of the undertaking, held that no explanation in a larger or general way was possible. The one camp bred socialism; the other narrow and helpless specialization.

At this point the modern university problem took its rise; and for over four hundred years the university has been striving to adjust its organization so that it may most effectively bend its energies to the solution of the problem as it is. For this purpose the university's scholars have unconsciously divided themselves into three types or classes: those who investigate and break new ground; and those who explain, apply, and make understandable the fruits of new investigation; and those philosophically minded teachers who relate the new to the old, and, without dogma or intolerance point to the lessons taught by the developing human spirit from its first blind gropings toward the light on the uplands of Asia or by the shores of the Mediterranean, through the insights of the world's great poets, artists, scientists, philosophers, statesmen, and priests, to its highly organized institutional and intellectual life of today. The purpose of scholarly activity requires for its accomplishment men of each of these three types. They are allies, not enemies; and happy the age, the people, or the university in which all three are well represented. It is for this reason that the university which does not strive to widen the boundaries of human knowledge, to tell the story of the new in terms that those familiar with the old can understand, and to put before its students a philosophical interpretation of historic civilization, is, I think, falling short of the demands which both society and university ideals themselves may fairly make.

A group of distinguished scholars in separate and narrow fields can no more constitute a university than a bundle of admirably developed nerves, without a brain and spinal cord, can produce all the activities of the human organism. It may be said, I think, of the unrelated and unexplained specialist, as Matthew Arnold said of the Puritan, that he is in great danger because he imagines himself in possession, of a rule telling him the unum necessarium, or one thing needful; that he then remains satisfied with a very crude conception of what this rule really is, and what it tells him; and in this dangerous state of assurance and self-satisfaction proceeds to give full swing to a number of the instincts of his ordinary self. And these instincts, since he is but human, are toward a general view of the world from the very narrow and isolated spot on which he stands. Only the largest and bravest spirits can become great specialists in scholarship and resist this instinctive tendency to hasty and crude philosophizing. The true scholar is one who has been brought to see the full meaning of the words development and history. He must, in other words, be a free man as Aristotle understood the term. The free man is he who has a largeness of view which is unmistakable and which permits him to see the other side; a knowledge of the course of man's intellectual history and its meaning; a grasp of principles and a standard for judging them; the power and habit of reflection firmly established; a fine feeling for moral and intellectual distinctions; and the kindliness of spirit and nobility of purpose which are the support of genuine character. On this foundation highly specialized knowledge is scholarship; on a foundation of mere skill, deftness, or erudition it is not. The university is concerned with the promotion of the true scholarship. It asks it in its scholars who teach; it inculcates it in its scholars who learn. It believes that the languages, the literatures, the art, the science, and the institutions of those historic peoples who have successively occupied the centre of the stage on which the great human drama is being acted out are full of significance for the world today; and it asks that those students who come to it to be led into special fields of inquiry, of professional study, or of practical application, shall have come to

89

know something of all this in an earlier period of general and liberal studies.

Emerson's oration before the oldest American society of scholars, made nearly sixty-five years ago, is the magnetic pole toward which all other discussions of scholarship must inevitably point. His superb apology for scholarship and for the scholar as Man Thinking opened an era in our nation's intellectual life. The scholar, as Emerson drew him, is not oppressed by nature or averse from it, for he knows it as the opposite of his soul, answering to it part for part. He is not weighed down by books or by the views which Cicero, which Locke, which Bacon have given, for he knows that they were young men like himself when they wrote their books and gave their views. He is not a recluse or unfit for practical work, because he knows that every opportunity for action passed by is a loss of power. The scholar, in short, as the university views him and aims to conserve and to produce him and his type, is a free man, thinking and acting in the light of the world's knowledge and guided by its highest ideals.

In this sense the university is the organ of scholarship, and in this sense it aims to be its embodiment. The place of scholarship has been long since won and is more widely recognized and acknowledged than ever before. The church and the state which first gave it independence are in close alliance with it and it with them. The three are uniting in the effort to produce a reverent, well-ordered, and thoughtful democratic civilization in which the eternal standards of righteousness and truth will increasingly prevail.

But a university is not for scholarship alone. In these modern days the university is not apart from the activities of the world, but in them and of them. It deals with real problems and it relates itself to life as it is. The university is for both scholarship and service; and herein lies that ethical quality which makes the university a real person, bound by its very nature to the service of others. To fulfill its high calling the university must give and give freely to its students, to the world of learning and of scholarship, to the development of trade, commerce, and industry, to the community in which it has its home, and to the state and nation whose foster-child it is. A university's capacity for service is the rightful measure of its importunity. The university's service is today far greater, far more expensive, and in ways far more numerous than ever before. It has only lately learned to serve, and hence it has only lately learned the possibilities that lie open before it. Every legitimate demand for guidance, for leadership, for expert knowledge, for trained skill, for personal service, it is the bounden duty of the university to meet. It may not urge that it is too busy accumulating stores of learning and teaching students. Serve it must, as well as accumulate and teach, upon pain of loss of moral power and impairment of usefulness. At every call it must show that it is:

"Strong for service still, and unimpaired."

The time-old troubles of town and gown are relics of an academic aloofness which was never desirable and which is no longer possible.

In order to prepare itself for efficient service the university must count in its ranks men competent to be the intellectual and spiritual leaders of the nation and competent to train others for leadership. Great personalities make great universities. And great personalities must be left free to grow and express themselves, each in his own way, if they are to reach a maximum of efficiency.

Spiritual life is subject neither to mathematical rule nor to chemical analysis. Rational freedom is the goal toward which the human spirit moves, slowly but irresistably, as the solar system toward a point in the constellation Hercules; and rational freedom is the best method for its movement. Morever, different subjects in the field of knowledge and its applications require different approach and different treatment. It is the business of the university to foster each and all. It gives its powerful support to the learned professions, whose traditional number has of late been added to by architecture, engineering, and teaching, all of which are closely interwoven with the welfares of the community. It urges forward its investigators in every department, and rewards their achievements with the academic laurel. It studies the conditions under which school and college education may best be given, and it takes active part in advancing them. In particular, it guards the priceless treasure of that liberal learning which I have described as underlying all true scholarship, and gives to it full-hearted care and protection. These are all acts of service direct and powerful.

The university does still more. It lends its members for expert and helpful service to nation, state, and city. University men are rapidly mobilized for diplomatic service, for the negotiation of important treaties, for the administration of dependencies, for special and confidential service to the government, or some department of it, and, the task done, they return quietly to the ranks of teaching scholars, as the soldiers in the armies of the war between the States went back to civil life without delay or friction. These same university men are found foremost in the ranks of good citizenship everywhere and as laymen in the service of the church. They carry hither and yon their practical idealism, their disciplined minds, and their full information, and no human interest is without their helpful and supporting strength. It is in ways like these that the university has shown, a thousand times, that sound theory and correct practice are two sides of a shield. A theorist is one who sees, and the practical man must be in touch with theory if he is to see what it is that he does.

What the future development of the great universities is to be perhaps no one can foresee. But this much is certain: Every city which, because of its size or wealth or position, aims to be a centre of enlightenment and a true world-capital must be the home of a great university. Here students and teachers will throng by the mere force of intellectual gravitation, and here service will abound from the mere host of opportunities. The city, not in its corporate capacity but as a spiritual entity, will be the main support of the university, and the university in turn will be the chief servant of the city's higher life. True citizens will vie with each other in strengthening the university for scholarship and for service. In doing so they can say, with Horace, that they have builded themselves monuments more lasting than bronze and loftier than the pyramids reared by kings, monuments which neither flood nor storm nor the long flight of years can overturn or destroy. Sir John de Balliol, doing a penance fixed by the abbot of Durham; Walter de Merton, making over his manor house and estates to secure to the others the advantages which he himself had enjoyed; John Harvard, leaving half his property and his library to the infant college by the Charles, and Elihu Yale, giving money and his books to the collegiate school in New Haven, have written their names on the roll of the immortals and have conferred untold benefits upon the human race. Who were their wealthy, powerful, and high-born contemporaries? Where are they in the grateful esteem of the generations that have come after them? What service have they made possible? What now avails their wealth, their power, their high birth? Balliol, Merton, Harvard, Yale are names known wherever the English language is spoken and beyond. They signify high purpose, zeal for learning, opposition to philistinism and ignorance. They are closely interwoven with the social, the religious, the political, the literary history of our race. Where else are there monuments such as theirs?

Scholarship and service are the true university's ideal. The university of today is not the "home of lost causes, and forsaken beliefs, and unpopular names, and impossible loyalties." It keeps step with the march of progress, widens its sympathies with growing knowledge, and among a democratic people seeks only to instruct, to uplift, and to serve, in order that the cause of religion and learning, and of human freedom and opportunity, may be continually advanced from century to century and from age to age.

Inaugural Address

by

WILLIAM PEPPER

President of the University of Pennsylvania

February 22, 1881

WILLIAM PEPPER (*August* 21, 1843 —*July* 28, 1898) *was born in Philadelphia, of a line of educators. His father occupied a chair of medicine which William Pepper held later. He received his early education in Philadelphia and in 1864 graduated from the University of Pennsylvania. In 1873, he married Frances Sergeant Perry, the great-granddaughter of Benjamin Franklin.*

It was largely through the efforts of Dr. Pepper that, in 1874, the first hospital in America was founded in which the faculty combined theory and practice. With the assistance of President Eliot of Harvard and others, Dr. Pepper led a reform for medical education in the United States.

It is according to time-honored custom, that, having received the keys of my office as Provost of the University of Pennsylvania, I am now permitted to address you as the official representative of this venerable Institution. It is, indeed, a custom sanctioned as well by illustrious precedent as by its apparent fitness, since it may reasonably be assumed that, under ordinary circumstances, the tenure of office of each Provost or President marks in the history of a university an epoch, characterized more or less strongly by the individual qualities of the man, and embracing the origin of important movements and the development or modification of plans already in operation. No opportunity can be found, therefore, so well fitted for submitting to the graduates and friends of a university a statement of its recent progress and of the measures contemplated for its future advancement, as that on which he, to whom has been intrusted the task of directing this development in accordance with the spirit and traditions of the past history of the Institution, first appears as its official representative. Such a statement should not be expected to contain matters of a startling or novel character. Just as the life-power of a great institution, with its hoarded wealth of the devotion of those who have faithfully served it and generously supported it; of the piety, wisdom, and learning of the teachers who have adorned it; of the achievements of its sons who have illustrated it, exceeds that of any individual, so much the more necessary is it that its life-history shall be one of natural and progressive development. Within certain wide limits the greatest activity and expansion are desirable, it is essential that there shall be a true continuous progress, and not a series of abrupt, violent, and ill-combined movements, inspired by caprice or uncontrollable restlessness.

In all vigorous organizations destined to perfect development, there are, however, occasional periods of extraordinary change and activity, when growth is rapid and when new and varied powers display themselves. This is true no less of nations and of great institutions than it is of individuals. Through such a period of rare developmental activity has the University of Pennsylvania been passing during the last decade: and the changes that have occurred in that time as affecting the condition of the various departments; the organization of the corporation; the relations of the University to the community; and the claims that it may fairly make upon its graduates and upon all friends of higher education, are so great as to demand our careful consideration. One who can recall the contracted space containing the modest University buildings of ten years ago need but turn to the new grounds, comparatively ample but still inadequate, where stand the group of spacious halls erected since that date, to appreciate what the development of the various departments has been. Even to enumerate the important advances that have been made in the educational system and position of the University would occupy too much space.

The methods of study in the Academic Department have been improved and its resources greatly strengthened; and since the adoption of the elective system to as great an extent as the policy of this University regards as desirable, it offers such advantages as must ensure it constantly increasing success.

The Towne Scientific School, endowed by the princely munificence of its founder, has attained such completeness of organization, and such abundant facilities in most branches of technical education, as fairly to entitle it to the prominent position it has rapidly acquired.

The Department of Medicine, freed from the trammels of an effete system, has strengthened its claim to be the foremost, as it is the oldest and most celebrated, of the Medical Schools of America.

The Law School, animated by an active and progressive spirit, has exhibited such gratifying evidences of its powers and capacity, and has gained in reputation so rapidly, as to justify the brightest hopes for its future.

98

While these older departments of the University have thus advanced, the new School of Music has acquired a creditable position; and the Department of Dentistry has at once assumed a leading position among the schools where this important branch of professional education is pursued.

The total number of students in attendance at the University has increased from 575 in 1870 to 969 in 1881, a gain of 60 per cent.; the number of professors has increased from 31 to 44 in the same time; and, to indicate the extent to which practical instruction has been introduced, the number of demonstrators has advanced from 2 to 25.

It is impossible to pass from this hasty summary of the advances in the strength and organization of the various departments of the University without pausing to pay a tribute of hearty admiration to the leader in this onward movement, to whose sustained enthusiasm and ceaseless energy its success is largely due. The task of inaugurating extensive changes in a long-established institution; of arousing widespread interest and zeal at a time when they had flagged; of organizing a complicated and yet thoroughly practical system of education in two of the most important departments of the University; of collecting a corps of highly competent teachers, imbued with earnestness and lofty aims similar to his own; of winning the confidence of the community, the cordial co-operation of his colleagues, and the respect and affection of the students;—this task was, indeed, one requiring rare qualities as an organizer, a leader, a teacher, and a man. As an alumnus of the University; as a teacher in one of its departments during the period referred to; and now as the representative of the Board of Trustees,—I can testify to the general feeling of admiration for the work done, and for him who bore so large a share of the burden. Well for our beloved University was it that at such a crisis in her history so able and devoted a leader was found. The good work he has done will long survive his departure from his official position; and when, in the distant future, the historian of this University shall record the services of those who have most contributed to her proud position, among the foremost must stand the name of Charles Janeway Stillé.

No less important changes have meantime taken place in the internal organization of the University; some of which are of such recent occurrence that, even before this audience, I may be pardoned for alluding to them.

The Board of Trustees, in which the corporate rights of the University are vested, owes its present composition to an Act of Assembly passed Sept. 30, 1791, which provided that the Board should consist of twenty-four members, with the Governor of Pennsylvania, for the time being; and that the Governor should be President.* For many years past, circumstances have prevented the Governors of Pennsylvania from occupying their official position in connection with the Board and the University. The link between the University and the State has thus been but little recognized; and yet it seems to me most important that it should again become a real and vital one. There is no question of the State interference or control, since the authority of the University is clearly defined and independent; but, on the other hand, the association that is implied by the fact that the Governor for the time being is President of the Board of Trustees of the University, shows that from the beginning this was designed to be, not a local institution of this city, but truly the University of Pennsylvania, the great central representative institution of a great and populous State. I must regard it as of good omen that, on this occasion, the highest function of the Governor in his official connection with the University has been performed in person; and by one whose scholarly attainments are no less conspicuous than are his public character and position.

* *The seat of State Government was transferred to Harrisburg in* 1812.

100

As time advances, the advantage of a large Board of Trustees becomes, and will become, more and more evident. It makes it more probable that a broad, catholic, and non-sectarian spirit will always animate the administration of the University. It renders it possible to secure the services of men, eminent in every walk of life, who may bring to the study of the questions that arise in the various departments the special skill and knowledge of experts, combined with sound practical judgment and general culture. Such a corporation will never be unduly controlled by the views or personal influence of any one man; and its slowly changing composition ensures a settled and abiding policy, faithful to tradition, and yet steadily progressive. Large as its numbers are, the duties developing on the members are onerous and responsible, and from the earliest days of the University to the present time they have been discharged, by successive generations of eminent citizens, with scrupulous fidelity and with singular devotion.

As regards the relations of the Faculties to the corporation, important and salutary changes have been made the past decade. It is of course impossible that in the various departments of a great University, an exact similarity shall exist in such points as the character of preliminary examinations, the mode of arranging and grading studies, the duration of the course of study; but it is vitally important that, in all that concerns its internal organization, and the relations of its Faculties to each other, to the Board of Trustees, and to the students, the greatest uniformity shall prevail; so that each department shall regard itself chiefly as a component part of the entire University. Without this, it is impossible for a vigorous and genuine University spirit to be maintained, pervading alike Faculties and students.

Equally essential is it that, as regards the special interests of each department, the greatest possible power and authority should be lodged in the hands of the respective Faculties. There can be no healthy or sustained activity on the part of any

101

public officials unless they are actuated by a high sense of their individual responsibility. There can be no intelligent sense of responsibility unless it is based upon the feeling that there has been conferred the power necessary for the successful discharge of duty. There can, therefore, be no question as to the wisdom of the recent amendments to the statutes of the University (January, 1881), which delegate to the Faculties of each department the administration of discipline; the approval of all requisitions for supplies; the decision as to applications for free scholarships; the care and supervision of the buildings and grounds; and the control of all employes. The Dean of each Faculty becomes the executive officer of that Department, and the practical autonomy of the Faculties is established. There will inevitably arise, under the continued discharge of these enlarged duties, a keener sense of individual interest in the welfare and progress of each department.

Spacious halls, rich collections and libraries, and munificent endowments are necessary adjuncts to a great University; but they do not and cannot render a University great. This can be done solely by the work of its teachers; by their learning; by their zeal and ability in teaching; by their personal influence over their students; and by their wider influence over the intellectual life of the surrounding community. No services rendered to a people can exceed in value those of the successful educators of its youth; and for services so responsible, so difficult, and demanding such rare qualifications, no honors or rewards would be excessive. Yet it would almost appear that the people imagine that these exceptional and valuable men are to be secured in any number, and for salaries barely adequate to support a decent existence.

The love of knowledge and culture for their own sake, and the fascination of teaching, do indeed lead many a man of the highest ability to neglect the lucrative occupations of life and to devote himself for long years to intense study and to the art of teaching. But the purest zeal might well grow languid, after years of labor, with no more adequate reward than the cheap title of Professor, and a salary—small in comparison with that of many salesmen—and pitiful in comparison with that of the officials of other large corporations.

I would not imply that the spirit actuating earnest teachers is often a mercenary one. Probably no more disinterested body of men exists in any community. But I would urge the wisdom and policy of securing only the best and most energetic men, of paying them liberally for their whole time and strength, and then of enlarging their duties and opportunities of teaching so as to develop and utilize their full powers. When this is done, let a community exact from those to whom is entrusted the education of its youth—from the lowest to the highest stage—the very best work; let them insist by the irresistible force of an enlightened and cultured public opinion that they who are set in the high places of learning shall be the most thoroughly fitted for their posts; the exaction will be cheerfully met, and the criticism be gladly borne, if at the same time the hands and hearts of the teachers be strengthened by the cordial appreciation of a community—competent to criticize because itself aiming at a high standard of culture, and authorized to exact because willing to reward liberally.

In no one particular are the changes concerning the Faculties of the University more important in establishing the eminently proper and necessary rule that each Faculty shall administer its own discipline. It is a matter that closely concerns the entire community, that the students of this University, already numbering nearly one thousand, shall learn thoroughly the various subjects to which they apply themselves. But it is also a matter of the greatest moment that they shall acquire, during their University life, due development of character, and a manly tone, self-reliant and vigorous, but yet deeply tinged with respect for law and for the rights of others. To know that the administration of discipline is tardy and indirect, and that an appeal may be made from the sentence imposed by a pro-

103

fessor or a Faculty to a Provost, or to any other authority, is directly provocative of insubordination; while the mere fact that the Professor or Faculty whose rules are infringed has full and conclusive authority to deal properly with such infractions, is a most potent guarantee against disorder.

But, after all, it is not to elaborate rules of discipline that we are to look for the prevention of truly reprehensible acts. The best safeguard against these is the cultivation of a high-toned University feeling, aided by the silent influence of the Christian spirit that pervades our Institution. Its organization has now reached a point where it is impossible for the students of one department to regard those of the other departments in any light save as comrades and members of the same college. All must feel themselves equally bound to protect her reputation, and to govern themselves by the best traditions of University life.

If, in the larger world outside, no force influences men so powerfully as that of public opinion, it should be the case in the lesser world of a University that the sustained sentiment of Class after Class against mean, ungentlemanly, or outrageous actions should render their repetition practically impossible. The passage, year after year, of a body of young men imbued with such feelings, as well as with a reasonable regard for intellectual pursuits, from the universities into the general community, must exert a constantly increasing and most beneficial influence upon the tone of society and of public life.

Such changes in the powers and duties of the various Faculties have at once made possible and necessitated important changes in the functions and position of the Provost, who is the official head of the University. Owing to peculiarities in its origin and development, his relations were with the undergraduate department alone, until within a few years past, when the Provost was declared the President of each Faculty, and was invited to a seat at the meetings of the Board of Trustees. Still, while this was an important step in the coordination of the various departments of the University, it added little to the real power of the Provost, or to his ability to influence the general policy of the Institution. At the same time, the addition of new departments, the erection of new and important buildings, the large increase in the corps of professors and instructors, and in the number of students, rendered it utterly impossible for any man to attend to the infinitude of details that formerly came under the Provost's supervision. But even if possible, such concentration of his time and attention upon matters of mere detail would of necessity divert him from those larger interests of the University which his peculiar official position would enable him to advance most successfully.

The recent amendments to the Statutes have finally placed the Provost in his natural relation to the entire Institution. The charter of the University* renders it impossible for him to be a regular member of the Board of Trustees; and after very careful reflection upon the advantages to be derived in this and in other directions from modifications in this charter, it has been generally conceded that they are overbalanced by the possible disadvantages involved in an application to the State Legislature, and an abandonment of the present independent position of the University. The same object has, however, been accomplished practically by declaring the Provost to be the President pro tempore of the Board of Trustees, with the power of appointing its committees.* Allusion has already been made to the enlarged duties and functions of the several Faculties, by which the organization of each department is rendered uniform and complete, and by which the Provost is for the future relieved from very much of the detail work that form-

* *Act of Nov. 27, 1779, Sec. 10, "Provided always, that if any trustee of the said University shall take any charge or office under the said trustees other than that of treasurer, his place shall be thereby vacated."*

* *Excepting the Committee on Ways and Means.*

105

erly devolved upon him. Not that this change of system has lessened his control over the working of each department, or his power of supervising and estimating the results of the work of each professor and of each student. On the contrary, it has for the first time rendered it possible for him to exert his proper influence; and by the establishment of a thorough system of reports from the various departments to secure an accuracy and scope of information unattainable while he was hampered with the details of discipline and of routine administration. It has always been thought desirable, though not essential, that the Provost should hold a chair in one of the departments, so that his practical experience as a teacher should be maintained; and if now, for the first time in the history of the University a teacher has been selected from the Medical Department to fill the position of Provost, it must be felt that the choice has been largely influenced by the brilliant record of that department, and by the admirable results that are attending its efforts in the cause of higher medical education.

The growth of the University during the past decade has been, it is true, highly satisfactory; but it is evident that, with the ample facilities now provided, and with the large opportunities that present themselves, there remains a far larger degree of activity to be attained. I prefer in the first place to address myself to the undergraduate department. Important as the professional schools are in the general scheme of the University, it is largely by the numbers and standing of its undergraduates that its strength must be judged. Their numbers have increased from 183 in 1870 to 283 in 1880, a gain of 65 per cent; but even this latter figure is far too small when the vast population of this city and State is borne in mind. I am confident that I am within the bounds of moderation when I say that, if this community were fully alive to the great practical benefits of a university education, and were fully aware of the advantages now offered by the University of Pennsylvania, the number of students in the undergraduate department alone would speedily reach 1000.

There is, I am well aware, a widespread feeling that a university course is not the best preparation for a business life; and as the great majority of the young men of Pennsylvania and the adjoining States are destined for such pursuits, it is notorious that a remarkably low proportion of them are sent to college. When a boy had no choice offered him but to follow the time-honored classical course at the University, it may have seemed that his acquirements would not assist him materially in a business career. With the introduction of many new subjects into the curriculum, the adoption of the elective system of studies, and the development of more direct, forcible, and practical methods of instruction, this objection became much less valid; and when, in 1875, the Towne Scientific School was established, such large facilities were offered for studies directly bearing on practical life that it was deprived of much of its remaining force. A striking proof of this is shown in the fact that while the students in the Department of Arts increased from 123 in 1870 to 142 in 1880, those in the Scientific School increased from 60 to 141 during the same period. There is reason to believe, however, that there is still demand, not merely a freedom of election between classical and scientific studies, but a complete course of study specially adapted for those who are destined for business or commercial life; and among the projects that will receive the careful consideration of the University authorities is one looking toward the establishment of a new department for this purpose.

But it has always seemed to me that this objection implies a mistaken view as to what really contributes most to a young man's success in life. Certainly the measure of his success is not to be the age at which he can earn enough to support himself. What if, in the eager haste to get an early start on the road to wealth, that development of character and that training of the mental powers which will be needed to grasp success when it offers itself have been forfeited? What if, when in the prime of life, the successful man, sated with the mere accumulation of wealth, finds his spirit restless and unhappy within him, and craves those cultured tastes that may no longer be acquired? We all admire success, and respect successful men; but it has been my lot to see so many instances where material success, secured by fierce driving activity from the earliest age without the counterpoise of careful mental training and sustained interest in intellectual pursuits, has brought with it unhappiness and mental disease, that I have been led to believe that there is no better preparation for a successful and happy life than a well-selected course at some large university.

I am aware, also, that there is a strong feeling on the part of many persons that a large city is not the best site for a great university. It is often asserted that it is necessary that the University shall be the main feature in the life of the otherwise insignificant place where it is situated; and historical precedents, such as those of Oxford and Cambridge, and some of the German Universities, are cited in support of the assertion. The facts of the case would seem to show, however, that this view is not a just one. I should rather infer from them that while a university may grow to be great and powerful in a small place, a great university in the midst of a great city will have many advantages over it. It is easy, of course, to mention illustrious cases in proof of this, as that of the universities of Paris, of Berlin, of Vienna, of Strasburg, of Leipsic; but it is more to our purpose to consider this question as it affects the interests of our universities in this country. An admirable classical and literary department may thrive anywhere that great teachers and good libraries are collected, but this is not so with the other departments of a University. When we consider the professional schools, the advantages of the great city are, of course, incontestable; but in any department, as soon as studies that bear on practical life are begun, it is desirable that the student shall have access to a sort of instruction that may be styled illustrative.

Look, for instance, at the unrivalled opportunities offered by Philadelphia to students in the Towne Scientific School, who are enabled to visit, study, and report on the vast and varied industrial establishments here maintained. It is impossible to supply, by any laboratory or museum, the practical advantages that may thus be secured.

The Law School can secure the services of the most eminent judges and lawyers whom it would be impossible to draw by a tenfold salary from the bench or bar to occupy the position of Professor in a provincial university.

Many of the teachers in the Medical Department must be active practitioners of medicine or surgery, with a familiarity with every form of disease and injury that can come only from daily work in the hospital and the crowded consultation-room. The laboratories where the student of medicine gains the most practical and important part of his education are the hospital wards where he is trained in the rudiments of his art, and the clinical amphi-theatre where he sees the best results that medical skill, aided by good nursing and all helpful appliances, can secure in its hard battle with disease.

If, indeed, we consider the numerous departments that are comprised in our idea of a University, it would seem impossible that it should be located elsewhere than in a large city.

It is, however, especially against the location of the undergraduate department in a large city that these objections are entertained; and as this is a matter of vital moment to our University, I may be pardoned for considering it in some detail, and especially with reference to the youth of our own city and State. It may be felt, for instance, that a student going to a distant university, and to one not in a large city, would have greater opportunities of becoming acquainted with students from other sections of the country, and thus of acquiring a wider knowledge of men, with the benefits that result from such intercourse.

It is not sufficiently appreciated, I think, that the University of Pennsylvania is truly a national institution, when all of its departments are taken into consideration together. Of the students now entered on its rolls, there are 873 from the Middle States (of whom 728 are from Pennsylvania); 26 from the Eastern States; 48 from the Southern States; 39 from the Western States; and 56 from foreign countries. What we need, therefore, in order to secure the fullest advantages of the intercourse of our young men with those of other sections, is not so much larger numbers, or greater variety of nativity, as it is a better university organization, and more adequate opportunities for communication between the classes of the different departments.

It is manifestly the duty of the Provost, as it certainly will be one of his pleasures, to do all in his power to promote these closer relations of a personal and social character among the university students.

Again, there are many who believe that it adds greatly both to the pleasure and benefits of a university life, as tending to create and perpetuate a stronger college spirit, that the students should, as far as possible, reside in dormitories. There seems, however, to be much to say on both sides of this question. Undoubtedly, in small towns,where the accomodations are limited and inferior, it must always be necessary to have extensive dormitories to accomodate any large number of resident students. But whether they are necessary when a university is located in a great city is a matter still under discussion. If it be found desirable to provide such halls, in order to attract and accomodate greatly increased numbers of students from a distance, it is certain that the University of Pennsylvania shall not long be wanting in this respect. But for the present it seems best to call attention strongly to the peculiar advantages which Philadelphia offers for the accomodation of students of every age from other localities. This city is essentially a city of homes; and all over its extent, and especially in the neighborhood of the University, are numerous private boarding-houses, well built and well kept. In order to test whether such exceptionally good accomodations may not be made to supply all that is elsewhere secured by dormitories, it is contemplated to form official lists of such boarding-houses as are worthy of the approval of the University, and of parents careful of the well-being of their sons. It may be questioned whether the moral tone, the healthfulness, and the economy secured by such an arrangement will not compare favorably with the conditions provided elsewhere.

The period of life between fifteen and twenty-two years, which embraces the ages of most students in the various departments of American universities, is undoubtedly a critical one.

Few, who recall honestly their own past, would not be fain to screen their sons from the trials to which they were then subjected; and I know well that many fear that, on the contrary, the life of a college student in a large city is one peculiarly full of temptation. I am convinced that these dangers have been greatly overestimated. It is true that many boys who go to college develop bad properties and habits; and we often hear such instances quoted as evidence of the injurious influence of college life. Who can determine what character those same boys would have displayed, what vices they would have contracted, had they been kept sedulously in the narrow limits of their villages, or, if city-born, had been educated in the strictest isolation? Nay, rather, who can tell in how many instances the development of ruinous habits or defects of character has not been averted by the healthful influence of that free intercourse with manly young fellows that college life ensures? Those who assert that boys educated in large cities are more disposed to be immoral, might well be more guarded in their assertions, if, like some of us, they were obliged to look into the inner life of those who have possibly never met their temptations, but who certainly have never enjoyed their advantages.

In one other important respect, indeed, the Christian influence exerted in a city may be rendered most valuable. No matter to what religious denomination a student may incline or belong, he will find its teachings fitly and eloquently represented. At a University in any small centre, there is a strong tendency for the religious element to acquire a narrow sectarian character. Even for those students who sympathize with this, it is a doubtful good as compared with the larger range of religious teachings furnished by the churches of the same denomination in a great city; but for all others it is an undoubted disadvantage. The strongly religious and the strictly non-sectarian character of the University of Pennsylvania has been its most distinctive feature from its foundation. The early Acts of incorporation clearly establish the fundamental principle that, while it was hoped the University, "through the blessing of Almighty God, would prove a nursery of wisdom and virtue, and be the means of raising up men of dispositions and qualifications beneficial to the public, in the various occupations of life," yet no religious body whatsoever should have any prejudice shown against it. Throughout its history, and never more truly than at the present time, the composition of the Board of Trustees and of the various Faculties, as well as character of the religious instruction given at the University, has maintained a broad and catholic spirit, untinged by the slightest prejudice or exclusiveness.

It seems impossible for any school which intends at the present time to exert its full influence in the intellectual life of the community to neglect the subject of the higher education of women. I do not refer to any such question as that of opening the University classes to young women, because I regard it as settled beyond dispute that the co-education of the sexes is inadmissable. The University has recently been making cautious advances in this direction, and persons of both sexes are now admitted to certain lectures and laboratory work. It may be that this comprises as much as is safe or desirable to be done in this particular direction; and as the special function of the University is not the education of women, it seems proper that further action should await the expression of some carefully matured wishes or plans on the part of those who may be assumed to represent the interests of women in this matter. It is evident, however, that some more definite provision is needed than now exists, to carry the education of women beyond the point generally attainable at present. The difficulty has been in part met by the establishment of special colleges, such as Vassar, Wellesley, Smith, or Taylor;* and recently by the system of Private Collegiate Instruction for Women, in Cambridge; but other arrangements than these are required to provide the necessary facilities for the large number of women who desire thorough and advanced education. This University will gladly witness and cooperate with all earnest efforts to secure such facilities. It recognizes the urgent need of Philadelphia, as of every other great city, in this direction; it realizes strongly the good that would follow from a more general diffusion of higher culture and increased activity in intellectual pursuits among our women; and the powerful influence which would be reflected upon its own future prosperity. There should be accessible, not only to those who desire to become teachers, or to those who are able or willing to take up their residence at a special college, but to all women who exhibit

*It has been decided that this Institution (founded by the late Dr. Joseph W. Taylor, of Burlington, N. J., who bequeathed $900,000 for the purpose) shall be known as the Bryn Mawr College. It is to be located near Bryn Mawr Station, on the line of the Pennsylvania Railroad.

the proper qualifications, a course of education in many respects the same as the usual University curriculum, in certain particulars different, but of equal excellence and thoroughness. Proficiency should be tested by rigid examinations, and satisfactory attainments should receive suitable certificates. The demand for such facilities is great and is constantly becoming more generally recognized. The particular arrangements for securing this object may vary in different places. If true to her traditions, Philadelphia will certainly assume a leading position in the movement; and while this University cannot take the initiative, it will watch with the deepest interest, and be ready to assist as far as possible, all well-considered efforts toward this end.

If the future of this University is to be worthy of its past, and of the wide opportunities that are offered to it, it must be largely through the cooperation and support of its graduates. I have no fear of being contradicted when I assert that, in spite of many notable exceptions, the general interest they have heretofore taken in the welfare of their Alma Mater has not been a consuming one. This is not true when we consider the work of the Alumni Societies of special departments. The deepest and most active interest, and a large liberality, have been frequently displayed. But this has been at special times and for special objects; while what is needed is, that there shall be a vigorous organization of the graduates of all the departments, and that the general prosperity of the whole University — which requires incessant care, because its needs are changing and enlarging incessantly — shall be the object of their constant and zealous concern.

This seems to me to be the greatest of all our needs today. The internal organization and the educational facilities of the University are, in most respects, all that can be desired; but we need more active and universal cooperation among her graduates, so that the entire community may be led to know and appreciate her true position. But if the Alumni are asked to thus unite in earnest support of the University, and to assist her now that her enlarged field of operations requires even more active support than ever before, it seems just and fitting that their connection with the University, and their interest in her affairs, shall not remain a matter of sentiment alone.

They are, it seems to me, entitled to the fullest information in regard to her real position, plans, and requirements, and, as far as may be practicable, to a share in the control of her affairs. The simplest mode of accomplishing this would seem to be by giving to the united Alumni of all the departments a definite representation in the Board of Trustees. How far this may be practicable under the restrictions of the Charter of the University is a question requiring careful consideration; but if no insuperable obstacles present themselves, I am convinced that the true interest of the University would be promoted by such an arrangement. There is, moreover, another way by which the Alumni could be admitted to a real and valuable share in the supervision of the University. I allude to the formation of a body bearing to the corporation something of the relation held by the Board of Overseers of Harvard College to that Institution. I do not conceive that it would be necessary for such a body to be called into existence by any special modification of the Charter, in order to give to it a positive and permanent value. Its functions would be purely those of supervision, criticism, and recommendation; and if it be deemed expedient by the Board of Trustees, and by the Alumni that some such body shall be called into existence, the high character of the men selected as its members, and the zeal they would display in promoting the welfare of the Institution, would speedily give it that importance which real utility alone can confer.

Still another means suggests itself for promoting the active and permanent interest of the Alumni in our University. If a special work was accomplished by their united efforts, a work that would be related to every department, and would influence and advance the prosperity of each, it would serve not only as a memorial of their affection, but as a constant incentive to further zeal. The opportunity for such an undertaking exists at this moment; and the work of erecting a spacious and imperishable library building, where the already large and constantly increasing collections of the University could be stored, where the students of all departments would meet in the common enjoyment of its bounty, and to which future generations of Alumni would look with gratitude as the most precious of the many advantages they had enjoyed — such a work is worthy of our united energies. The University has other urgent needs at present; but none more imperative than this, and none that can so strongly solicit the cooperation of the graduates of every department.

There are, indeed, other and urgent needs, for when a great Institution ceases to require constant and liberal assistance, it is only because it has ceased to grow, or even to be actively alive. It is a proud privilege of our University that it can point to a career distinguished by spotless integrity, and by a scrupulous discharge of every trust; and that it can now offer itself to this vast and wealthy community as the most fitting agent for the adoption and execution of its educational and charitable purposes.

The experience of all countries has shown conclusively that institutions created for special purposes rarely carry out the original intention of their founders.

But in the case of a great institution, each separate trust confided to it must act only as an incentive to more and more vigilance in the discharge of former obligations, because closer public scrutiny is invited, and because the operation of every such trust will, in the course of time, breed new demands upon the confidence and generous approbation of the community.

Large as have been the gifts to the University of late years, they have only enabled her to lay the deep and broad foundations of her future prosperity. We still need more and larger endowments for existing professorships, that will perpetuate the name and munificence of their founders. We need the establishment of many free scholarships, by aid of which poor but meritorious students may be supported and educated and fitted for careers of usefulness. We need generous additions to the general funds of the Institution, so that every department may be maintained in the highest state of efficiency. These are some of the pressing needs of the University; and those who supply them may be assured of the largest returns on their bounty, and of the most faithful observance of their intentions. The net income of the University and Colleges of Oxford was ascertained, in 1874, to be $2,000,000 a year; and though generations must pass before the endowments of our American Universities approach this in magnitude, the fact that such vast sums have elsewhere been given for the advancement of learning may well stimulate and encourage us. It is a hard matter to over-estimate the capacity for growth and achievements of a man, even with his limited faculties and brief span of life; but it is impossible to form an edequate conception of the future power of a great University like ours, deeply rooted in the fertile soil of a peaceful and thoughtful people; growing with their growth, and strengthening with their strength; increasing its Faculties and its facilities as the mass of knowledge multiplies; and diffusing its illuminating and purifying influence, through ever widening circles, until, like the sweet light of Sirius, it reaches the furthest confines of humanity.

Inaugural Address

The College of the Future

by

ERNEST MARTIN HOPKINS

President of Dartmouth College

October 6, 1916

ERNEST MARTIN HOPKINS (November 6, 1877—) was born in Dunbarton, New Hampshire. He graduated from Worcester Academy and Dartmouth College. He has received honorary degrees from a number of leading universities of America. Dr. Hopkins had wide experience in the business world as an organizer before accepting the presidency of Dartmouth. He was a lecturer for the Jayne Foundation and, at one time, was in charge of industrial relations; he has also been a member of the Rockefeller Foundation.

College is means to an end. This statement of fact, even if, perchance, it be lacking in originality of conception or novelty of form, is so fundamental to all right thinking in regard to college administration as to demand constant consideration and not infrequent reiteration—and rarely if ever has it required emphasis so insistently as now. If read aright the purposes of our ancient foundations, or of the devoted lives of those whose work has made our colleges what they are; or if I interpret aright the overwhelming need of times to come, the end is constructive idealism interpreted in terms of service.

Civilization is being shaken to its deepest foundations, and agnosticism is rife in regard to much that has been accepted as axiomatic in life. Many a conclusion has been abandoned that until recently has been held rigidly, and it is yet impossible to know what premises may be established from which the conclusions of the future shall be drawn. We hardly know more than that a great winnowing of human affairs is in process, separating the essential from the incidental and attaching to each its rightful value in symbols that all may read. Matters formerly of little more than speculative interest,—such for instance as those concerned with the conservation of wealth through personal and national economies,—have all at once become of the most practical concern.

Peoples in convulsion and governments narrowly escaped from death will never resume life on the basis of customs and sufferances extant but so little time ago in our academic calendar, as the freshman year of our seniors now in college. This suddenness with which conditions have changed is matched only by the extent to which they have been transformed. Never has an epoch in the world's history been so plainly differentiated to the men of its generation as is this time in which we live. We stand on the threshold between two eras, and it is given to those of thoughtful minds to comprehend in some measure the significance of this vantage ground.

121

It has been said that an enduring college always dwells on the mountain top, that its face may first reflect the light of the coming day. As yet we fail to see the dawn, but we can seek to establish ourselves upon the heights and to hold ourselves in readiness for the sun's first gleam. There is no time for sleeping. That which shall come will come quickly at the last, and those things which are to be done will be doubly well done if done on the moment,—and this is no less true for the colleges than for other institutions of mankind. Meanwhile, in the darkness which surrounds us we have consciousness of certain changes which are being wrought.

A wide and rapidly increasing seriousness is abroad in the earth, to the effects of which we as a nation must respond as definitely as we respond to the economic tendencies among numerous peoples or to the policies of statecraft of great governments of the world. It is, moreover, a circumstance of the utmost consequence that when we, who crave so much for our national life, are called with other nations of the earth to make response to these world tendencies, we must make it without the spiritual uplift or the purification of purpose which is so plainly developing among those nations which have staked all for their ideals. Neither does it appear that we, as a people, are vitally absorbed in carrying through to completion any of these projects so aptly called by Professor James "the moral equivalents of war." Herein for the college are great obligation and great opportunity alike, and upon the contribution which it shall be equipped and prepared to make will depend the relative importance of the college to life at large in years to come.

It is a certainty that such a revaluation of customs and institutions is imminent as has heretofore been unknown; and no sentimental consideraton can be expected for such as cannot prove their worth. Under these exigencies the historic college must submit itself, without arrogance, to searching audit; and, as it offers the exhibit of its honorable past, it must show its potentiality for the future. Such a requirement presupposes complete receptivity of mind and of self-respecting humility that makes impossible didactic statements or *ipse dixit* assertions. We who engage ourselves in college work cannot well do more than to review what seem to be the enduring principles of our respective foundations and our subsequent achievements, and attempt to define the spirit and the aspirations with which we approach the overwhelming problems of the future so immediately before us.

It seems probable that the first point at which we shall be called upon to define our attitude is on the contention that all education, to be worth while, must be made utilitarian. One finds generally in the English periodicals of the present the argument that classical education is a luxury which has outlived any possible usefulness, and which must go the way of all those other luxuries which have been foregone; and that new obligations and responsibilities can only be met by an education of which every branch shall be designed for direct application to immediate needs. Likewise, there come back to us accounts of meetings of groups of German schoolmasters in the trenches, for instance, where resolutions are adopted to the effect that when the war shall be over these teachers will return to their homes with determination to make the German system of education more practical. These occurrences cannot be dismissed as sporadic. The evidence abounds that the national tendencies in these great nations is in the direction of an educational system of pure utility.

No tribute is fitting, for none is needed, to those institutions of higher learning in our country which have been founded for, and are giving, that vital training of a highly specialized technical curriculum. They have merited, and won, the highest commendation. The liberal colleges, with all other types of educational institution, owe the technical schools a great debt of gratitude for their insistence upon the scientific method in the approach to scholarship, which has had its effect throughout the educational world. We are a wide-spread people, with numberless needs, and we could not do without that which such types of education have afforded. The realm of higher education, however, is of too great area for any kind of institution to occupy it all, and least of any should the traditional cultural college have ambition to attempt it. The function of the cultural college has proved to be of the utmost importance; its work has been of distinctive service throughout the nation's history; and its future success, in my opinion, will be more marked,—if change is to be made,—by reverting to a curriculum of fewer subjects better taught, than by spreading its efforts constantly thinner until its attitude takes on unfortunate semblance to a sprawl.

It is not likely to be, at any time, that without loss to itself the world can close its mind to the influence of the past. The institutions for the beautiful and the understanding of the logical which have come down to us from civilization which have risen and lived their allotted lives are foundations for that appreciation of philosophy, art and literature without which the world would lose its breadth and depth.

There has been no better expression of this belief than is included in the "Memorandum on the Limitations of Scientific Education," issued by a group of Englishmen of world-wide fame, headed by Lord Bryce, and published as a protest against the prevalent propaganda for the monopolization of the field of education in England by technical subjects.

"It is of the utmost importance that our higher education should not become materialistic through too narrow a regard for practical efficiency. Technical knowledge is essential to our industrial prosperity and national safety; but education should be nothing less than a preparation for the whole of life. It should introduce the future citizens of the community not merely to the physical structure of the world in which they live but also to the deeper interests and problems of politics, thought and human life. It should acquaint them, so far as may be, with the capacities and ideals of mankind, as expressed in literature and in art, with its ambitions and achievements as recorded in history, and with the nature and laws of the world as interpreted by science, philosophy and religion. Some of its most distinguished representatives have strongly insisted that early specialization is injurious to the interest they have at heart, and that the best preparation for scientific pursuits is a general training which includes some study of language, literature and history. Such a training gives width of view and flexibility of intellect. Industry and commerce will be most successfully pursued by men whose education has stimulated their imagination and widened their sympathies.

"What we want is scientific method in all the branches of an education which will develop human faculty and the power of thinking clearly to the highest possible degree.

"In this education we believe that the study of Greece and Rome must always have a large part, because our whole civilization is rooted in the history of these peoples, and without knowledge of them can not be properly understood."

I am emphasizing certain convictions about the older humanities, not from any lack of confidence and belief in the sciences, but simply because the sciences will not be subject to attack in the newer movements in education as will be the humanities. And in regard to those essential subjects of the curriculum which we know as the newer humanities. it is simply to be said that they will be open to much the same sort of attack as has been the older group once the agitation against this latter shall prove successful.

There is no law of physical science to which more exact analogy can be found in the realm of movements social, economic, philosophical or religious, than that which states action and reaction to be equal and opposite in direction. As one studies the swing of theory from one extreme to another in mental and spiritual realms, he comes to the understanding that the influence of the college on these must be a steadying influence, like the force of gravity on the pendulum, tending constantly to shorten the arc of motion and influencing toward an eventual stable equilibrium. It is for this reason that the college cannot be inherently either radical or conservative, for the same principle which impels it to pull back from one extreme today will tomorrow lead it to endeavor to correct the overswing of the reaction.

I have said that the college exists as means to an end, and that the end should be constructive idealism interpreted in terms of service. It well may be added that no particular form of service is so vitally essential today as high-minded consecration to the needs of the state. The development of our national life has been shown to be far short of the standard to which it was supposed to have attained, and in many of our attributes we have proved more a group of peoples than a nation. It remains for the living of our time as truly as for those of the generation of half a century ago to be dedicated to the great task remaining before us, of developing unity and forcefulness of conviction in our national life, that, from the heritage of the past and the needs of the future alike, we take increased devotion to the cause for which such sacrifices have been made and in the success of which we firmly believe humanity to be so much concerned.

To this endeavor the colleges should be commited by their every instinct and by all the influences which have shaped them; and solemn responsibility rests upon them now that they shall be sensitive to the new note which is beginning to sound in our national affairs, as parochialism becomes less and less a characteristic, and as we come to recognize our inevitable responsibility among the nations of the earth.

The periods before us will demand clearly defined national consciousness and forceful leadership of rarest sort if we are to be important agents in the world's trend towards democracy. Mental processes must be clarified and thinking must be less muddled. It will not be a time when the destructive genius of critical analysis will be of maximum worth; and the necessity will exist that the susceptibility of modern college life to this process of thought shall give place to a genuine passion for constructive thinking and constructive planning, which is the only motive under which truly great things are ventured and done. Montaigne's statement still has point,—"The discharge of a present evil is no cure, if there be not general amendment of condition. Whoever proposes only to remove that which offends him falls short; for good does not necessarily succeed evil; another evil may succeed, and a worse."

Democracy is a very precious thing to us who wish to live our own lives with the minimum of outside interference. But it is possible to defeat the very ends for which it exists if we concede the utmost claims of individualism which have been urged to such extremes. It is important for the college at this point to study the type of its accomplishment and to understand the change which the needs of the immediate future must work in its methods if it is to make its vital contribution to meet these needs. In training for leadership its influence in years past, unconsciously perhaps, has been to set college men apart in the communities in which they have lived. The requirement now is emphatically the reverse. At a time when, almost without exception, the college man went into a profession, and when the professional man was inevitably a college man, the leadership of the community gravitated towards its advisers, who were the ministers, lawyers, doctors and teachers,—in short the college men of the community. These men were necessarily individual workers, and it came to be that the stamp of college training, as a matter of course implied individualism.

127

But whether it be that business and industry began to summon the men from institutions of higher learning, or that college men began to seek careers in the field of production and distribution, the change has been wrought very quickly that the men going into the professions from our colleges are far outnumbered by those seeking the newer career.

Figures prepared at Dartmouth a decade ago show that, for the first twenty-five years of the College, 40 per cent of its graduates entered the ministry; 25 per cent entered the law; 12 per cent entered teaching; 7 per cent entered medicine; 16 per cent were untraceable. For the first fifty years the legal profession led with 36 per cent; the ministry was second with 30 per cent; and only 10 per cent, classed as untraceable, have the possibility of having been outside the professions. In the half decade from 1900 to 1905, 52 per cent of Dartmouth's graduates went into business and industry, and that figure has increased until, from 1909 to 1913, it runs above 60 per cent. Like changes, in varying degree, have been going on in other colleges.

All this requires definite modification of some of the theories about individualism as compared with group action; for cooperation is the basis of accomplishment outside the professions, and in ever increasing degree within them. Thus individualism that either fails of ability or interest to express itself through helpful influence on group action is, at the best, of restricted worth; and, at the worst, is positively pernicious. Individual success attained for selfish ends is an unworthy goal for the colleges to set for their men, but the colleges are not entirely free from indictment on this count. The brilliancy of the halo which has been set about the theory of individualism and all that it implies, in some of our college teaching, has been too often responsible for dulling in the student's mind the conception of the beauty of service. The way must be found to stimulate the desire of our student bodies for supreme service within the group rather than outside it. The inscription in the Worcester County Courthouse, in Massachusetts, — "Here speaketh the conscience of the State, restraining the individual will,"—could well be placed, with slight adaptation, in our academic halls, and made descriptive of one great function of the college.

We have as a people specialized so completely in recent years on claiming rights, that our senses of obligation responsibility have become atrophied. Authority has been weakened, not only in state and church but in home and school, until it commands less respect even than obedience. Amid all this, somehow, the conviction has begun to grow that dilettante philosophizing about rights, and claims to opportunities which have not been earned offer too little compensation in constructive accomplishment for what society is called upon to sacrifice in the character of the individuals who compose it, through their being so little called upon to acknowledge any authority of any kind whatsoever.

A proper understanding of the needful limits upon the theory of individualism is important in defining the relations between the college and the undergraduate body. In a large way the college exists for the individual student; but it does not exist so truly for the individual student as for the generation of college men, and it does not exist for either as definitely as for the social group which is the state. It is an easy and pleasant thing to say to an undergraduate member of the college what properly interpreted is true,—that the institution is established and maintained for his benefit. If, however, application of this statement is interpreted to mean that the college lives to meet his personal convenience or to enhance his personal success, as apart from the needs of society and his ability to contribute to them, wrong is done the man, and the college trust has been maladministered.

The service which the college should render to the nation includes, very definitely, the inculcation of an idea of the value of discipline in the minds of those men who have conferred upon them the advantages of the college endowments. And this cannot well be instilled if the college abjures all responsibility for maintaining a code of discipline. This is one of the vital reasons for the existence of certain standards of intellectual competency and moral inclination for membership in the college. Admittedly, many of these are awkward, and some may be badly designed for the purpose sought; but, even so, they should stand until they can be replaced with methods better devised. This is the answer that must be made not infrequently to some earnest and loyal friends of the college, who, from the best of intentions, seek to neutralize its standards by reiterated requests that exception be made to regulations of proved worth, and who are prone to contend that all human attributes have disappeared from college teaching and college administration because the avenues to special privilege have been closed. The same reason exists for saying to the undergraduate that his preferences, either concerning modifications of the curriculum or in regard to administrative policy, cannot necessarily prevail unless, in the opinion of the best intelligence derived from experience, such modifications are for the ultimate accomplishment of those ends for which the college exists as a means. Thus, in the not infrequent student query as to what benefit he derives from certain curriculum requirements of non-utility, the attempt should be made to have him understand that the cultural heritage handed down through the ages, and now particularly entrusted to the historic college, is worthy of preservation. But the requirements cannot be abolished even if he remains unconvinced, for the college is more responsible for his ultimate satisfaction than for his immediate contentment.

I recently chanced upon a quotation from the London Journal of Education on the relation of education and character, which clearly expresses the thought that is becoming more largely held in regard to our colleges particularly, as well as in regard to education at large.

"To turn out boys with pleasant manners, generous hearts and good animal spirits is not enough; we want boys and girls with trained intelligence, who have been made to use their brains and taught that not to use them is a sin. Every boy and girl who grows up mindless, ignorant or intellectually undisciplined, is so much dead weight hanging around the neck of the community, and ought to be made to feel it. When we discuss character and education, therefore, let us give the fullest possible meaning to each word."

I believe that it is worthy of more emphasis than has sometimes been given that the development of character is distinctly one of the great responsibilities of the college. The introduction of university methods into college teaching, the influence of professionalized scholarship in the chairs of instruction, and the marked disinclination of men of the present generation to consult together concerning the deeper phase of life have, all together, so altered the once existing relationship between teacher and student that the old-time formative influence of the college faculty on student character has too greatly disappeared. It is still, however, not to be forgotten that our colleges were founded and sustained through years of drastic toil by men of religious fervor, who, in self-sacrifice, literally gave their lives for the perpetuation of institutions designed no less for spiritual inspiration than for intellectual command. Forms of expression change from generation to generation, and manifestations of spiritual instinct differ widely from those of a century-and-a-half ago. But the initial obligation rests upon us to make the college influential in the development of those traits vital to well-proportioned goodness.

Scholarship as a product of the college is incomplete except as it be established on the foundation of character which is not only passively good, but which is of moral fibre definite enough to influence those with whom it is brought into contact. By as much as evil directed by intelligence is more dangerous than brainless badness, by so much is the college open to the danger of doing the country an ill turn if it ignores its responsibility to safeguard and develop character as it undertakes to stimulate mentality.

The demands which will be made upon the college in the years immediately before us will be insistent and heavy. The knowledge of this compels us to strive with unwonted effort to realize all our resources and to have all our assets quick assets. There will be few such possibilities of added vigor to the college as in the development of what has come to be known as the alumni movement until, in far greater measure, the solicitude and the intelligence of the alumni,—more truly even than their financial means,—are directed to furthering the true interests of the college.

Such strength as the American college lacks it lacks, in the main, because of the too great confinement of interest among its men to the college of their undergraduate days. Many a man, through lack of opportunity for anything else, draws all the inspiration for his enthusiasm for his college from his memories of life when an undergraduate, and feeds his loyalty solely upon sentimental reverence for the past. The mis-fortune of interest thus confined falls alike upon the individual and upon the college. In general, the alumni of our American colleges have little knowledge of educational movements or college responsibilities on which to base any interest that they may be disposed to give to the evolution of college thought. It is needless impoverishment for a man to be the recipient of the bounty of his college for the brief season of his membership and thereafter to miss being a participator in its affairs as a going concern.

The ability of Dartmouth to continue to justify its existence in a large way will be greatly increased or seriously curtailed by the degree of willingness of the alumni to seek knowledge of what the function of this College should be, and how its function should be accomplished. Any college which could have the really intelligent interest and cooperation of a large part of its alumni body in working out its destiny to major usefulness would become of such striking serviceableness as to be beyond comparison. I am a great believer in the desirability of organized effort to get every individual alumnus enrolled as a financial contributor, but I believe in this most largely because of my conviction that, as a people, we are so constituted that where a man gives his money he there gives his interest.

There has been no phase of college activity which has been of such personal interest to me as has been the alumni movement; there has been none in which I have believed greater possibilities of good to exist. I am convinced, however, that this movement will fail of major usefulness unless it bases itself, and is based by the intelligent understanding of the problems which education must face. This movement may indeed become detrimental to any given institution if it accepts the privilege of reviewing college actions without accepting responsibility to review them with the utmost discrimination, and without accepting accountability for opinions which it may express. Knowledge of conditions in the time of a man's own undergraduate course will not be sufficient. He must know the problems of today, and foresee the general characteristics of those of the future, and his efforts at all times must be rigidly to hold the college to its highest ideals. The age of a college is one of the rights of every undergraduate; but, as truly, to every alumnus should belong the spirit of her eternal youth. It is a recollection to be cherished to know the glorious days that have gone, but our boast is incomplete unless we can say of the present that we crave the privileges and claim a share in the responsibilities of our brotherhood and of our sonship.

In urging that the alumni make a special effort to have their relations with the College based on continuing intimacy of contact I do not forget that a share of the responsibility for developing the alumni movement aright belongs to the College. I give most unqualified support to the attitude already taken by the Trustees of Dartmouth that the request of the Alumni Council of the College for some definition of the educational intent of Dartmouth should be answered in the fullest possible manner. I likewise am very sure that the contribution of the College to its graduates ought to be continued in some more tangible way than exists at present. The tendency of college men to seek careers outside the professions, the tendencies of the professions themselves to become so highly specialized as to necessitate the complete engrossment of thought of the men who follow them, and the ever increasing demand of the age on all, requiring constantly greater intensity of effort and more exclusive utilization of time in men who wish to do their respective shares of the world's work, impose a duty upon the college which formerly belonged to it in no such degree, if at all. Contacts with what we broadly classify as the arts and sciences are less and less possible for men of affairs. In many a graduate the interest in or enthusiasm for these which the college arouses is, therefore, altogether likely to languish, or even die, for lack of sustenance. If the College, then, has conviction that its influence is worth seeking at the expense of four vital years in the formative period of life, is it not logically compelled to search for some method of giving access to this influence to its graduates in their subsequent years? The growing practice of retiring men from active work at ages from sixty-five to seventy and the not infrequent tragedy of the man who has no resources for interesting himself outside the routine of which he has been relieved, make it seem that the College has no less an opportunity to be of service to its men in their old age than in their youth, if only it can establish the procedure by which it can periodically

134

throughout their lives give them opportunity to replenish their intellectual reserves. It is possible that something in the way of courses of lectures by certain recognized leaders of the world's thought, made available for alumni and friends of the College during a brief period immediately following the Commencement season, would be a step in this direction. Or it may be that some other device would more completely realize the possibilities. It at least seems clear that the formal educational contacts between the College and its graduates should not stop at the end of four years, never in any form to be renewed.

As we approach the demands of the future of the college at this particular stage in the world's history, however, there seems to me a single word of caution which should be uttered. At a period of such violent readjustments, when the values which shall be accorded to things physical, intellectual and spiritual are undergoing so much revision, it is more to be desired that institutions as well as individuals shall safeguard openness of mind than that they shall prejudice future action by the too definite recording of preconceived notions toward which subsequent policies are bound to be bent. We are like travelers over unfamiliar trails, who know the point of the compass along which their ways lie, but who are without knowledge as to the exact spot at which they will make their camp.

We cannot reasonably attempt at any specific time to solve the whole problem of the relations of the college to a future whose needs we do not know. We should rather recognize the general attributes of our task and attempt to define the spirit in which the college shall make its approach to them. The college has always stood for fullness of life for the individual and has thus by indirection benefited the group. It must from now on, to such extent as it has not done before, have as its first aim, fullness of life for the group, depending for this largely upon the advantage it can afford the individual.

135

The practical operation may not be so very different in the one case from what it has been in the other, but the modification of motive will be one of those intangible but vastly important influences which will be certain to have much to do with the quality of the spiritual product of the college.

A little less than a century and a half ago, Eleazar Wheelock, fired with a great missionary impulse, fared forth into a physical wilderness, overcoming difficulties, offsetting lack of acquaintanceship with his new environment and rising superior to discouragement, and here, in the forest-clad plain of Hanover, reapplied those principles of education, of religion and of service to country and to God for which he had laid the foundations in a land of security and comfort. It is the propulsion of this spirit down through the decades that has resulted in the Dartmouth that we, her sons, so love and reverence.

Today we are summoned forth along uncharted ways into the mazes of a changed life, of a rapidly transforming world. We are summoned into a wilderness of thought. May we not pray with faith that under the guidance of God, working from principles that are among the verities, we may give effectually the service most needed to add depth to the shallows of life, breadth to the straitened places of mind, and height to the lowlands of character. Thus, in truth, shall we be justified in the new life, as we have been in the old, and continuingly we can claim the ancient motto of the College,—*Vox Clamantis in deserto.*

Inaugural Address

by

MARK HOPKINS

President of Williams College

September 15, 1836

MARK HOPKINS (February 4, 1802— June 15, 1887) was born in Stockbridge, Massachusetts. His father was a farmer in humble circumstances. With inadequate preparation Mark Hopkins entered Williams College as a sophomore and graduated in 1824. After graduation he began the study of medicine but was called to Williams College as a tutor. Later, he resumed the study of medicine and received his degree in 1829 after which he practiced medicine in New York City. Hopkins returned to Williams in 1830 as professor of philosophy and rhetoric. He was not trained as a theologian but was licensed to preach. His fame rests mainly upon his skill as a teacher.

Connected as the cause of Education is, in this country, with every thing that we hold dear in our social, civil, and religious institutions; and sustained as our Colleges are by public and private benefactions, it is desirable that the principles and feelings of those who conduct them should be fully known by the community. That much is constantly said on the subject of education, only shows that much still needs to be said; for the public will can act efficiently only in view of principles which are regarded as settled, and in favor of institutions in which it has confidence. It may not, therefore, be inappropriate for me, on this occasion, to make some observations on the nature and objects of education in general; and more particularly upon collegiate education as adapted to attain those objects, and to meet the wants of the community.

To all the productions of nature there belongs an ideal perfection of which they are fully capable, and beyond which, under the most favorable circumstances, they cannot go. We may so plant a particular seed and cultivate its shoot, that it shall attain the highest perfection of which the species is capable; or we may so plant and neglect it, as to cause it to be dwarfish and deformed. The elm, for example, if its soil and situation are favorable, may attain in size the limit of its species, and may leave, in the figure of its graceful boughs, nothing for the eye to desire. It would be the object of culture to produce such a tree. And so it is with man. There is a strength and beauty of physical structure, a compass and accuracy of knowledge, a soundness of judgment, a readiness and retentiveness of memory, a richness and grandeur of imagination, a refinement of feeling, a correctness and strength of principle, and a promptitude of action, which it is possible should be combined in the same individual, and which, if we are to cultivate man as man, it must be the object of education to produce.

By education, I mean not merely formal instruction, but any system of excitement or restraint the object of which is to effect some definite change in the physical, intellectual, or moral character of man. The term, I know, is often used in a broader sense to include every thing in external nature, and in the circumstances of the individual, which can exert an influence upon him, whether intended to exert such influence or not. That there are circumstances in local situation, and in the structure of society, the influence of which cannot be avoided, and which yet often control the character and destiny of the young, there can be no doubt. Climate, the form of government, childhood spent in the city or in the country, in luxury or in poverty, and perhaps more than all, early and casual impressions caught from first associates, operate imperceptibly, but irresistibly, in modifying and giving variety to character. But though the influence upon the mind of causes beyond our control, may be an interesting subject of speculation, just as is the influence of gravity on matter, and though these causes may form a part of that tutelage under which in the providence of God his creatures are put, and we may, if we please, call it the education of circumstances, yet if we regard the common use of language, or if we would define a practical science, we must include in the term education, only those circumstances over which we have a control, and which we can and do bring to bear upon man with the intention of effecting a particular end. The simple fact that the parent is rich, will have an effect upon the mind of the child; but that effect is, as I use the term, no part of education—it is often something which it is the business of education to counteract. According to any other use of the term, one individual is as much educated as another, since all are equally under some influence by which they are formed to some particular character.

But besides those circumstances which act upon the mind, and over which we have not control, there are others over which we have; and education may be said to consist, according to its most general division, first, of those influences which we may bring to bear upon the mind aside from direct instruction; and second, of direct instruction.

Of these two, the first is, no doubt, the more important, and will be most regarded by a wise parent. A child may be an inmate in a family, and form virtuous habits from the general influence by which he is surrounded, without having a word directed especially to him in the way of advice—indeed it is perhaps in this way that he would be most likely to form them; and we all know that it needs no positive instruction to render children vicious where the general influence by which they are surrounded is bad. When direct inculcation is obliged to struggle againt such an influence, it finds a current which it cannot breast. Among the circumstances which can be controlled to some extent, and which ought to be desired, are opportunities and inducements of physical exercise, a healthy situation, fine scenery, proper books, a suitable example on the part of instructors, companions of correct and studious habits, and above all, a good religious influence. On this subject, the apathy of many parents is astonishing. They do not seem to consider this a part of education for which they are in any way responsible. If their children are in a reputable, it may be in a fashionable or celebrated institution, they live in contented ignorance of the rest. In regard to this part of education, perhaps no system can be formed; but wise and good men need to consider it more deeply, and the public mind needs to be awakened, and the public conscience stimulated respecting it. It may be doubted whether by the combined influence of parents, and of teachers and of those students who are governed by principle, and who know the moral power which is exerted by one young man who pursues throughout his course of study a consistent and holy course, our seminaries of learning, and especially our colleges, may not be made places where vice and indolence cannot remain. Instruction may form the intellect, influence moulds the moral character.

But whether we consider education as comprising more

141

or less, or whatever division we may make of it, the general principle which we are to regard, especially in its second part, which is positive instruction, is now settled among all thinking men. It is, that we are to regard the mind, not as a piece of iron to be laid upon the anvil and hammered into any shape, nor as a block of marble in which we are to find the statue by removing the rubbish, nor as a receptacle into which knowledge may be poured; but as a flame that is to be fed, as an active being that must be strengthened to think and to feel—to dare, to do, and to suffer. It is as a germ, expanding under the influence certainly of air and sunlight and moisture, but yet only through the agency of an internal force; and external agency is of no value except as it elicits, and controls, and perfects, the action of that force. He only who can rightly appreciate the force of this principle, and carry it out into all its consequences, in the spirit of the maxim, that nature is to be conquered only by obeying her laws, will do all that belongs to the office of a teacher.

That there has been so much mistake respecting this fundamental principle, obvious as it appears, and conformable as it is to the analogies of nature, can have arisen, only as most practical mistakes do, because men were "willingly ignorant." There is indeed, great temptation on the part both of teachers and scholars to pursue a course not in accordance with this principle. It is far easier for a teacher to generalize a class, and give it a lesson to get by rote, and hear it said, and let it pass, than it is to watch the progress of individual mind, and awaken interest, and answer objections, and explore tendencies, and, beginning with elements, to construct together with his pupils, so that they shall feel that they aid in it, the fair fabric of a science with which they shall be familiar from the foundation to the topstone. It is far easier also to induce students to get particular lessons, than to induce to study subjects. The one they may do from any transient motive—from fear of disgrace or mere ambition; the other is seldom done except from interest

142

in the subject. This is a point that needs attention, for it is astonishing how often even intelligent young men content themselves with being able to appear well in particular recitations without ever tracing relations, and carrying out principles, and taking a wide and comprehensive survey of the whole subject.

This course is also more fruitful in immediate results of a certain kind, and there are especial temptations to it in rival seminaries, and where examinations are made the test of what is done. There are not wanting schools in this country in which the real interest and progress of the pupils are sacrificed to their appearance at examination. But the vanity of parents must be flattered, and the memory is over-burdened, and studies are forced on prematurely, and a system of infant school instruction is carried forward into maturer life. Nature, however, will not be hurried, and if it is desired to enter upon a study for which the faculties are not yet ripe, if, for example, as is often done of late, Intellectual Philosophy is attempted before the reflective faculties are somewhat mature; the only honest course is to advise its postponement, and not to attempt to satisfy ignorance, and really to foster conceit by substituting memory for investigation. I will not say that studies so pursued invariably perplex, and discourage, and disgust, because the student often remains in such happy ignorance of the subject as not to be aware of its difficulties, and thus a little that is valuable may be picked up, and the memory be improved; but I do say that whenever a mind, proceeding in the true method, is brought to wrestle with a subject which in the nature of things it is not yet competent to master, and it has only discernment enough to see difficulties, it must be perplexed and discouraged, and its progress retarded. A great part of the complaints which we hear of studies as hard and dull and dry, is no doubt the result of sheer indolence; but they may also result from an injudicious attempt on the part of parents or teachers to push a really good mind too fast.

But thus it is that indolence and interest in teachers have conspired with vanity in parents to sustain a false system. And the reasons are equally obvious why it should find favor with the mass of pupils. The habit of patient attention, that to which Newton attributed all his superiority, is perhaps formed with more difficulty by mankind at large, and especially by the young, than any other. But it is only by means of this that they can investigate for themselves, or proceed in the spirit of the principle we are now considering. Innumerable are the expedients which are resorted to on all sides to avoid this, and yet obtain an education. The rich may employ tutors, and purchase apparatus, and procure lectures, and still, if they cannot inure their children to intellectual toil, they will not be educated. The young man may get another to prompt him, or may slily read from a book and cheat his instructor——but he is cheating himself still more. There is a strange slowness in assenting practically to that great law of nature, that the faculties are strengthened only by exercise. It is so with the body, and it is so with the mind. If a man would strengthen his intellectual faculties, he must exercise them; if he would improve his taste, he must employ it on the objects of taste; if he would improve his moral nature and make progress in goodness, he must perform acts of goodness. Nor will he improve his faculties by thinking about them and studying into their nature, unless by so doing, he is enabled and induced to put them into more skilful and efficient action.

We hear much said about self-educated men, and a broad distinction is made between them and others; but the truth is that every man who is educated at all, is, and must be, self-educated. There are no more two methods in which the mind can make progress, than there are two methods in which plants can grow. One seed may be blown by the winds, and cast upon the southern, or perchance on the northern side of some distant hill, and may there germinate, and take root, and do battle alone with the elements, and it may be so favored

144

by the soil and climate that it shall lift itself in surpassing strength and beauty; another may be planted carefully in a good soil, and the hand of tillage may be applied to it, yet must this also draw for itself nutriment from the soil, and for itself withstand the rush of the tempest, and lift its head on high only as it strikes its roots deep in the earth. It is for the want of understanding this properly, that extravagant expectations are entertained of instructors, and of institutions, and that those who go to college sometimes expect, and that the community expect, that they will be learned of course—as if they could be inoculated with knowledge, or obtain it by absorption. This broad distinction between self-educated men and others has done harm; for young men will not set themselves efficiently at work until they feel that there is an all-important part which they must perform for themselves, and which no one can do for them.

And here I may mention, that from this view of the subject, it is easy to see what it is that constitutes the first excellence of an instructor. It is not his amount of knowledge, nor yet his facility of communication, important as these may be; but it is his power to give an impulse to the minds of his pupils, and to induce them to labor. For this purpose, nothing is so necessary as a disinterested devotion to the work, and a certain enthusiasm which may act by sympathy on the minds of the young. It is from the decay of this that courses of lectures and of instruction once attractive, often cease to interest. When a teacher has advanced so far beyond his class, or has become so familiar with his subject, as to fell no interest in its truths, then, however well he may understand them, and however clearly he may state them, he is not all that a teacher ought to be. He who carries the torch light into the recesses of science, and shows the gems that are sparkling there, must not be a mere hired conductor who is to bow in one company, and bow out another, and show what is to be seen with heartless indifference, but must have an everliving fountain of

145

emotion that will flow afresh as he contemplates anew the works of God, and the great principles of truth and of duty. This is no more impossible in regard to the beauties and wonders which science discloses, than it is in regard to the more obvious appearances of nature, and the instructor may adopt in spirit the words of the poet:

"My heart leaps up when I behold
The rainbow in the sky,
So was it when my life began,
So is it now I am a man,
So let it be, or let me die;
The child's the father of the man;
And I would my days should be,
Bound each to each in natural piety."

It is such an one alone who can know the pleasure of carrying forward a class of ingeneous youth, and watching them as they gain new positions, and take in wider views till the whole prospect is at their command. And when, as sometimes happens, he has a class of an opposite character, and his instructions fall dead, and no interest is excited, it is he alone who can know the anxiety, I had almost said agony with which, as the prophet of old upon the dead body of the child, he once and again as it were puts his mouth to its mouth, and his eyes to its eyes, and stretches himself upon the class, and finds no life come. And he alone knows how cheerless and hopeless, and slavish is the dull routine of his labors after that. There are, it seems to me, few modes of gaining a living short of actual villainy, which a man of sensibility would not prefer to it.

With such an object, and such a method, our further views respecting education will be determined by the opinions we may have formed respecting the faculties of man which are to be perfected, and the relative attention to be bestowed upon each. On these points there are different views, and views substantially the same may be involved in different classifications. I may however, remark briefly, as my limits compel me, that a wise system of education will regard man.

First, as possessed of a body which is to be kept in health and vigor. It is now agreed that the health of the body is to be one great object of attention, not only for its own sake, but from its connection with a sound state and vigorous action of the mind.

Second, a wise system of education must regard man as possessed of intellectual faculties whose object is truth. It is upon these faculties that education has too often spent all its force. In cultivating these, we are to point out the great sources of prejudice to which mankind are liable in their search after truth, to strengthen the memory, to exercise the judgment, to teach the mind both to comprehend and carry on general reasoning, and to descend to details; we are to make distinctions, and go back to first principles, being always careful to quicken and keep in exercise all that there is of that most uncommon quality, good common sense. As far as possible, knowledge is to be communicated; but we are not to aim so much at giving the world men whose minds are already full, as those who have the power of attention, and habits of analysis, and of accurate investigation, and of intellectual labor, and the power of communication.

Third, a wise system of education will consider man as having faculties whose object is beauty. That part of our frame whose object is beauty and sublimity, (for no one word expresses it exactly,) does not probably receive its due share of attention, and is sometimes wholly overlooked. The cultivation of these emotions is by some powerful, though dry intellects, rejected as effeminate, and they are often buried up amidst the pursuits of ambition and of wealth. But it is not for nothing that nature addresses herself to this part of our constitution in a thousand forms, and with a thousand voices; that

147

she has so frequently united beauty with utility, and even stamped it with an independent value by often setting it alone. It is not for nothing that she has consulted the appearances by painting the flower, and turning the glossy side of every leaf to the eye, and dipping in gold the plumage of the bird, and bathing in its pomp of hues the coming and the parting day. Nor was it merely to impart a transient pleasure; but it was that the exercise of this part of our nature might throw a refining and softening influence over the rest, and to teach us to carry the principles of taste into our manners and outward conduct. If there is nothing morally good in these emotions, yet are they naturally allied to goodness, and seem to be its twilight; they are the transition step in the creation, from mere matter, to moral worth and beauty. And if but little can be done, which is by no means certain, to cultivate directly this part of what may be called the emotive or affective part of our frame; we at least need not overlay it, and carry forward education as if it did not exist. We may appreciate it, we may dwell upon it, we may favor to some extent the operation of circumstances in eliciting it.

Fourth, it is hardly necessary to say that a wise system of education will regard man as possessed of a moral nature, the object of which is goodness. This implies the combined action of the rational and affective nature of man, and is their consummation and final cause. The union of cultivated intellect and refined taste with moral corruption, however common it may be, is monstrous; and if there are institutions the legitimate tendency of which is to produce that result, they are a curse to the community. As in the intellect we endeavor to form the mind, if I may be allowed the expression, to self-progress, so in morals we are to endeavor to form it to self-government. This gives us our principle in moral education. Evil is in the world, and must be met. This world was intended to be a place of trial, and if a scheme of optimism can be made out upon any supposition, it is upon this. Temptation

148

cannot be excluded. It leaped the walls of paradise, and the frontier which we have to guard is far too wide to enable us to prevent its incursions. Our main reliance must lie in strengthening the citadel. There should be no needless exposure; there should, if possible, and this is the point to be attended to, be none till there is strength to meet it. The youth must, if possible, be prevented from tasting the cup of Circe till we have shown him the swine that had once been men; he must be kept from the fascination of the serpent, till we have shown him its fangs; and having done this, we must commit him to his own keeping, and to God.

According to this division, we shall have physical vigor, knowledge and intellectual power, refined taste, and moral excellence; or in other words, we shall have formed the mind to the love and pursuit of truth, of beauty, and of goodness.

I might here close this enumeration, but I should not feel that it was complete, unless I were to add that a wise system of education will regard man as susceptible of the influence of habit. The susceptibility to habits is to the mind, what the system of voluntary muscle is to the body—for as it would require our whole time to cause the heart to beat, so there are modes of voluntary action constantly recurring, which would engross life if they did not, by being often repeated, pass to some extent beyond the sphere of deliveration and immediate volition. But in passing from the sphere of conscious volition, they also pass from that of observation, and it is this fact that renders it so difficult to correct habits that are wrong, and so important to form those that are right. Few, probably, practically estimate as they ought, the power of repetition to give facility of action, and the decrease of susceptibility on repeated impression. It is through these that man may, on the one hand, come to perform with ease the nicest operations of art, and on the other, become gradually reconciled to almost any situation; and the system of education that should disregard these facts would be highly defective. A regard to them will lead us to look at an act in its connections, and when a habit is in question, as that of punctuality for instance, to insist upon some things with a particularity which would not be justified by their intrinsic importance.

From these general views I now pass to consider how far the course pursued in our colleges is adapted to attain the ends mentioned, and to meet the wants of the community. Time however will permit me to do this only so far as will be necessary to meet some of the objections that are made against them.

And first, it is objected that colleges destroy physical vigor. There has, no doubt, been ground for this objection. From its local situation, this college has probably suffered less in this way than some others, and there has been here, especially of late, comparatively little failure of the health. Something has been done, but there is still room for improvement. It ought, however, no more to be expected that the student should have the same robustness of frame and muscular vigor as the laboring man, than that the laboring man should have the same intellectual cultivation as the student. There is no use in undertaking to combine things that are incompatible, and however useful and desirable on many accounts and in many situations manual labor institutions may be, I believe they may be both; still there always have been, and probably always will be institutions not on that plan, and yet compatible with perfect health. If we were to regard the general voice on this subject, we should suppose that a want of exercise was the great, if not the sole cause of the failure of health among our literary men. But there is a power of adaptation in the human constitution which fits it for different occupations. It was never intended to lay down, in this respect, a railway from which, if man deviated, he should be dashed in pieces; and experience shows, that if other things are attended to, the range of safety to health is comparatively wide. It is not a fact that students in Germany exercise more than those in this country, and yet they are healthy. But the truth is that students, in common with other classes of the community, not only do not exercise enough, but they live in the constant violation of all the rules of dietetics. Some have used, and still do, intoxicating drinks; a much larger number use tobacco, many of them are constantly loading their stomachs with raisins and almonds, and various kinds of confectionery. They eat too much, they sit up late under the excitement of novel reading, and perhaps for study. Let their food be of proper quantity and quality, let them avoid poisonous substances, let them keep regular hours, and shun the predominance of an excited or polluted imagination, and they will find that there is an elasticity in the human frame that requires exercise. Nor need it be aimless exercise. Let them saw their own wood, let botany and mineralogy lead them over the hills, let them cherish a love for fine prospects, let them cultivate the taste and manly spirit that have originated and carried forward so happily in this college, the Horticultural and Landscape Gardening Association, and there will be cheeks as fresh, and limbs as agile, and animal spirits as buoyant, as if they spent three hours a day in a workshop, and, which would be necessary in some of our institutions, as if a thousand dollars a year were expended to enable them to do something useful. It has been a fault, which I trust will be avoided here, that this subject has not been sufficiently urged upon students in the early part of their course.

Again, it is objected that colleges are not practical. There are some who seem to be slow in understanding what is meant by the discipline of the mind, or mental training, as if it were different in its principle from a military drill in which a series of actions is performed, not so much for its own sake as a preparation for the future battle. It is true the discipline must be such as will fit them for the combat. We must not put bows

151

and arrows into their hands when they will have to use the cartridge-box and the musket——but discipline there must be. We are indeed to consult utility, but it must be in its highest and broadest sense——not that eager utility which would cut down the tree for the sake of sooner getting its fruit, its unripe fruit, but that farsighted utility, which would plow under a crop for the sake of benefiting the soil, and which would look forward to the coincidence of its plans with the high purposes of God in the creation of man. But if there are any who never make a distinction between general and professional education, who look upon man solely as a being who is to be fitted to make money in some particular sphere, and not as one who has faculties to be perfected, to them I have nothing to say.

Again, it is objected that colleges do not keep up with the spirit of the age. This objection probably does not always assume a definite form in the minds of those who make it. But if it be intended that improvements in the sciences are not ingrafted, as they are made, upon the scientific courses, or that new sciences are not introduced as the wants of the public demand; if it be intended that there is an adherence to things that are old because they are old, then, however much there may have been for the charge formerly, and especially in England, from which this complaint is mostly imported, I do not think there is any ground for it now. It is within the memory of our older graduates that Chemistry, and Geology, and Mineralogy, and Botany, and Political Economy were either not taught at all, or scarcely at all in the college course. These have been introduced as fast as the sciences have become so mature as to furnish good text books; and now, if the public will furnish us the means we shall be glad to introduce more of Modern Languages, and something on Constitutional Law, which we intend to introduce, and Perspective and Civil Engineering. In regard to those things which are retained, there is not, that I am aware of, much complaint except respecting the Latin and Greek languages. But this subject is of so wide a compass, and the propriety of retaining them has so often and so fully been shown, that I shall not enter upon it here.

Again, it is objected to colleges, that they are aristocratic. Besides those who form no theory of society, there are two classes who would be thought to aim at the perfection and perpetuity of republican institutions, but their methods are directly opposite. The one can conceive of no improvement except by levelling every thing down——and probably there always will exist in every community a sediment of such people, whose uneasy malignity, manifesting itself in a pretended zeal for republicanism, nothing but a return of society to a savage state could satisfy. The other class do what they can to level up. And if there be one of these who imagines that colleges are not co-operating with him, it is because he is entirely ignorant of the facts. Must men be told at this day that the diffusion of knowledge is the only safety of republican institutions? Or are they ignorant that without higher seminaries the lower can never be sustained in any efficiency? Or that if there were not some institutions like colleges to make education cheap, we should soon have an aristocracy of knowledge and refinement as well as of wealth? On this subject there is a mistake in regard to two points. One respects the class of persons who go to college. While a portion of these are sons of wealthy men, the great mass are the sons of clergymen, and farmers and tradesmen, who feel that an education is the best patrimony they can bestow upon their children, and who are unable to give them even that, unless they assist themselves in part by teaching. The most of those therefore who graduate at our colleges spend no inconsiderable portion of time, either before or after graduating, in teaching, and thus diffusing the blessings of general education. The other point on which there is a mistake, respects the real extent to which the cost of education is diminished. At this college a young man receives instruction, and has the use of the buildings, and library, and apparatus, and cabinet, and pays the college but about $33 a year. The whole necessary expense per annum is less than $100; a sum quite insufficient to maintain a boy in a common family school. In addition to this we have funds bestowed by benevolent individuals which enable us to appropriate something to meet the bills of those who promise to be useful, but are not able to pay so much. Still, the whole expense is greater than is desirable, and if our funds would permit it we would gladly make it less. It is thus that the poor man who has no farm to give his son, can give him an education, which, if he is a suitable person to be educated, is better, and will enable him to start fairly in the race of competition with the sons of the wealthy. In a class in college each is on a perfect equality with the rest, and must stand on his own merits, and if the son of the rich should happen to have the advantage in previous training, he may yet find that he will have as much as he will care to do to maintain it in the field of open competition; and often when he does his best, much more if he become vain or frivolous, or self-indulgent, will he find himself left behind by the stern efforts of those who feel that they must depend on themselves alone. Surely he who would tax and cripple colleges, would tax and depress general education, and keep down the people.

The last objection against colleges which I shall notice, comes from another quarter, and is, that they do not teach manners. And it must be confessed that this is not one of the things for which we give a diploma. Good manners certainly ought to exist, and to be acquired in colleges, and more to be done on this point than is done. Still there are difficulties in the way which will be appreciated by every sensible man. In the first place, manners cannot be taught by direct inculcation; they must mainly depend on parents and on associates during the earlier years of life. Again, many of those who come to college are of such an age that it would be impossible to re-model their manners entirely under the most favorable circum-stances. They seem to have lost the power, which indeed some never had, of perceiving the difference between the easy inter-course of good fellowship which is consistent with self-respect and respect towards others, and a coarse familiarity which is consistent with neither. There is further apt to be a sentiment prevalent among young men, than which no mistake could be greater, that manners are of little importance, and that to be slovenly and slouching, and perhaps well nigh disrespectfull, is a mark of independence. After all, college is not, in some respects, a bad place to wear off rusticity and break down timidity. And if those who make the complaint could see the transformation and improvement which really take place in many, I may say in most instances in a college course, they would perhaps wonder that so much is accomplished, rather than complain that there is so little. Still, when a young man comes with a frame of granite rough from the mountains, or as rough as if he came from them, and has seen perhaps noth-ing of polite society, and knows nothing of polite literature, it cannot be expected that he should learn during his college course the manners of the drawing room, or the arbitrary forms of fashionable etiquette. If he shall possess, as perhaps such men often do, that higher form of politeness which con-sists in respecting the feelings of others and consulting their happiness, and we can send him into the world with a sound head and a warm heart to labor for the good of the world, we shall be satisfied, and the world ought to be thankful. Such men often become the pillars of society.

I now proceed to make some remarks on College Govern-ment. In regard to this, the principles on which we are to pro-ceed are very simple. As in a community, so in a college, gov-ernment ought always to be regarded, not as an end, but as a means to a further end. The end of a college being education, there should be no regulation or restraint which is not subservient to that; and when it becomes necessary to enforce those that are thus subservient, it would be treason to the cause of education not to do it at any sacrifice. If it should be necessary for this purpose to send away the half or the whole of a class, it must be done without hesitation. It is, however, always unfortunate when much comes to be said or thought about government. There should be among young men an ardor of study, a sense of propriety and self-respect, a strength of moral principle which would render government unnecessary, and cause every thing to move on as it ought, spontaneously. That college is in the best state in which the least government is necessary.

Closely connected with the government of a college, is the manner of intercourse between the officers and the students. In this respect a great, and no doubt a beneficial change has taken place. It is within the memory of some who hear me, that seniors had well nigh despotic authority over freshmen, could send them on errands, exact their obeisance, and settle authoritatively their disputes; and when the distance within which a student might approach an officer without taking off his hat, was prescribed by law. All this was as little in accordance with the nature of man, as with the spirit of our institutions, and we have no wish for its return. Nor do we desire any form, except so far as it is useful in fitting men for society, and in keeping alive in the minds of the young that respect towards others which ought to be cherished for their own sakes. He who has no respect for those qualities which fit men for responsible situations, can have no proper sense of appreciation of them, and he who has no sense of those qualities can never attain them. As he alone is fit to command who knows how to obey, so he alone who knows how to pay respect will ever come to deserve it. Hence it is that pertness and self-conceit, and disregard of those who ought to be respected, are so very unpromising symptoms in the young. There is indeed, between the officers and students of a college, something of official intercourse, and all the usages of society require that when this is the case there should be something of official respect. But in general the intercourse between the officers and students ought to be free and unrestrained, and precisely that which takes place between one gentleman and another in good society.

But the great point here is, and it is absolutely necessary in order to carry forward the principle of instruction of which I have spoken, that there should be such an intercourse and state of feeling that the officers and students can go on harmoniously together, and feel that they have a common object. This is all-important, and there is in respect to it much need of reformation. A young man often enters college with the impression that the faculty and students are opposite parties with opposing interest. As long as he has such a feeling, it would be better for him and for the institution that he should be away. On this subject, I have recently met with a letter from Fellenburg, in which my sentiments are so fully expressed that I shall quote a few sentences from it. "They," says he, referring to this class of young men, "consider teachers and pupils as opposite parties with distinct interest, or at best as rulers and subjects, the former seeking for power, and the latter having the right of resistance. They cannot understand our desire to act as parents, who seek to direct and restrain their children in order to improve their character, and secure their happiness. They attribute to the lowest and most sordid motives all that is done to furnish an education truly christian and entirely disinterested; an education liberally provided for in reference both to science and the arts. Pupils of this character often find their greatest pleasure in defeating all the efforts which are made for their improvement, instead of co-operating in them, and considering their own best interests as identified with the success of their teachers." If such a state of things must exist in our colleges, they ought not to be sustained.

It was my intention to consider at this point some of the obstacles in the way of our success; but as I have already occupied so much time, I shall only indicate them.

One is, want of preparation on the part of many. Much of what is done in colleges, especially in the languages, ought to be done before entering.

Another is, the necessity of so much absence for the purpose of teaching. This breaks up and retards a class, and makes general scholarship meager.

Another is, the want of interest in parents. If parents would come with their sons, or occasionally visit them, or let us know by letter, their peculiarities and tempers, we might sometimes avoid mistakes.

Another is, the diversity of ages, capacities and tastes. Many enter too young.

But the great difficulties which we have to contend with result from influences that flow in from the community; and if they would have colleges what they ought to be, they must be what they ought to be themselves. A college is not an isolated community. No place sooner feels the undulations of public sentiment, and it is impossible that it should not partake of the tone of feeling, and adopt the practices of the community in which it is. The young man does not forget, on coming to college, the associations and habits of home, and if smoking, or drinking, or profane swearing, or gambling, or any other habit is prevalent in a community, then it cannot be entirely excluded from the colleges. They can never be what they ought, till the general tone of moral feeling in the community is elevated.

The remarks already made may suffice to indicate my views of the general course of instruction and government that should be pursued in our colleges. In carrying out these views, I have the happiness to know that I shall not have to labor alone—that I shall have associates in whom I can confide—some of them of wider experience, and maturer views than myself—who will not merely second my endeavors, but who will go abreast with me in bearing the responsibilities, and sustaining the labors which are inseparable from a faithful performance of the important trusts committed to us. But with all their aid, and the indulgence which I may hope for from the public, it is with much diffidence and self-distrust that I enter upon the office to which I am called. Whether I remember the venerable men who have preceded me, and especially my distinguished predecessor, to whom this college is so largely indebted, or the high reputation of this institution or the standing and influence of its alumni, or the standard of education now demanded, or the character of the times for excitement and change, and reckless attack upon those who conduct our publc institutions, I feel that the responsibilities and labors and inquietudes of the office will be fully equal to its honor. I enter upon it with no excitement of novelty, with no buzz of expectation, with no accession of influence to the college from abroad, and with no expectation of pleasing everybody. I have no ambition to build up here what would be called a great institution; the wants of the community do not require it. But I do desire, and shall labor that this may be a safe college, that its reputation may be sustained and raised still higher, that the plan of instruction which I have indicated may be carried out more fully; that here there may be health, and cheerful study, and kind feelings, and pure morals, and that in the memory of future students college life may be made a still more verdant spot.

But deep as is my anxiety when I look at the connection of this college with the interests of science and literature; it is far deeper when I look at its connection with the immortal destinies of those who shall come here, and with the progress of the cause of Christ and the conversion of the world. The true and permanent interests of man, can be promoted only in connexion with religion; and a regard to man as an immortal, accountable and redeemed being, should give its character to the whole course of our regulations, and the spirit of our instructions. This college has, for a long time been regarded, and not without reason, with interest and affection by the churches. Of its whole number of graduates, as many as one third have devoted themselves to the ministry, and recently a larger proportion. It was on this ground that American missions had their origin. It was here that Mills and Hall prayed, and their mantle has so descended on the institution, that now we can hardly turn our eyes to a missionary station where one or more of its sons are not to be found. Others are on their way, and there is remaining behind an association devoted to the same glorious work. This college has also been the scene of revivals of religion, pure, and repeated and mighty, which have caused, and are still causing, joy on earth and in heaven. It is upon these, and upon the higher standard of consistent piety that follows in their train, that we mainly rest our hopes for the distinguished usefulness of this college. For these let the churches pray; and let them join with us, in the words of my venerable predecessor when this building was dedicated, "in devoting this College to the Holy Spirit as a scene of revivals of religion, and to the blessed redeemer as an engine to bring on the millenial glory of His church." This would we do, not only as the friends of religion, but as the friends of science, and of a pure literature, and of the freest spirit of inquiry. We would do it that we may disabuse the world of the absurd prejudice that the knowledge of God cramps the mind, and disqualifies it for the study of his works —that we may hasten that day, which must come, when it shall

160

be seen and felt that there is a coincidence and essential unity between reason and religion; when the spirit of literature and the spirit of science shall minister before the spirit of piety, and pour their oil into the lamp that feeds its waxing flame; when study shall be nerved to its highest efforts by christian benevolence, and young men shall grow up at the same time into the light of science and the beauty of holiness.

Inaugural Address

The Relation of Learning and Religion

by

JULIUS HAWLEY SEELYE

President of Amherst College

June 27, 1877

JULIUS HAWLEY SEELYE (*September 14, 1824—May 12, 1895*) *was born in Bethel, Connecticut. He graduated from Amherst College in 1849 and received the degree from Auburn Theological Seminary in 1852. His forceful personality and vigorous mind placed him in great demand as a public speaker. He had a profound influence upon his college community. He was the author of a number of books dealing with citizenship and christianity.*

Amherst College was founded by Christian people and for a Christian purpose. It was an association of Christian ministers, who, at Shelburne, May 10, 1815, started measures for the foundation of the College, and it was the Christian men and women of Franklin and Hampshire Counties by whom these measures were carried to their consummation. The inspiring sources of the whole movement were devotion to Christ and zeal for His kingdom. When the first college building was dedicated, and its first president and professor were inaugurated, September 18, 1821, "the promotion of the religion of Christ" was declared to be the special object of the undertaking, and the prayers which were then offered for "the guidance and protection of the great Head of the church, to whose service,"—in the language then used,—"this institution is consecrated," have been since repeated with undiminished earnestness and faith, on every similar occasion. At the first meeting of the trustees after the legislative act of incorporation, steps were taken for the organization of a Christian church, which, when formed, was named the Church of Christ in Amherst College, as indicative no less of the Catholic than the Christian spirit which should here reign.

It was the original purpose, from which the friends and guardians of the college have never swerved, that there should be here furnished the means for the highest attainable culture in science and literature and philosophy. The college was not to fall below the best in its intellectual provisions. But the constant and chief aim of its founders was to establish here an educational institution in which Christian faith might dominate, and whose power might subserve the knowledge of Christian truth. From President Moore, in whose saintly zeal the earliest students of the college found both instruction and inspiration, to President Stearns, whose purity and faith surrounded his presence like a halo, ennobling him and enlightening and elevating all who had contact with him, the controlling purpose of the college has been to provide the highest possible educational advantages, and to penetrate these with a living faith in the Lord Jesus Christ, and a supreme devotion to His kingdom.

In all this Amherst College is not peculiar. Other institutions of learning have been founded and carried forward with the same purpose. Indeed, here is the source from which directly and obviously, or indirectly, all our influences of education flow. The schools of the Christian world trace their actual historical origin to the Christian church. As early as the third century we find it recognized as a Christian duty to plant schools for the nurture of the children and youth whereever churches were planted. In subsequent centuries, by recommendations and decrees of councils and synods, the attention of Christian ministers was everywhere directed to the establishment of town and village and parochial schools "because,"—as the third council of Latern in 1179 decreed,—"the church of God as a pious mother is bound to provide opportunity for learning." It was under this influence that England, in the time of Edward III., was called the land of schools, every cathedral and almost every monastery having its own.

The precise time and way in which the oldest universities of Europe arose cannot be definitely ascertained, but the evidence is clear that they directly owed their origin to the church, and were subject to her control. The University of Paris, the oldest of them all—with the possible exception of that at Bologna—was designated as "the first school of the church," and the oldest public documents extant respecting it are ecclesiastical decrees for its management. The thousands on thousands who flocked to these seats of learning during the Middle Ages, exceeding by far,—whether we take their actual number or their relative proportion,—the classes since attending the same, were drawn thither,—so far as we can judge from the results,—not so much by zest for study as by zeal for the service of the church. When kings and emperors added their efforts to those of synods and councils for the advancement of learning, as when Charlemagne extended schools through his empire for the education of the clergy, or Alfred, according to the old Warwick Chronicler, erected the first three halls at Oxford in the name of the Holy Trinity, they sought for learning as the handmaid of religion, because they saw that religion was the conservator of the state. When the Reformation arose, its great religious quickening was a wide-reaching inspiration toward education, as well. The great reformers were well nigh as zealous in the work of education as in that of religious purification. "It is a grave and serious thing," says Luther in his Address to the Common Councils of all the Cities of Germany in Behalf of Christian Schools, written in 1524, "affecting the interest of the kingdom of Christ and of all the world, that we apply ourselves to the work of aiding and instructing the young. I entreat you in God's behalf not to think so lightly of this matter, as many do." Melancthon equaled Luther in his zeal and surpassed him in his practical activity for the advancement of learning. He wrote textbooks on dialectics, rhetoric, physics and ethics, which were more widely used in schools than any other books of his time. No man, not even Erasmus, contributed so profoundly to the culture of the age as did Melancthon. It was through a visitation of the churches and schools of the electorate of Saxony in 1527, in which more than thirty men were engaged through a whole year, that the so-called Saxon school system, which may properly be termed the basis of the modern German system of education, was drawn up by Luther and Melancthon. The great universities of Konigsberg, Jena, Halle, Gottingen, and afterwards Berlin, owed their existence directly to the reformation, while those of Tubingen, Wittenberg and Leipsic received their character and power from the same source.

All our educational frame-work owes its corner-stone and informing law to the interests of religion. Our oldest college,

founded less than sixteen years after the landing of the Pilgrims, and six years after the first settlement of Boston, had,
says Johnson in his Wonder-Working Providence, "its end
firmly fixed on the glory of God and good of all his elect
people the world throughout in vindicating the truth of Christ
and promoting His glorious kingdom." The original charter of
Yale college declares the motive for the undertaking to be
"a sincere regard to and zeal for upholding and propagating of
the Christian Protestant religion." The first order made upon
this continent for the establishment of common schools, was
issued by the united colonies of Connecticut in 1644, and
copied and re-declared by the colony of Massachusetts Bay in
1647, in these remarkable words:

"It being one chiefe project of yt ould deluder, Satan, to
keepe men from the knowledge of ye Scriptures, as in formr
times by keeping ym in an unknowne tongue, so that in these
lattr times by pswading from ye use of tongues, yt so at least
ye true sence & meaning of ye originall might be clouded
by false glosses of saint seeming deceivers, yt learning may not
be buried in ye grave of or fathrs in ye church & commonwealth, the Lord assisting or endeavors, -

"It is therefore ordred, yt evry towneship in this jurisdic-
tion aftr ye Lord hath increased ym to ye number of 50 householdrs, shall then forthwth apoint one wthin their towne to
teach all such children as shall resort to him to write & reade,
whose wages shall be paid eithr by ye parents or mastrs of
such children, or by ye inhabitants in genrall, by way of supply, as ye maior prt of those yt ordr ye prudentials of ye towne
shall appoint; provided, those yt send their children be not oppressed by paying much more yn they can have ym taught for
in othr townes; & it is furthr ordered, yt where any towne shall
increase to ye numbr of 100 families or householdrs, they shall
set up a gramer schoole, ye mr thereof being able to instruct
youths so farr as they may be fited for ye university, provided,

yt if any towne neglect ye pformance hereof above one yeare, yt every such towne shall pay 5L to ye next schoole till they shall prforme this order."

Though all our colleges and systems of common schools do not start so obviously from a religious impulse, though it is claimed for some that their source and aims are purely secular, there has not yet appeared any prominent and long continued educational influence, among us or elsewhere, wholly dissociated from a religious origin and inspiration. "I have always despaired," said a superintendent of public schools in Ohio, "of maintaining even a good common school, where there is not a Christian church to help it."

Is this wide-reaching relation of religion and education after all only accidental and temporary, or has it a rational ground, which is therefore abiding and on which, if we are wise, we shall still continue to build? There is at the present time no graver or more practical question relating to education than this, and none also on which more hasty and inconsiderate answers apt to be given, perhaps, on either side. It will help us to a clear view and correct conclusion, if we divest ourselves at the outset of the very common but quite superficial notion that there is an inherent law of progress in human nature, by which it is constantly seeking and gaining for itself an improved condition. Such a notion is not supported by the facts, either of history or of human nature itself. The facts of history certainly show a far more prominent law of deterioration than of progress. Over by far the larger portion of the globe today, and with by far the larger portion of mankind, retrogression reigns instead of progress, and this is true as we look back through all ages. Progress not only has never been universal, but so far as records reach, it has always been confined to the few; wherever yet its fertilizing streams have flowed, they have been rivers in narrow beds, never covering the earth as the waters cover the sea. Moreover, in unnumbered

169

instances where progress has begun, it has died out and disappeared. The evidences of this are as striking as they are mournful. No historical fact is clearer than that human progress has never revealed any inherent power of self-perpetuation. Arts, languages, literatures, sciences, civilizations, religions, have, in unnumbered instances, deteriorated and left a people to grope in the shadow of death, whose progenitors seemed to rejoice in the light of life. There is as yet no induction of facts sufficiently broad, if we had nothing else, to warrant the conclusion, that any progress that the world now knows is certain to be permanent or likely to be universal.

But these facts of history would not surprise us if we did but see that they represent, on a broad scale, only a deep-seated fact in human nature itself. Strange, and startling, and sad as it is, the fact will not be doubted by a close observer, that there is a much deeper impulse in human nature to throw away its privileges than to retain them. Endow a man with any possessions you please, give him any kind of degree of culture, let his culture be clothed and crowned with virtue till he shines like the sun, and lesser stars fade in his light, and then leave him to himself; take away the restraints and incentives of society, free his thoughts from the claims of God and duty, and let only the dictates and desires which are bounded by his individual will control him, and how long before his glory will be gone, and you might search in vain among the ashes of his wasted privileges for a single spark of his former fire? The influences which perpetuate a man's culture, which give it strength and growth and fruitfulness are not of the man's own creation. They are not his in any sense, save as he receives them, and he can no more retain them than he retain tomorrow, the light of the sun by which he walks today, and without whose continued shining he walks in darkness.

And it is no more within the power of human nature to originate than it is to perpetuate its progress. There are many

170

current notions upon this point which a clear discernment would at once dispel. We crudely talk as though human nature by the evolution of its own inherent forces could lift itself from a lower to a higher plane, but in no case was this ever done. The historical fact has always been that the higher has first descended upon and breathed its inspiration into the lower before the latter has shown any impulse to improvement. In our processes of education, the higher school have not grown out of the lower and do not rest upon them, but the higher school is historically first, and the lower one is not its precursor but its product; there is no law of evolution by which the common school grows up into the college, for as an historical fact, the college is actually first, and gives birth to the common school. It is not by the lower education of the many that we come to have the higher education of the few, but the exact converse of this is the universal rule.

A great man who leads his nation or his age to a higher state is no mere product of forces belonging to the time of his appearance. What forces belonging to his time produced Moses, or Confucius, or Sakya-Muni, or Zoroaster, or Socrates? A great man is a God-bestowed gift upon his time, giving to his time a new day for which there is no approaching dawn, and whose coming is as unexplained by the conditions when he came, as it was unexpected by the people to whom he came. They are lifted by him to a higher plane, because he stands already, and from the outset, on a higher plane than they. So far as records of history go, no nation ever originated its own progress. No savage has ever civilized himself. The lamp which lightens one nation in its progress, has always been lighted by a lamp behind it.

But whence, then, does progress originate, and by what means is it perpetuated? A general answer to this question is not difficult. Divesting ourselves of all theories which prejudice the facts, and looking only at the facts themselves, it is quite

171

clear that the prime impulse toward human improvement, is not any desire for what may be called the arts or advantages of civilization. These have no attraction to a people which does not already possess them. They are not attractive to a savage; on the contrary, he finds them repulsive. This, in fact, is what makes him a savage, that he hates the very condition in which the civilized man finds his joy. He is conscious of but few wants, and these of the simplest sort, which it needs but few efforts to satisfy; and the gifts of civilization for which he feels no necessity, offer him, therefore, no advantages which he can appreciate, and can excite in him no efforts to obtain them. The first impulse to any improvement of a man's outward condition must come from the quickening of some inner inspiration, without which all the blandishments of civilization could no more win a savage to a better state than could all the warmth of the sun woo a desert to a fruitful field.

But the seed of this inner quickening can never be planted in the soul of the savage by advancing knowledge. He does not desire knowledge any more than he desires the power which knowledge brings. He is not only indifferent to his ignorance but he is unconscious of it, for ignorance is first of all and always ignorant of itself. An ignorant people has never yet leaped from its ignorance into advancing knowledge without some other impulse than the knowledge furnished. In order that knowledge may be attractive and thus attained, the soul must be kindled by some inspiring sentiment, and thus we find as an historical fact that the quickened heart is the precursor of the enlightened intellect and the origin of progress with any people.

In the history of human knowledge, science is always preceded and quickened by art, yet art does not spontaneously originate. While the mother of science, she herself is the child of religion. These sentiments of the soul in which art finds its fountain, and from which all the streams of science spring, are the deep convictions of the soul's religious wants and its

172

religious capabilities. Take to illustrate this any of the arts which mark the culture of a people and trace their origin and history. It might be crudely supposed that architecture arose from a natural necessity man has of furnishing himself a shelter and a dwelling-place. But allowing this natural necessity to exist, and supposing it to have found its natural expression, the result need have no more resemblance to architecture than have the huts of a Hottentot kraal to the palaces of Vienna and Versailles. Man's natural want of a shelter can be supplied, and if we look simply at numbers, is supplied by a great majority of men, with as little beauty and as little architectural skill as are found in the habitations of the ant or the beaver. But, aside from this, the truth is that the history of architecture does not begin with the history of human homes. The oldest remains of architecture are symbols and monuments of religious faith. Columns and colonnades and temples, structures erected for worship, or to symbolize some object or doctrine of religion,—these, and not human dwellings, are the earliest indications we have of the dawn of architecture. Looking now, not in the light of any theory which prejudges the facts, but only at the facts themselves, we are obliged to say that it was not the construction of his dwelling-house that taught man to build his temple, but exactly the other way.

The same is true with sculpture, painting, poetry, music. It was a religious impulse which gave to all these their first inspiration. The oldest monuments we possess of any of these arts are associated with some religious rite or faith. But more than this, we must also notice the undoubted fact that the arts have grown in glory just as the religious sentiment has grown in power. The period of decadence in art is always indicated by a prior decline in religion. There is no high art, as I suspect we may also say there is never a great genius uninspired by some sort of a religious sentiment and impulse. As the seed whose growth shall fill the fields with plenty, and clothe the earth with beauty, slumbers in the earth in darkness, and with no signs of life till the warmth of the sun comes nigh, so all the thoughts of men, with whatever capabilities of art and science endowed, lie dormant in the soul until some divine communication stirs the soul with the sense of its accountability and its sin, and kindles it with a longing for the favor of its God. If, as all the facts would indicate, even if we had no evidence from Scripture, man originally started on the high plane of these divine communications, from which he fell, all his subsequent degradation has had its stages exactly marked by the prior degree in which his knowledge of God has been clouded. The knowledge of God is the light of our inner life, and when this light grows dim or dies, the glory of great thought and noble deeds fades also and expires. I know not elsewhere so profound a statement of the law of history when men do not retain God in their knowledge, as Paul's in the first chapter of Romans: "Because that when they knew God they glorified Him not as God, neither were thankful, but became vain in their imaginations and their foolish heart was darkened. Professing themselves to be wise they became fools, and changed the glory of the incorruptible God into an image like to corruptible man, and to birds, and four-footed beasts and creepings. Wherefore God also gave them up to uncleanness through the lusts of their own hearts."

All this is quite contrary, I am well aware, to many current theories. I read in a late book by a noted author, "To believe that man was originally civilized and then suffered utter degradation in so many regions, is to take a pitiably low view of human nature." But, alas, this is exactly the view which the sad facts of history oblige us to take, and we must square our views of human nature to the actual facts of the case, whether or not it would better suit our desires and our theories to have them otherwise. All the facts of history point backward not to an original savage state, but, as the deep thinkers of antiquity in the pagan world were constantly declaring, to an original golden age of peace and purity.

174

Aureus hanc vitam in terris Saturnus agebat.

Man became corrupt and degraded instead of being originally such, and as all his degradation comes from the darkness into which he plunged when he turns away from God, so it is not strange that his purity and upward progress are restored to him only as the light of God's communications shines again upon his soul. Here is not only the first impulse to human progress, but the only one which in our time, or previously, has shown any permanent power. Wild, uncivilized, barbarous, savage people are changing today to a state of peace and purity and advancing civilization, not by commerce or conquest of arms, not by letters, or science, or the knowledge of the so-called useful arts, but by the simple preaching of the gospel, by the story of God's grace, which makes a man feel that he is a sinner, and gives him his first longing for a better state. He who does not see the exhibitions of this now taking place on different parts of the globe is blind to some of the most obvious and most important events of the present age. A naked, filthy savage, who has heard the story of the gospel and been brought to a living application of its strange truths, wishes at once to be clothed and clean, and becomes thus for the first time conscious of wants which his industry must relieve. Civilization, education, all progress starts with this inner quickening, which they could no more themselves originate than could the brooks which beautify the meadows, originate the mountain springs from which they flow. Clear observers now acknowledge the mistake of attempting to civilize a savage people through any other process than by a prior religious renovation. Plato saw this when he argued in the Sophist, that men merged in sensualism need to be improved before they can be instructed, they must first become virtuous before they can be made intelligent.

The basis and life of all our present civilization are clearly seen to be in the Christian spirit and the religious quickening it has wrought. It was not the capture of Constantinople by the Turks, and the consequent scattering of Greek scholars over Europe, which led to the modern revival of learning. And is was not the grander proportions which the natural world assumed through the discoveries of Columbus and Kepler, nor the new method furnished by Bacon for the instauration of the natural sciences which has led to so vast an increase of the study of nature in these modern times. The light before which the Dark Ages rolled away, and in which all the germs of our modern life have been quickened, was the dawn of the Reformation, which, long before the time of Luther, was falling on the vision of Tauler, and Eckhart, and Nicolas of Basle, and the Gottesfreunde, and the saintly men who wrote the Theologia Germanica and the Imitation of Christ.

And not only the dawn but the day of which we boast, has proceeded step by step from the clearer shining on the human soul of some truths which the Bible first revealed. It is a simple but most significant truth, that every stage of our modern progress has been preceded and inspired by a closer study of the Scriptures and a deeper reverence for them as the word of God.

These historical facts will not surprise the profound student of human nature. To such a student not only are the religious feelings seen to spring from the deepest susceptibility of the soul, but they are seen also to form the very ground work of intellectual development. The first impulse to know is always a feeling. The thoughts of the intellect are started and sustained by the sentiments of the soul. But

"These first affections,
These shadowy recollections,
Which, be they what they may,
Are yet the fountain-light of all our day,
Are yet a masterlight of all our seeing,"

do not have their object, do not find their source in finite

176

things. The knowledge of the finite, instead of producing, presupposes the knowledge of the infinite. The disposition to measure and grasp the finite is not derived from the finite, for the finite, with no standard to measure, and no power to grasp itself, can originate no impulse to attempt these achievements. The first movement of thought, in so far as it differs from the thoughtless preceptions of the brute, is a movement to learn the ground and meaning of things. The first question asked by the human mind, and which also marks the mind's progress in all its stages, is the question, Why. But this question never could be asked save for the deep conviction that it could be answered. The disposition to seek the explanation of things could never arise but for the ineradicable conviction that the explanation can be found. But what does this imply when thoroughly considered? An explanation needing itself to be explained does not answer the mind's inquiries. These inquiries cease only when an ultimate and self-sufficient ground is reached. The mind rests only on what is itself at rest. But nature does not rest. Nothing in nature rests. Life in unnumbered generations rolling like a flood, light and heat penetrating space in perpetual pulsations, the winds, the waves, the stars sweeping, swelling, circling in ceaseless change, mark the restlessness of nature everywhere. Up and down this realm of things the human thought wanders in its inquiries, seeking rest and finding none. One inquiry only answered by another, one fact of nature expounded by a farther fact, which needs itself an explanation by something still beyond, keeps thought ever baffled, keeps its products of philosophy and science ever tossing to and fro, and makes the mind in its thirst for truth like the traveler thirsting for water in the desert, before whose eye floats the distant mirage of flowing fountains and shining streams, which keeps beyond him as he travels toward it, and still mocks him with its delusion as he sinks exhausted in the sand. Only reason rests, only the supernatural rests, and the human mind in its inquiries into nature in its eager search for the unseen meaning of the things it sees, finds joy and peace only when it finds the supernatural.

But the supernatural marks the end no more than it does the beginning of the mind's inquiries. The supernatural is the alpha as well as the omega of the human thought. We never should be impelled to seek it but for its own stirrings already within us. That which the thoughts of our intellect are striving to formulate is already present in the sentiments of the soul. The mind's pursuit of science and philosophy is only its impulse to know what it already feels, is only its effort to become conscious of what is already its unconcious possession. The saying of Lessing is often quoted, "If the Almighty should hold out to me in His right hand all truth, and in His left the search for truth, and deign to offer me which I would prefer, I would say, Lord, pardon the weakness of thy servant, yet grant me the search for truth rather than all truth." But could the human mind ever take such an attitude as this? Could we ever choose a progress which has no goal save the endless repetition of its own steps,—a way like that of Sysiphus rolling his stone up the steep mountain side, only to find it slipping from his grasp before it reached the summit, and ever rolling back into the valley again? No, no, we seek that we may find. The hope without fruition dies, and the hopeless search would not be undertaken by one who knew its hopelessness. The search for truth is excited only by the love of truth, and the love of truth bears witness to the presence of the truth within the soul, whose face that soul alone desires to see which has already felt its quickening embrace. But truth is inconceivable without God. Neither truth, nor beauty, nor goodness would have any meaning, or be anything more than words, which the unthinking brute might speak as well as man, unless they point to Him and come from Him in whom all beauty, truth and goodness find alone their exhaustless and eternal source and sun. They are not God; they are not parts of Him;

178

but they are revelations of Him in whom we live and move and have our being, who is not thus far from any one of us, and who declares something of His glory to the eye which he has opened to behold it in these radiant expressions of Himself. We call him glorious, whether artist, sage or hero, who has seen and made known to us the glory of these divine manifestations, and we link his name with immortal renown. But the glory is not in what he is, but in what he beholds. This it is which has furnished him his exaltation, and his fame, and which continually suffices to

"Disturb him with the joy of elevated thoughts,
A sense sublime of something far more deeply interposed,
Whose dwelling is the light of setting suns,
And the round ocean and the deep blue sky,
And on the mind of man."

Thus the whole intellectual life hangs on what, in the most comprehensive sense, may be termed the religious life. Its original impulse comes from the religious life, and it will be strong and fruitful, only as this is profound and penetrating. That self-consciousness wherein we are distinguished from the brute, and in which the very being of reason consists, has not only as its constant attendant, but as its essential prerequisite, the consciousness of God. "To know God," says Jacobi, "and to possess reason, are one and the same thing, just as not to know God and to be a brute are one and the same thing." This knowledge may be very vague; its first dawnings may be so dim that they can hardly be discerned from the feelings out of which they rise; it may often remain quite obscure, and may even be denied or derided by the very intellect which has derived all its light and life therefrom, but the truth, still and forever remains that there can be no illumination of the intellect without a prior inspiration of the heart, and this inspiration of the heart is as meaningless and groundless without a divine impulse, as would be the light and warmth of earthly nature

179

without the quickening presence of the sun.

In all this I have only uttered what the deepest students of human nature have, in all ages, seen and acknowledged. The truth I have stated is, I think, exactly what Plato saw when he said, in the Republic, "In the same manner as the sun is the cause of sight, and the cause not merely that objects are visible, but also that they grow and are produced, so the good is of such power and beauty that it is not merely the cause of science to the soul, but is also the cause of being and reality to whatever is the object of science, and as the sun is not itself sight, or the object of sight, but presides over both, so the good is not science and truth, but is superior to both, they being not the good itself, but of a goodly nature."

It is therefore not accidental that the actual historical progress of mankind in art, science, philosophy or virtue should depend, as we have seen, upon some religious impulse for its beginnings and continuance. Nor is it strange that schools and systems of education should have had no other source. It is only surprising when we fancy that the currents of progress can now be made to flow from any different springs, or that the lamp of learning can be lighted or kept burning with any other flame. If we are wise we shall not only learn, but be guided by lessons which history and human nature both teach, that education divorced from religion is like a tree severed from its nourishing roots, which thereby falls to the ground, leaving its leaves to wither, its fruit to perish, and itself to decay. From such folly we turn, leaving the blind to lead the blind, not doubting what the end to them both will be.

What then are the practical consequences of this truth? What adjustments does it require in the processes of our higher education? It requires, obviously, that the corner stone and the top stone and the informing law of our whole educational fabric should be Christian faith and Christian freedom, the faith in which the true religious life finds its only sufficient root, and the freedom in which that same life finds its only adequate expression. We need Christian faith to perpetuate and perfect what Christian faith has begun. For, even if the fabric built upon this basis could be kept standing when its foundations were removed, its increasing beauty and living growth would then be gone. A Christian college, therefore, looking not at transient but at permanent ends, sowing seed for a perennial harvest of the farthest science and the fairest culture, will be solicitous, first of all, to continue Christian. If it is to be in the long run truly successful in the advancement of learning, it will have the Christian name written not alone upon its seal and its first records, but graven in its life as ineffaceably as was the name of Phidias on Athene's shield. It will seek for Christian teachers and only these,——men in whom are seen the dignity and purity and grace of Christ's disciples, and whose lips instruct, while their lives inspire. It will order all its studies and its discipline that its pupils through the deep and permanent impulse of a life by the faith of the Son of God, may be led to the largest thought and kindled to the highest aims, with an energy undying and an enthusiasm which does not fade. It will not be ashamed of the Gospel of Christ, nor remiss in preaching that gospel to its students "till they all come in the unity of the faith and of the knowledge of the Son of God unto a perfect man."

But this is to be taken in no narrow sense. Christian faith does not fetter, it emancipates the mind. Just in proportion to its depth and power is its possessor liberated from prejudice and superstition and all narrowness of thought. Christian faith is not only not hostile to free thought, but it finds its normal exercise and expression in this very freedom. It is itself in such exact accord with all the original endowments and deepest instincts of the soul——whose foundations were not laid in falsehood——that it is only settled more firmly in its seat by free inquiry. It is only when the thought becomes fettered and is

181

no longer free that it fails to return——over whatever field it may have ranged——to the faith which has inspired it.

In Raphael's famous School of Athens the great artist has represented Plato looking upwards and pointing to the heavens, but holding in his hand as his most characteristic work, the Timaeus, wherein he seeks to bring upon the created earth the light of the uncreated heavens, while Aristotle, standing by his side, his eye lost in thought, but his fingers directed toward the earth clasps as his most significant treatise, the Ethica, wherein he would find the heavenly principle which should regulate the earthly life. The representation is worthy of the great genius who made it. Philosophy, where its inspiration is highest, and its investigations are deepest, reaches the same result, no matter in what direction it starts. Plato beginning with the heavens, looked so comprehensively that he saw the earth shining in the light of the skies, and Aristotle beginning with the earth, looked so deeply that he saw the heavens beneath it, the same heavens which Plato saw above. It is a mistake, though one often and easily made, to suppose that Plato and Aristotle only represent the opposite poles of idealism and empiricism. They differ in their method rather than in their end, for the idea, as Aristotle apprehended it, was just as much the object of his search, as of Plato's. They both agreed that the essence of the individual thing is in the idea, and that only ideas can be truly known. And it is because of this original agreement,——this original unity of insight and aim——that in the end which each reached, the method and results of the one were justified by the method and results of the other.

In like manner Christian faith, if that be the object sought, may be reached by divers methods of inquiry, and we shall wisely welcome any tendency of thought, starting from whatever source and moving in whatever direction, which has this faith for its presupposition and is zealously bent upon discovering and declaring its sufficient grounds. Only that tendency of thought which divorces itself from God and the supernatural and the Christian atonement shall we wisely discard from our processes of education, and this not simply because such a tendency is untrue, but because it is necessarily empty and vain, because it has no power of permanent progress, and because the schools and systems of education left to its control, will become first superficial and formal and then barren and dead. We discard it just as Plato and Aristotle would both have discarded any speculations which did not presuppose and seek the idea as their starting point and goal, such speculations belonging, as Plato would say, only to a world of darkness and shadows, and being, as Aristotle would say, of necessity fruitless and dead. A philosophy which should expend itself upon the natural and ignore the supernatural and the spiritual world, would be, according to Plato, only a phantasm deluding our vision and vanishing at our touch, and a science which should content itself with looking into the earth without looking through it unto the heavens, would, according to Aristotle, be buried in Cimmerian darkness or lost in Tartarean fires.

Gentlemen of the Trustees and the Faculty, Students and Friends of Amherst College: I take up the work assigned me, in the spirit, and with the aims I have thus endeavored to express. Far distant be the day when one intrusted with the interests of this institution in any degree, should set before him any other than the lofty aim which has prevailed in the history of Amherst College from its beginning to the present time. To Jesus Christ, the Son of God, the Savior, the College was originally dedicated, and to Him be it now again presented in a new consecration, ever living and all embracing. May He reign and ever be acknowledged in all its affairs! May He keep the College strong and progressive, and give it increasing power through the increasing strength of its faith in Him! May this faith be so firmly fixed, and so intelligently

183

held that it shall be free and fearless in its exercise, emancipated from all intolerance and bigotry, showing itself in largest charity and sympathy, and giving speed and cheer to whatever seeks the knowledge of Christ, in whatever avenue the search be made, and yet, because it is a living and not a dead faith in Jesus Christ and his atonement, tolerating nothing which makes its aim to set aside His claims! May He guide continually the guardians of the College, and live in the life and speak through the lips continually of every teacher, and may all the students who, from the east and the west, the north and the south, shall throng these halls, be made complete in Him who is the head of all principalities and powers! As the wise men from the East came and laid their gifts in adoring homage at the feet of the babe at Bethlehem, so may Amherst College ever show that the learning of the world, where it is highest, and deepest, and widest, and best, is content to sit at His feet and receive instruction from Him, who is not only wise but Wisdom, not only a true teacher but Himself the Truth, and whose words, which contain the sum of our faith, reach also, and ever beyond the summit of our philosophy!

Inaugural Address

Relation of Metropolis and University

by

HENRY MITCHELL MacCRACKEN
President of New York University

February, 1885

*HENRY MITCHELL MacCRACKEN
(September 28, 1840—December 24, 1918)
was born in Oxford, Ohio. MacCracken prepared for the ministry at Presbyterian Theological Seminary. He was at one time pastor
of Westminister Church, Columbus, Ohio. His
pastoral duties were interrupted by a year's
study in Europe. Upon his return, he resumed
the pastorate at the First Presbyterian Church,
at Toledo. In 1881, he accepted the chancellorship at Western University in Pennsylvania.
He instituted a number of reforms during his
administration of three years.*

The environment of this platform—a lively reception on the right hand and an approaching collation on the left—dictates to me a practical subject, a prompt entrance upon it, and its plain, off-hand treatment.

The theme I have chosen is The Relation of Metropolis and University.

In history it appears as the relation of whole to part, of body to member. Where ever the metropolis has risen, there as a rule has risen also the university. It is an interesting fact that when the word metropolis was first written by old Herodotus, it was of a city that was founding a university. Athens was not only taking the commercial headship of Greece, bringing home the grain and wools of the East, the iron and copper of the West, and manufacturing them as well, but she was founding a school, the first in the world, to image the modern university—a school that has deservedly been painted, in the persons of its leaders, by Raphael in the chambers of the vatican, by Kaulbach on the walls of the Berlin Museum—the school of Athens, which was indeed a university.

Was it not a university where the faculty included Socrates teaching philosophy; Protagoras, law; Prodicus, rhetoric; Hippias, natural science; or in the following generation, when the faculty enrolled Plato in theology, Aristotle in philosophy, Antisthenes in ethics, while natural science, under Theophrastus, brought together two thousand young men from all quarters of the world?

Take either definition of the university—the theoretic, which requires it to be a place whither teachers and scholars come from every quarter, for giving and receiving every kind of knowledge, or the modern historical, which requires it to be a school of several faculties, embracing in their circle the sciences, human and divine, which they impart in order to prepare students for the learned professions and other higher

187

walks of life——and is not the School of Athens found to be indeed a university?

When Athens found a successor in Grecian leadership, her University found a successor also. In Alexandria, the noble town created by Alexander, whither his dust was born over the desert from far-away Babylon, and whither Eastern and Western civilization flowed, mingling their streams, there rose, more quickly than in Athens, through kingly favor, an extended faculty.

As the University of Athens had its specially named places of instruction——its Porch, its Lyceum, its Academy—— so Alexandria had its Museum, that vast building that gave comfortable homes to the professors, as well as spacious apartments for teaching, and for gathering the famed Alexandrian Library. Nor were its professors behind the Library in renown, when chairs were filled by the geographer, Ptolemy, the mathematicians, Euclid and Appollonius, the physicist, Archimedes, the philosopher, Philo, or in the later faculty by Clement and Origen, Gregory and Athanasius.

Scant justice has been done the University that rose in metropolitan Rome, simply because Rome demanded of teachers that they make men able for professional usefulness rather than for mere professorial amassment of learning, or for manifestly unfruitful speculations. The theorists now who are ready to rule out from the university proper the special professional instruction that fits for the ministry, the law, or for medicine, will contemn the Romans, who cared, as Dr. Zeller, of Berlin University, says, "little for the scientific establishment and logical development of a philosphic system, much for the strengthening of moral principles and the training for the calling of orator and statesman, and much for physics. Rome suggests that the law that every metropolis will include the university should be expanded to read: Every metropolis will

188

include a university partaking of its own characteristics. 'Like people, like priest'."

When cities came to an end universities came to an end as well—at least in the Western world. The fact is to me ever a warning not to overestimate the teaching done by the formal faculties of great universities. There is better teaching in the world than ever done by learned faculties. It is the teaching of the commandments of Heaven, which is done by a single powerfully-moved mind; by Paul or by Ulphilas, by Columba or by Columban, by Boniface or by Methodius, by whatever solitary heart and tongue Heaven has taken into union with the Triune Faculty and commissioned to teach men the commandments of the Master. When university faculties fail to help men as they did fail at last in Athens and Alexandria, in Carthage and in Rome, the Trustee of Heaven and Earth dismisses those faculties from their offices, and raises up some one to do the needed work.

It was not more of scientists, lawyers, theologians, physicians, the world was wanting in those days. It wanted pure homes, good men and women; and the Almighty Trustee of the world forced the best men of earth to leave teaching the choice youth in colleges and go teaching the savages the first elements of the Gospel.

There met a Christian council in the midst of what some men call the Dark Ages, which I hold to have been dark in contrast with former ages only when viewed from the standpoint of university learning, which were not at all dark when seen from the standpoint of moral effort. This council, in answer to an appeal to cultivate science, declared that they had no science save the knowledge of how to be Christians and how to make others Christians.

There came a day, three-quarters of a millennium ago, in which Christian intellect found that it need not employ itself chiefly either to conquer or to convert the Pagans, and

189

then it went to building cities. No sooner did Europe rear the metropolis Paris than it organized in Paris the University; no sooner did any nation or principality agree upon building a chief city than it builded in the city a university. Take the kingly or princely capitals of Germany in the last five hundred years, and you will have, with hardly an exception, the names of the German universities, from Heidelberg, Leipzig, and Tubingen, the oldest, down to Berlin and Munich, the youngest.

The metropolis must sooner or later include the university. Even far-off Edinburgh and Glasgow obeyed the law. England long resisted the natural course in this as in many another thing. Not till within the recollection of most of us here did the metropolis of London build the University of London. We are told that the very processes which made the geologic layers of limestone in England may be seen going on at this hour in the coral reefs of the Southern Ocean. So the very processes which formed universities five centuries ago in Europe may be seen going on under our eyes at this hour. While this city, the metropolis of this continent, is building professedly two great universities, the metropolis of each great State—Boston, Philadelphia, Baltimore, Cincinnati, St. Louis, and Chicago— each is building its own, albeit the name, in more than one case, expresses less an accomplished fact than a confident expectation.

History thus proves the law, that the metropolis included the university. What is its philosophy? What is it in the chief city of each people that compels it to erect the university? It is not chiefly that the city furnishes the youth to be trained. I do not find that Paris furnished the twenty thousand youth who five centuries ago rushed to the University of Paris. I do not find that this city furnished last year half the youth that were in the Union Theological Seminary, or under the university, medical, and law faculties. It is not the law of demand, as commonly understood, that creates a supply of learned faculties. Rather the philosophy of the creation of the university in a metropolis is this: Intellect comes to the city to carry on business, to govern great corporations, to preach, to practice law and medicine. It concentrates in the city. Its activity is whetted in the city by the severity of the work to be done and by the large contact of bright minds one with another. Mind, when stirred to its largest activity, must impart of itself to others. It is made in God's image, and cannot acquire without giving. It cannot acquire money without giving money. It cannot acquire knowledge without giving knowledge. Stirred by kindred minds, it organizes for the bestowal of knowledge upon others, either in person or by proxy. Thus it is explained why Plato in Athens, stirred by his interviews with his neighbors, founds a school. This explains why the wealthy Cimon and Epicurus give grounds, and building, and money to encourage the learned faculties. They find it easier to give than not to give. The quality of their giving is not strained, but is as the dew from Heaven.

In the same way did it come to this metropolis to have higher faculties—aye, and to have its nobler libraries, which are an especial part of a university—and its scientific, art and historical museums. To confine myself to the New York University, and to quote words found in the address of Mr. Charles Butler, fourteen years since: "A few leading and public-spirited citizens associated themselves together and determined to lay the foundations of an institution of learning, to be erected by private liberality, which should bear the name of the University of the City of New York, and which should be in every way worthy of the metropolis."

Such spirits do not wait to have youth beseech them to found a faculty. They hardly ask themselves whether there are many who are ready to accept the instruction. They offer the teaching, knowing that sooner or later the supply will make the demand. Though no plants or shrubs are on the alkali plain, calling for the irrigation of the streams from the mountains, none the less the streams irrigate, knowing that after a little while the plants will call for it. They will spring up by the water-courses. They will bless and reward the beneficence. The philosophy upon which men found higher faculties and proffer learning, is that upon which John Chrysostom, according to his own accounts, preached his wondrous sermons. "I speak," he says of himself, "as the fountains bubble and still continue to bubble, though no one will come to draw. I speak as the rivers flow, the same though no one will drink of their flood of waters."

"Sooner or later each metropolis does find wise and cultivated souls rising up, and urged by the necessities of their own constitutions, each saying, "I must give to others, and I will give the best gift in my power: I will give knowledge; I will give sound instruction'."

Granting then that the metropolis must include the university, and that full faculties of every science will arise here sooner or later from the constraint to give that must be felt by the wise and cultivated minds, the third point which I present is *some conditions peculiar to the university in America.* The first condition is, that it must follow American tradition in its view of the Complete School, and in taking care of what is known among us as the College, what in Germany is comprehended under the Gymnasium, with its rival, the Real School.

The complete school is to the American an edifice which resembles this stately edifice of the New York University, in that it is divided into four distinct stories. There are, on the lowest floor, the broad and numerous apartments in which are pursued what are known as the common school studies. Here is ended the school-life of at least nine-tenths of the boys of America. Second is the academy floor, where are the academies, high schools, and schools preparatory to college. Here are found perhaps one-twentieth of the boys of our country. Third is the college floor. Here the boys remain four years, pursuing languages and mathematics, with the elements of natural and mental sciences. There are possibly forty thousand young men in this division. Last is the university floor, which, as in old times, is divided into the four faculties of theology, law, medicine and philosophy, though the last named begins in our day to be subdivided, as for example, in Tubingen into the faculties of philosophy, natural science, and political science. This fourth floor has in our country perhaps as many students as the third, not all of them, however, going up by the stairway through the college but many climbing up some other way.

Now, while Germany places the third floor——the gymnasium or the college—— under the same corporation with the second or academy division, and while England does the same in a measure, America, with more reason, either sets up the college as a distinct foundation, or places it under the same management with the professional or university courses. We demand of every corporaton that attempts advanced philosophy that it carry on also a college. Even Johns Hopkins, which above all our other foundations has attempted to copy the German model, has felt obliged to furnish a course to undergraduates. There are two strong arguments for the American rule; first, the economy which suggests that the teachers of the advanced courses, can, without serious diversion of their minds from their specialties, give instruction also to undergraduates; second, that the line between the college and the university is not a line between young men of diverse aims, since all as a rule are thinking of professional careers. The line between the academy and the college, which is emphasized in America but almost ignored in Germany, is a line beyond which a majority of our academy or high school students do not venture. The American tradition, that the university in the metropolis must care for the college, is a wise and wholesome tradition.

The next condition resting upon the university is that it keep this third story under old-fashioned college discipline and instruction, and in order to do this must keep it limited in the number of its students. Unfortunately, there has been of late a marked ambition in colleges to gather undergraduates in large numbers. The College Catalogue is thought most of as a "Book of Numbers," when it ought rather to be a "Book of Genesis," giving the genesis of better modes of training, or a "Book of Exodus," showing an exodus made out of the land of superficiality and house of stupidity, or a "Book of Leviticus," recording a high culture, exalting God and His service. But the chief point of the catalogue is, How many Freshmen have you? It is the American demand for bigness.

There is a school at West Point that can have just as many students as there are members in the Lower House of Congress, and ten students for the nation at large. Who thinks that West Point would be as good a school, if she were required to obtain all the students possible, and to be rated according to the numbers attracted? That college which gathers as many in her four classes as West Point enrolls has all the students any college should undertake. The college, with overflowing classes, which first sets up the rule that only a definite number can be admitted into each class, and this in obedience to the law of the survival of the fittest, will erect for herself a lasting monument. No college in Oxford, England, enrolls three hundred undergraduates. Who thinks that it would improve Oxford to place all her colleges under one corporation? The solution of the problem of governing students, which is so serious in some colleges, is to be found in the word "Divide." With limited classes there will be good discipline, and the faculty hardly know that it is governing, or the students that they are governed.

194

The third condition resting upon the American university is that it multiply its faculties of graduate instruction just so far as there are precious sciences to be explored and taught, able men to explore and reach them, and money to support the explorers. Unlike other nations we will not allow our central Government to fix the standard of what is the university. But, in one of our great States, the best colleges are settling practically for that State by an association, the standard of what is a respectable college, so ere long there will be an association of the leading candidates for the title of university that will settle substantially the standard of the American university. It will demand that there be certain faculties and courses of study, and it will demand, I doubt not as essential in every case, the ancient faculty of philosophy, perhaps distinguishing it, as is done in Tubingen, from the faculties of political and natural sciences. It behooves every would-be university to prepare for admission to the approaching University Association.

I am happy in finding that the New York University has nothing serious to undo in order to fulfill the conditions resting upon the American University. Like most other foundations, she has enough work to do in order to be ready when the competitive examination comes for the foremost places in the future association of universities in America.

I believe that you purpose doing the work. I believe that you purpose speedy effort in behalf of the cause which I feel at liberty to magnify, inasmuch as you commit it especially to my care, the cause of mental and moral philosophy. May I not give reasons for this hope that is in me? I find that only a year ago, at your fiftieth anniversary, it was indicated by our Chancellor, Dr. John Hall, that you were fixed in your resolve to carry out the provisions of your laws, and I find that your laws say, "The first general department of this University shall comprise professorships and faculties for instruction in the higher branches of literature and science," while the second general department is to embrace what is usually deemed a full college course. The laws contemplate, then, instruction in advanced philosophy.

Further I find, that at that same date, you announced that your charter was so changed that you were at liberty to marry yourself to certain religious bodies, which happen to be the religious bodies that have always cultivated philosophy, and thriven by philosophy. But there will be proof positive that this union has taken place—I mean the marriage of the New York University to the metaphysical Presbyterian, Reformed, and Puritan bodies, when there appears offspring in the form of a faculty of graduate philosphy.

I find reason for hope in the kind of college for undergraduates which you maintain here. It does not, like certain wealthy and honored colleges that ought to have known better, enthrone Young Americanism, saying to the profound sophomore: "You are to judge whether you will need the elements of logic, ethics, and psychology; if you judge that they are unneccessary, discard them." This college utters no such nonsense. It knows that logic, psychology, and ethics are necessary for every thinker, and hence it lays them down for even the candidate for the degree of Civil Engineer.

Further, this college is strong, I find, and ever has been strong on behalf of the "Humanities." When I find Latin and Greek taught as they have been taught here, I find a hand pointing to such advanced courses as will bring students into more intimate acquaintance with the thoughts of the best men of the ancient ages.

I take encouragement from the prosperous faculties of law and medicine for an advanced course in philosophy, whether the latter is to be regarded as propaedeutic to law and medicine or as in some measure an application of the same. The honored Deans of the faculties of law and medicine will agree that whatever thorough grounding in philosophy can be given

196

their students will benefit them in their school, while on the other hand, philosophy was never so much as now sending students to certain chairs of the faculty of medicine with grave questions to be answered.

The fact that this corporation ordains that instruction shall be given by the University in apologetics is to my mind an ordinance in favor of advanced work in philosophy. For if philosophy be suffered to receive her retaining-fee and chief employment from non-Christianity, it will fare hard with Christianity before the tribunal of educated mind. If I were asked how a few thousands of dollars each year can best serve Christianity here in the way of education, I could conscientiously say, by causing that it be used to imbue our future professional and cultivated minds with a sound Christian philosophy. I have met here in this immediate vicinity the Institute of Christian Philosophy presided over by a member of the Council of the University. The lectures and magazines it gives each year are themselves almost a Faculty of Graduate Philosophy for the whole country. But before young men can fully profit by them they require the work of the class-room and the living specially devoted to mental and moral philosophy.

The ready helps for its establishment are offered here. The books are in your libraries for free reference. The men who have read the books are here and often in positions which may allow them to offer their aid to the school without requiring full compensation. If Mr. Garfield really said that it was college enough for him to have a bench in a cabin, himself on one end and an honored teacher upon the other, I am sure that he meant a college of philosophy, for no other can prosper with such very inexpensive accessories.

Finally, ladies and gentlemen, this is New York—the heart and metropolis of America—and I offer this as a reason for the hope that is in me. When old Solomon describes Wisdom as teaching, as he does often, he portrays her in every in-

197

stance as uttering her words in the city, as crying at the entering in of the gates and in the high places of his own metropolis. New York City has self-forgetfully endowed colleges and schools here and there over the land, and she has done well. But now that we have reached the point in our national growth where full universities' faculties begin to be thought of, I am sure that the wise men of New York City will decide that it is their duty to invite Wisdom to utter her words in the city, to cry at the entering in of your own gates—in the high places of this metropolis of the United States of America.

198

Inaugural Address

by

SAMUEL PALMER BROOKS

President of Baylor University

September, 1902

SAMUEL PALMER BROOKS (December 4, 1863—May 14, 1931) was born in Milledgeville, Georgia. He had an A. B. degree from Baylor University, an A. B. and A. M. from Yale, and pursued graduate work at the University of Chicago. He received honorary degrees from the University of Richmond, Mercer University, Georgetown College and Austin Texas College.

Dr. Brooks was a popular lecturer. He organized the Texas Peace Congress, was Vice-President of the Southern Baptist Convention in 1910, President of the Baptist General Convention at Texas 1914-17, and was President of the Southern Sociological Congress in 1915.

It is a trite saying that a horse rarely pulls well in a new collar, nor does he usually work so well in the lead as in the team. Transitions are hurtful in government or administrative affairs. They always create friction somewhere, though it may in the end be the best for the enterprise in which the transition has been made. This institution has gone through a period of changing, now high, now low, for at least ten years, from the time it began to rise in curriculum to meet the requirements for scholarship. And it remains yet to be seen whether the present administration shall be able to maintain the high standard that has been kept up in the years that have recently gone by. As you all know, of recent years that under my immediate predecessors the University has gone forward by leaps and bounds, and possibly we may not be able to keep up with the pace already set, but I have never, even in the darkest days of the institution, since I came here as a student, doubted that each transition would result in its best interests. All for which this institution was founded, we bear and hold up to the people of today, and the work and co-operation of the men and women of this state cannot fail, because underneath it, and in it, and over and about it is God, in whose name all of its work has been done and always must continue to be done.

The question has been asked over and over again of me, as might be expected, from one end of the state to the other, what will be the policy of the new administration with reference to this and to that? Naturally you expect me to answer some of these questions. I may not answer them according to your judgment; I may not answer them according to my own future judgment; but I shall undertake to answer them on the basis of my own experience as a student, and as a teacher in Baylor, coupled with my observation of the work of other institutions with greater endowments and larger scholarship.

The question naturally arises as to what our policy is with reference to the founders of the institution. It will be to honor them, to study them, to know more of them, to know those who worked in Baylor at Independence, in old Waco University, and later in the combined institution. It will be not only to study, but to honor them one and all—presidents, faculties, boards of trustees—who have shaped the University since its founding. We shall think of the old Baylor and its presidents; we shall think of Dr. Crane, and the long years through which he served the institution. We shall not forget to honor Dr. R. C. Burleson, who stood so long for Christian education at a time when there were greater difficulties than this state has ever since seen.

We shall hope to see in the University life-sized portraits of Dr. Burleson and Dr. Crane, so that all of the former students of these two institutions may come together and have their interest quickened by seeing the lineaments of those to whom they are so deeply indebted.

Our policy with respect to the alumni, not only of Baylor, but of Waco University and Baylor University at Independence, will be to come in personal contact, as far as possible, with every alumnus and alumna, and we hope to see them give us their co-operation, their money and their patronage, and honor us by frequently visiting the institution. I have sent letters to all of the alumni bespeaking their hearty co-operation. We have had it in the past to a gratifying extent, and we hope and believe that in the future every one will stand by Baylor University.

We shall have a definite policy with respect to the correlated and affiliated schools. We hope to see the various Baptist colleges organically united not only in theory but also in fact. When we shall come to know more of each other we will love each other more. Then we will help them and they will help us, until the universal standard shall be high scholarship and the book of God. We shall achieve that of which the Texas citizenship shall be proud.

There is not a man in Baylor University but stands for the public schools of the state. We stand for them emphatically and positively. Their good work, wherever done, we shall recognize. Such has been our attitude in the past, and such shall be our attitude in the future.

The question is asked, as to what our relationship shall be to our competitors. As a matter of fact, there is no real competition in culture. There is room in Texas for every reputable institution it now has. I speak not of short cut schools; I speak not of schools that live on paper, or that are built to sell real estate; but I speak of bona fide schools that have been founded by men of business, and I wish godspeed to them, and we shall be helped by them in return. Yale University has 932 students from Connecticut alone, and you might take Connecticut and put it over McLennan County, and it would lap over it only a little. There is no limit to the growth of this state, and we think the population will enable us to have at least 2,000 students from a territory of a hundred miles radius within the lifetime of the people who now hear me. The possibilities are unbounded. We glory in the State University for the good it may do, and for other competitors, whether they be state, secular or Christian. We pledge them our co-operation and emulation, but with absolutely no strife. This state is big enough for us all. Every Christian denomination must have its university. Let the state institutions grow as they will, and they will grow. State institutions will be supported by Christian men and women as well as by non-Christian, but we shall not forget equally to support our own. We shall stand with all the power of our might in disapproval of frauds. One of the worst things, as Prof. Tanner once said, is to let a boy or girl graduate from a short cut school; for it makes one immune to higher education even to the third and fourth generations. Every member of this faculty will in every way possible give the stamp of his approval to the high scholarship that may be produced and the good service that may be rendered by public and private schools.

We shall have a very definite policy with respect to the citizens of Waco. We are citizens here, we pay our taxes to the city, we glory in its prosperity, and there shall never be a new building, or bridge, or railroad, or any other good enterprize, but shall have our moral and financial support. It shall be my purpose, while I am in this position, to connect myself with every business organization that will have me. It is to my shame that I know so few of the business men; but, if they will let me, I will cultivate their acquaintance, so that we may know each other better. I glory in the work of Waco, and all of us shall glory in it.

It is the wish of the faculty that the students should be amenable to state and municipal laws; and when the students conduct themselves as men should not, they will get no protection from this faculty. They must stand as men and though we love them, they must suffer the penalty of every violation of the law. I am sorry to say it has come to pass that boys in college think they may be riotous and run over the citizens. It is the policy of this institution never to attempt to shield a disorderly student, and it shall be the work of the faculty to eliminate this lawless element from the student life.

What shall be the relation of the president to the faculty? To give each one the largest possible freedom, but always with the understanding that each instructor shall work in harmony with the general policy of the institution that has come down to us as a heritage; and any man who goes in with a view of revolutionizing our traditional policy, will find that the climate will agree with him better in some other locality. While we stand with the old institution and shall continue to stand with it, we shall be ready to adopt all real improvements in educational methods that commend themselves to us as such. The ladies and gentlemen of the faculty have their homes here, they have come to stay, and they are going to work with us in this general policy, conduct this work as Christian men and women ought to, thinking what they will, teaching what they will, and amenable only to the general policy of the institution.

What shall be our policy in regard to social life? We shall have a social life, but mark you, students, the school is for work, and, if you have come here simply to learn how to appear in society, you should go to another institution. We stand for social development, but I left the farm and workshop too recently to be in a position to teach you all the rules of fashionable society.

What shall our policy be towards the beneficiaries? The Baptist preachers, and their sons and daughters will be welcome; but it must be understood that they must give us their living co-operation for the extension of the life of the institution, and I believe that they will do so, as the majority of them have done in the past. It is necessary for the Baptists of this state to provide a fund for the adequate support of a faculty that is worthy of the denomination and the institution.

It shall be our policy, as far as possible, to help students to secure work, whereby they may wholly or in part defray their expenses. There is a great deal of work which can be done here by beneficiaries, and it is better for them as far as practicable to earn their way than to stand as drones. A great many of the sons and daughters of preachers may give us help in the clerical force, whereby they may earn their tuition and save us money.

As to discipline, we shall have it. I have already hinted at it. We shall have discipline that is discipline for certain, when necessary, but it shall be the discipline of love and advice always until the last resort, and then we will meet it frankly and flatly, and violators will find that the climate suits them better at their homes. There is not an army under the sun that ever did a great thing that was not subject to its head. There was never a battle won by a debating society.

What about athletics? It has been known to some that I am a conservative in athletics. Dr. Burleson was strictly against athletics, and there he was wrong, I thought at one time. I stood out against athletics later when the responsibility fell on the faculty, because I saw there was dynamite in it and it would give us trouble. Later when we had a president to bear the burden of it, I stated in faculty meeting that, because he was so ardent an admirer of it, if this institution adopted it, he was welcome to all the glory that came of it, and if it brought trouble he would have to bear it. I frankly acknowledge my cowardice in not being willing to bear my joint share in the one case, and in throwing it upon the president in the other. There will be those in the house who will misunderstand me now. My experience has somewhat changed my views. I am for athletics but as a conservative. If this institution sets a rule whereby a man must have a given grade in scholarship to play on the teams, he may expect that this rule will be carried out. I tell you that this institution is not above reproach in the history of its athletics, and the greatest shame that ever came to me here was when our boys played men on our team who were not members of our school. I am against that kind of athletics. It may be a surprise to some, but we had to bear the burden, because we could not help it; but it shall not occur again and hereafter every man shall pay the penalty of his fault. We shall have clean athletics, and our boys must be men enough to go down in honorable defeat. If we are defeated on the foot-ball field this year and next year, and every year, we will honor the institution that defeated us. It will set the pace for clean lives and healthy bodies. If we have that kind of athletics, I am for it. I know that some men, whose influence has gone into my life are altogether against foot-ball, but with all due deference to their judgment, I shall have to give my support to healthy athletics, football included; for there are always bad boys among the students and some of the wildest boys in this school are Baptist boys, from Baptist homes, and are difficult to control, and I will let them kick each other half to death, rather than run around town living lives of shame. Their time must be occupied, I believe there is less sickness among the boys who give a reasonable amount of time to athletics and military drill than among those who do not. I well know that there is some harm connected with the former. I am altogether against going over the state with special trains to intercollegiate football games or debates, as we are here to work. We will do what we can to get the other institutions of the state to co-operate with us for the discontinuance of the practice of running these excursions. I acknowledge I have heretofore asked the last one of you to go, because it was the custom; but I have now come to see that it takes up too much of your time and prepares some of you for play rather than for work.

I am not going to discourage football or athletics in general, and you boys may depend upon it. I will help you when I can but if you practice any fraud, we will be against you with all our power, and the public of this state will be against you.

What are some of our needs? In attempting to get students, in publishing our advertisements, in sending out our representatives, it is but natural that we should discuss with all our might the merits of the institution and cover the demerits. We need some things so badly that we are hampered without them. We need endowment. It must come, for as certain as the college shall grow we shall need increased clerical force, increased teaching force, and we appeal to the citizenship of this state to respond heartily and liberally when the appeal for endowment shall be made. Do not wait to hear it but respond at once with your money and help us to employ teachers on pay instead of promises. It is well known that the Baylor faculty have done a higher class of work, more hours a day, more work in an hour, and at less pay than the professors in any other high grade institution in the land, and there have been the fewest possible number of them that have begrudged the time and strength expended, so wrapped up have they been in the work they are doing here. When men and women come into the faculty of this institution they work with all their might, and the students pass their desks and ask them thousands of questions, and they always receive the help they seek. This has been true and it will be true, and I have not written any man asking him to come here this year, without telling him that for the least possible amount of money he would be expected to work himself to death. We have the finest type of material in the rough out of which the pure metal may come and be polished. I never saw its like elsewhere in this world.

We need dormitories. One of the difficulties I have had to meet this summer was in placing some of our boys in homes at rates they could afford. Food products have gone up, which, of course, could not be helped, and it is exceedingly difficult to get first class board at the prices paid ten or twelve years ago. So there is a problem that must be solved. Some arrangement must be made by which the girls and boys that cannot meet the prices charged may be provided for.

We need greater facilities for enabling students to find opportunities for self-help. The announcement at the First Baptist church the other day had the effect of giving homes to two or three students. If we could keep that announcement before the people, there would be more homes opened. We need to have some organized plan and it will be our purpose to provide it. We will take the names of all needy students. Those who can give them help or afternoon employment will be found out, and we will inform the boys and girls that, even if they have not the money, they may come here and by the courage of their countenances demand places in the houses, and they will get them.

We need libraries. It will be a standing joke if we have a magnificent library building and nothing to put in it. We have some old books, but they are not sufficient. We want you to give us books, and what is more important, to give us money to buy the books that we need. We need modern books representing the most advanced work in every department of study.

We need now, it seems to me, a law department, and I cannot see why we could not organize it in the very near future. I have asked some of our old boys whether they would have taken their law course here if Baylor had had a law school, and they have always answered that they would. I do not see the way clear just now, but I believe it can be done.

We need a gymnasium for the girls. The boys have a gymnasium of fresh air, but the girls are sadly limited in their opportunities for physical culture.

The campus of this institution needs to be beautified. I believed when I was a boy that whoever spent his or her time at anything else than digging fence-post holes or some other form of utilitarian labor was wasting time. I have long ago come to see that things of the mind are as much the work of God as anything else can be, and we want the students who come from the country to know that a campus well kept, with beautiful shade trees, will shed an influence on those boys and girls that will be helpful in their homes, and will beautify their minds.

Some of you expect me to speak on another line. I remind you again, as I look back over the history of the institution, that the wisdom of our fathers has been well proved. It took a great deal of faith long years ago, for men to build a house on a hill top in the prairie, and consecrate their lives to the institution out of which this should grow. Faith in God, faith in our power to do our part, faith in the people that should co-operate with us in our efforts to fill this state with a citizenship of which we should be proud, is what we now need.

It is wise that a theological department should be established in this institution. It is natural that the preachers should get their training here, and go out into broader fields with Baylor University behind them. The library building that is now in progress of erection will, when suitably equipped with books, suffice for both theological and literary students. It is altogether rational that we should have a theological department. I glory in the start so well begun.

It is also wise that this institution should have a session in the summer months. Some can come only in the summer. There are students now who come summer after summer, and a lady will graduate next year whose studying has all been done in the summer sessions. Many of the public school teachers make up work in the summer, and that this institution should be idle during the summer months seems to me the veriest folly. There is no more reason why a school boy or girl should do nothing in the hot summer than that anybody else should.

It seems to me wise that under the influence of this institution the fine arts should be cultivated. It seems to me that it is about time for the Baptists of this state to take the highest possible rank in art and music, so that we may be in a position to do as good work as is done in Germany, and supply our own institutions with teachers.

The wisdom of our fathers has been shown in the keeping up of an academic department. I believed when I first got through with the college course, with a diploma in my pocket and not much training in my head, that we ought to abandon the preparatory department. Illogical, of course. And so I now see that there is no better place to give the lessons of the high school course than in close relationship with a Christian University. The results of the work of this department have abundantly justified its continuance and increase. I hope to see the time in the very near future when we shall have more buildings and more and better equipment, and then there will be rules made for the academy that will not be necessary for all the college students.

I believe with all my heart, without any reflection upon any of the men or women who differ from me, that it is wise that we should have co-education, and the history of the past has justified it.

I believe that this institution should be for Christian education, and last and best of all that this institution stands for Christianity. Popular education has been defined as the full development of all our faculties and has to do with mind and body and soul as well, and he who has the education of mind and body and leaves the soul out will leave out the greatest of all. I must be measured by my soul, and I believe with all my heart that the soul of the student must be trained in keeping with his mind and body, and you shall never have a symmetrically trained individual unless the three in one shall be observed. Some people think that we are a lot of pious frauds here, and that we spend our time in prayers and never do any work. We do endeavor to induce the fear of God, but we teach the students to work over their lessons and pray over them as well. We also teach them that prayer alone will not prepare them to recite their lessons. They must work over them, think over them, and dream over them, and use the same sort of methods as in other things.

We shall have Christianity; we shall have piety; we shall reserve the right to put God into our words; but we shall not ask or require anybody to reject his former faith for that of the Baptists, and we do not seek to interfere with the religious convictions of others. In my judgment, there is no real education that is not essentially Christian. All education is moral, but not all moral education is Christian. The question, of course, comes with force, whose morals are you speaking of? The morals of Jesus Christ, or of Cicero, or of the man of to-day? We stand for the morals of Jesus Christ, and it seems to me that the work of this University should be done with a view to the production of Christian character. To make it perfectly clear, there is no real attainment in life, except to recognize the complementary nature of sin and redemption. Secular education can never go beyond the grave; it has no reference to the future; it cannot tell when life is done.

Christianity is not the church. The college is not the church, but I believe with all my heart that the college may become the servant of the church, doing work for the church. A church is an educational institution in an exceedingly high degree. The highest kind of training stops not short of regeneration, and I believe we ought to say it.

What is the function of the church? It is the saving of souls. In Mexico, I saw a painting representing the Indians being converted. There were the soldiers of Spain with their bayonets bringing them up to the cross and written under the painting was, "The Conversion of the Indians." My heart sank within me to think that in any part of the world such a proceeding should ever have been called a conversion. Salvation must come by instruction, and I believe that there is no salvation without instruction. Man's idea of right is of God. Man's idea of what is right is of instruction.

Christian education seeks to find the whole truth. It is not limited by any constitution. Christian education goes to the grave and looks beyond it, and no system of secular education can do as much. It seeks the whole truth, whether applied to the home, or marriage, or paternity, or life, or death; things present or things to come—all come under the purview of Christian training.

212

There is as much mental gymnastics and real culture, as well as scholastic value, in a knowledge of Moses crossing the Red Sea as Caesar's crossing the Rubicon. We may know Christ an emperor as well as Napoleon, Christ as king as well as Henry VIII. Christian education is sectarian; so is the truth sectarian. There is absolutely no truth but what is sectarian, and the man who is not sectarian is a straddler of all creation.

Let it be understood well and once for all, that freedom of religion does not mean no religion. It means that you can believe what you please, but it does not mean you can hamper me in teaching what I believe; and there are those who get on a foundation so broad that they mistake religion for Christianity. Christian education is never anti-State. Secular education in its last analysis is anti-Christian.

Men of Waco, men of Texas, students of this institution for which I would give my life, if necessary, I appeal for your co-operation in putting it on an enduring foundation with God as its supreme director. I appeal to you to help us in building an institution that will win the respect of business men. Let us work heart to heart with one purpose, and we shall make all Texas bristle with the glorious work of Baylor. If you are true to your Alma Mater, if you are true to the history of this institution, you will give us your support; and though you may differ with us occasionally it may be for our mutual good both now and hereafter. We are engaged in a life work. We are teaching you for tomorrow as well as for today. We are striving to prepare you for an appreciation of that kind of training that ends in the spiritual reformation of your own soul.

Inaugural Address

The Modernizing of Liberal Culture

by

RUSH RHEES

President of the University of Rochester

October 11, 1900

*RUSH RHEES (February 8, 1860—
January 5, 1939) was born in the City of Chi-
cago. He received the A.B., A.M. and LL.D.
degrees from Amherst College. The LL.D. de-
gree was also conferred on him by McMaster
University (Canada), University of Toronto.
He received the Doctor of Divinity degree from
Colgate.*

*Dr. Rhees was President of the University
of Rochester from 1900 to 1935. After he resigned from the Presidency he continued to
serve the institution he had contributed his life
to by accepting membership on the Board of
Trustees. He was an administrator of distinction. He increased the endowment of the University and earned the title of University
Builder.*

Mr. Chairman and Gentlemen of the Board of Trustees: — I accept the trust you have this day formally committed to me with a deep sense of its dignity and seriousness. I pledge to you my most earnest and diligent endeavor to realize the broad hopes of those who secured this charter, to guard the honor of this seal, to be watchful for the most efficient use of these buildings, and in general to advance in every possible way the usefulness of the University over which you have called me to preside.

And now, Mr. President, distinguished Friends, Gentlemen of the Board of Trustees, Alumni, and Ladies and Gentlemen:

In obedience to the custom which asks for my confession of educational faith on entering this office, I invite you to consider with me this afternoon some of the facts and problems involved in "THE MODERNIZING OF LIBERAL CULTURE."

There is good reason why we should admire the high ideals and large hopes which prompted the founders of this institution to secure for its liberal charter, and in some measure influenced the choice of its name. Men have reached practical agreement, however, that a name does not constitute a university. The difference between a college and a university is a clear difference of aim. The college aims to give to its students a liberal culture, which has in view no special calling or profession, but simply the fullest development of their intellectual powers and the widest practicable information of their minds. A university, on the other hand, seeks to train specialists; for its proper work it demands that its students shall have completed their college training; and carries them on to advanced degrees in philosophy and other fields of knowledge. Rochester has not developed, in its past history and in its present aim, those higher faculties which are essential to university work. It seeks with seriousness and frankness to do the work of an American college, and to meet the demands which the new

217

century makes upon its schools of liberal culture. It is not necessary for me to discuss the meaning of liberal culture, nor to state in detail how it is to be attained. It will be sufficient for our purpose, if we remember that a liberal education seeks first, to train a man in the use of all of his intellectual powers; and secondly, to inform him, as widely as may be, concerning himself and his world. Of these two aims the first is generally recognized as the more important. It is a comparatively slight matter that we should be able to prove that the square on the hypotenuse of a right triangle is equal to the sums of the squares on the sides; or that we should have the power to determine by the use of reagents the constituent of a given chemical compound. It is of supreme importance that we have our reasoning powers in such control that when confronted by the practical problems of life these powers will render prompt and sure service. It is of slight importance, comparatively, that a man be familiar with the precise shades of meaning of the Greek prepositions or of the Latin subjunctive; it is of the highest importance that his powers of discrimination be so trained that he may be able to distinguish, in practical life, between things essentially different but superficially alike. Mere intellectual discipline, however, may secure no more than a scholastic acuteness like that which, in the days of the later schoolmen, busied itself with the profitless discussion of subjects unworthy of serious consideration. Matthew Arnold's conception of culture, — "Acquainting ourselves with the best that has been known and said in the world, and thus with the history of the human spirit," emphasizes a highly important truth; for intelligent exercise of judgment, broad knowledge is as essential as disciplined powers.

The many subjects of study offered by the college curriculum are not intended to satisfy the cravings of an idle curiosity, but to give men that knowledge of nature and life which will enable them to perceive the practical bearings of a question when they meet it; to know whether past experience has condemned or approved a given project. There is an appetite for knowledge which passes little beyond an eagerness to dabble in all sorts of learning for the mere pleasure of it. With this dilettantism the college has no patience. Genuine culture results when information is acquired and digested by the well disciplined mind. Such culture is a preparation for the most effective work in any line of activity which a man may choose. His discipline enables him to apply his powers with the least waste to the task presented; his information enables him to estimate with the least margin of mistake the actual significance of his task.

When we consider the present status of liberal culture, two facts indicate an attained modernization; First, the successful demand for recognition by what may be called the new learning. In the days of our fathers the study of the classics, mathematics, and so-called mental philosophy, constituted the largest part of the work of our colleges. Early in the century new interest in learning presented their claims; the history of mediaeval and modern times, the languages and the literature of modern peoples, and the manifold branches of modern science, called for a place in the college curriculum. The educational history of the middle and later decades of the century, has been one of successive surrender to this demand. One after another the sciences have won their place. Little by little the scope of the teaching of history has been broadened and enlarged. The modern languages and modern literature, including our English heritage, have gained recognition. Furthermore, the introduction of so many new subjects of study early necessitated the offering of the liberty of election to the students, and gradually the elective system has extended. until a large proportion of the work in college is done with classes that have definitely chosen their courses. Along with this surrender to the demand of a new learning and extension of the elective system, a strong educational conservatism has insisted that the palladium of liberal culture is in the keeping of the old group of disciplinary studies: the classics, mathematics, mental philosophy. The study of the sciences, history, and modern literature, was introduced in response to the demand for a wider and more modern information. As experience grew, however, even the advocates of the older culture were forced to recognize the disciplinary value of the scientific and historical methods, and of the analytic study of literature, so that today the new learning rivals the old as a means of training, while with many students it surpasses the old as a means of broad and interesting information.

The second noteworthy fact in the present status is the revolution in the method of teaching the classics and mathematics. Most of us, familiar with the old drill in Greek grammar and Latin prosody, would hardly recognize the same studies, had we the good fortune to sit under our modern instructors in classics; and some of us, who developed nice skill in the recital of Euclid, would be much put to it to pass the modern tests in original geometrical demonstration. The new interest in the classics find in them the monuments of a people's life. Men used to read Homer to learn the peculiarities of the Ionic dialect, and to be impressed with the beauty of classic literary form; Horace was their text-book in Latin metres, and the classical pattern of poetic beauty. Today our students read their Homer to learn how the men of ancient Greece lived, and fought, and died; they read their Horace and become acquainted with the life of the literary set in Rome in the Augustan period. Syntax and grammar they learn, to be sure, but as a means to an end. The centre of interest has shifted. Reading these classics now, the students "acquaint themselves with much of the best that has been known and said in the world, and thus with the history of the human spirit," — to adopt Matthew Arnold's phrase. The old study takes on modern interest. These peoples, who attained the highest perfection in beauty and in law which our race has ever seen, live again to add their experience to our modern equipment, and make us wise in our daily tasks. I have instanced the new classical teaching alone. A similar modernization is apparent in mathematics and so-called mental philosophy.

Turning now from the accomplished modifications, let us consider some of the questions still pressing for attention. Among these, first the problem of yet further expansion of the curriculum. With the increasing recognition of science, history, and literature, the colleges have found it necessary to open their doors to many students who have made no preparation in Greek and Latin. For these students courses in Science, and in Philosophy or Letters, have been arranged, although regarded as rather inferior to the so-called regular, or classical, course. Some of the students in these courses discover, after entrance to college, that the old learning has advantages and charms that they did not suspect. The college of today provides elementary instruction in modern languages. Must not all our colleges in the near future offer also opportunities to beginners in Latin and Greek? The question is not novel. Some institutions have already taken this step and have found eager welcome for this opportunity. If the modern liberal culture recognizes the new and living value of classical study, it is due to college students that they have opportunity to obtain the classical advantages after entering college, if they have not had them previously. The wide recognition of history has already been noticed. Within this field, however, there are new developments which are demanding, and will more and more demand, a place in college teaching. Men turn from the story of dynasties and constitutions to the records of the under-currents of life. The development of trade, the history of domestic customs in succeeding generations, the study of social organization, and the manifold kindred topics, are rich with fascinating information and full of opportunity for effective discipline.

221

There is also a demand for the serious study of aesthetics. Apart from literary art, our college training has been content to neglect the cultivation of the sense for beauty, as too far removed from the practical side of life. Passing with simple mention the place given to music in the medieval curriculum, art has been recognized as a subject of study by few institutions except technical schools and some of the larger universities. It is clear that our colleges have no call to teach the technique of art; but, if it is true that the sense for beauty is one of the subtlest qualities in the human soul, that education is partial which is content to leave the Aesthetic side of life without discipline and information. A liberally educated man should have his sense for beauty trained, he should have his knowledge of beauty enlarged, by familiarity with the best. To-day, as never before, such discipline and information are possible with moderate expenditure of money. The great marbles of the world are reproduced for us in plaster; the great paintings and works of architecture, in photographs. If the artistic expression of the human soul were a passing phase of life, its claim for recognition in college training might well be disregarded. The fact that attempts at such artistic expression are found among the earliest monuments of civilization, and persist in varying form through all the stages of the history of mankind, shows the fundamental character of aesthetics, and its value as a means of culture. One reason why the formal recognition of the study of art seems so desirable to me, is that the college might in this way begin a ministry to the community which would grow into one of great value. If its illustrations of art were chosen with care and properly placed, they would readily form a nucleus about which might gather in the course of years a collection of original paintings and sculpture, loaned to us or owned by us, which would be an honor and a boon to the city.

If it is true that the traditional curriculum has neglected the study of aesthetics, it may not be so apparent that it has failed to give due emphasis to the study of religion. Most of our colleges were established with a distinct religious purpose, — the love of learning being linked in the minds of the founders with their love of God. Religion in college, however, has generally found recognition in an atmosphere of reverence and spiritual earnestness. The curriculum has not often made place for any systematic study of the facts of spiritual life. Our day is one of fresh recognition of the reality of religion. From an attitude of indifference or opposition, begotten partly by misapprehension of spiritual truth, partly by unreasonable opposition on the part of organized religion to the advancement of science, the student of history and life is coming to recognize that religion has been a most potent factor in human evolution. Define religion as we may, the fellowship of the soul with that unseen power not ourselves that makes for righteousness is the most real experience in human life, — the richest in influence, the fullest of vitality. If it is desirable that a liberal culture should discipline and inform the sense for beauty, it is essential that the cultivated man should not be left unmindful of this most subtle and most significant phase of life. Such study of religion will not, in any wise, rival the appeals of the pulpit or the varied means of religious culture. It properly sets before itself two tasks: first, the study of the history of religion in all times and among all spiritual life; and second, acquaintance, in some measure, with the most significant parts of the Christian Scriptures. In this the college will not seek to do the work of the Sunday School or the theological seminary, but simply to secure for its graduates such an acquaintance with the most potent of spiritual forces as will justify its claim to have given them a genuinely liberal culture.

These demands for expansion of the curriculum to include work for beginners in the classics, new phases of historical study, culture in aesthetics, and in the facts of religion, may represent the constant calls for recognition of new or neglected branches of learning. They also emphasize a different problem which seriously presses for solution. We may call it the problem of adjustment. The crowding of our curriculum with new studies has forced the adoption of the educational principle of free election of studies. This in itself is a distinct advance. At present, however, the result is confusion. Few of our institutions have taken steps so to regulate election as to preserve that balance in education which is essential to a broad culture; few have taken steps to prevent the idle man from seeking his degree by means of work which will cost a minimum of effort. In as much as a college does not aim to train specialists, and as it assuredly does not purpose to reward indolence, we are face to face with the problem of a new estimate of the educational significance of different studies—their work for training and information—and with the demand for such a regulation of election as will leave the students' freedom essentially unimpaired, while securing from every candidate for graduation work sufficiently broad to warrant sending him out into life as an educated man. Some of our colleges have studied this problem and are attempting a solution. We have it before us and will take it up courageously.

Readjustment brings with it the problem of educational economy. There is complaint that our present system involves too much waste—waste of time and waste of energy. The graduate finds that much of the work he was compelled to do is of little service in his after life. His text-books lie in dust on his upper shelves—or on those of some dealer in second-hand books—and their contents are forgotten.

The extension of the elective system may do much to silence this complaint of waste of time. The ground for the complaint may be largely removed by the continuous modernizing of the work of the college. The readjustments of the curriculum now in progress should provide such guidance in elections that immature students will have least cause to regret the courses chosen by them. There is no more serious obligation resting on our shoulders as educators than this of reducing educational wastes to a minimum.

Economy is called for in another direction. There is a wide-spread demand for the reduction of the time necessary for securing advanced degrees in our universities. At the same time professional schools are finding it necessary to increase their courses by a year, while it is manifestly impossible for the college to reduce its course to three years with so many new subjects pressing for recognition. A response to the demand is possible, however, if we can reduce somewhat the duplication of work in the college and university courses. Universities— like Harvard and Columbia and Chicago—which have colleges allied with them, solve the difficulty by opening to undergraduates certain courses in the professional schools, which are in some cases credited towards both the bachelor's degree and the higher one which follows it. This simple solution is not yet practicable for the isolated college. In order to give a liberal culture it must offer to its students courses which are closely akin to the professional studies which some of these students will afterwards pursue. Economy of the student's time and the reduction of duplication of work may be secured in two ways, if the college will seek a closer understanding with the university. On the one hand, it may prove wise for us to arrange, under certain conditions to recognize a year of work in the university as counting towards the bachelor's degree, in place of one spent in residence. This might be done in connection with the readjustment of the curriculum noticed already. On the other hand, the college may arrange to give courses of an introductory and general character in subjects pursued further in professional schools, and may ask the universities to recognize this work,—in the measure of its excellence,—so reducing the time necessary to secure the advance degree. There is no reason why students who have no intention of specializing in medicine, for instance, should not gain their training in scientific method and information concerning scientific attainments, by the pursuit of studies that will contribute directly to the special end the aspirant for the degree of medicine has before him. Specializing and general culture can go hand in hand for a time with distinct advantage to both. Whatever the ultimate solution may be, this demand for the reduction of waste in education presses for early attention.

A fourth problem confronting the modern college administration, is the question of the degree which shall be granted for the successful pursuit of the college course. The degree of bachelor of arts is the traditional and suitable of a course of liberal culture. The granting of this degree corresponds with the ceremony by which, in the middle ages, a student at Paris or Oxford was recognized as a candidate for the master's degree in arts, law, theology, or medicine. Our educational conservatism has reserved this degree in arts for those who have included in their training the study of the Greek and Latin classics. The demand for full college work for students not in the classical course has consequently led to the offering of a degree in science, and in philosophy, or letters. The so-called bachelor's degree in philosophy, or letters, represents in our American life that a student has pursued a course of liberal culture which includes one ancient language. The degree of bachelor of science often indicates little else than that the student has pursued a course of liberal culture which includes no training in classics. The degree of bachelor of science properly should mean that the student has completed the first stage in a course of special scientific training; it is not suitable evidence of liberal culture in any sense. The dominance of the classics as a means of liberal culture dates from the time of the renaissance. During the medieval period the student at the University of Paris learned Latin as a means of communication between cultured men; of the Latin classics he had the slightest knowledge, if any. With the renaissance the literature of Greece and Rome came to the old world as a means of new and enriched life. The new learning was then this classical literature. These studies obtained their place in the curricula of the older institutions as a fresh and enriching means of mental discipline and information. It is historically justifiable, therefore, that the new learning of our recent times, insofar as it is fitted to give to students that discipline and information which are essential to liberal culture, should be recognized by the degree of bachelor of arts. This new learning will not in this way displace the classics. It will simply take its place beside the older culture as a means of liberal education, fitted to enable a student to enter upon his life work with broad views and disciplined powers.

These educational problems are not to find their solution in a day. All permanent growth is gradual. The opportunity of this afternoon has invited me to consider these features of the prospect which opens before me, as I enter upon this work to which I have been called. Little by little the present will change into the better future. Little by little this vision will be chastened, corrected, and disciplined by those larger views which will come with a larger experience; but always the aim before the college, in so far as it remains a college, will be to give to its students a culture genuinely liberal, by means of an education which is modern and economical.

Today you have honored the college by your presence, citizens of Rochester. The prospect for our future is bright in the measure of your interest. We are here to serve a wide constituency reaching many cities and neighboring states, but our closest, most intimate relation must be with the city which gives us hospitality. Our students come in large measure from your homes, the ties which link our interests with yours grow stronger with each year. It is our ambition to serve you most fully. We would give you here the opportunity for the most thorough modern education, which shall neither despise the past, nor be blindly tied to it; an education of the widest scope possible with our resources. As new demands arise and new resources are found, we pledge to you that we will meet the demands most eagerly, and use the resources with the broadest wisdom we can attain.

The fathers did not see our present day, but they saw larger things than they knew, which included and surpass any present attainment or definite prospect. The hand engraved on the college seal points onward toward ever "better things." We follow those courageous souls in studying with unresting earnestness for the modernizing of the culture which we offer you in their name.

Inaugural Address

by

GUY E. SNAVELY

President of Birmingham-Southern College

December, 1921

GUY EVERETT SNAVELY (1881—
) *was born in Antietam, Maryland. He received the A.B. degree and the doctorate from Johns Hopkins University. He is the recipient of five honorary degrees from leading institutions of the country.*

Dr. Snavely was Dean of Converse College before accepting the presidency of Birmingham-Southern College, where he served with distinction for seventeen years. Since 1937 he has served as Executive Director of the Association of American Colleges in a most effective manner.

In accepting the keys from President Warren G. Harding, Dr. Snavely spoke as follows:

President Harding and Friends:

In accepting through you, sir, this symbol of authority as the president of Birmingham-Southern College, we are not unmindful of the largeness of the task and our insufficiency in many respects. We realize that we succeed to the standards set by great educators and leaders, some of whom have become famous in Church and State. We recall that at least one who presided at Greensboro became a bishop, as did one who was president in Birmingham.

Stimulus to best effort and highest endeavor comes also when we recall the brilliant achievement and prominence of position attained by the great majority of our alumni. In preparing for the Christian education movement, which culminated last June in the drive for funds for additional endowment and buildings for our colleges, an investigation was made as to the product of our educational factory. It was found that the gift of Birmingham-Southern College to the country has already included 2 governors of States; 1 member of the United States Senate; 3 members of the National House of Representatives; 8 college presidents; 32 college professors, as well as numerous other teachers; 200 preachers and 6 missionaries to the foreign field; 90 lawyers, 3 of whom have become judges; 76 physicians, and a host of bankers, business men, planters and others who are rendering more or less conspicuous service in their various walks of life.

Such a record seems all the more admirable when it is recalled that the college began its work on the eve of the Civil War and had to weather the terrible set-back incident to the reconstruction period. With the more recent accessions to its list of friends and additions to its resources the responsibility for producing a proportionately larger number of leaders in all fields of human endeavor becomes correspondingly greater.

231

In order then to prepare men and women for better and nobler services to God, country and fellow-man the administration and the faculty need the utmost cooperation of trustee, alumnus and friends of education. In the confident hope that this support will be freely given, we accept this token of our responsibility.

"Dreading to leave an illiterate ministry to the churches" is part of an inscription on one of the gates at Harvard University. This is the spirit that prompted the establishment of the first American College at New Towne, now Cambridge, Mass., in 1636. The same idea was doubtless in the minds of the founders of William and Mary College in 1693, and practically all of the other colleges that had their origin in the colonial days. In other words, the early colleges in the United States were avowedly vocational in their aim.

The spirit of conservatism, however, which underlies educational progress, has caused the so-called liberal arts' subjects of the curriculum of the early colleges to be maintained with slight modifications almost up to the present. On the other hand, very few students enter the Liberal Arts' departments of the original colleges or their successors with the set purpose of entering the ministry.

This somewhat anomalous position maintained at present by the liberal arts college is discussed quite at length in a recent number of the Educational Review by Dr. S. P. Capen, Director of the American Council on Education. There is, indeed, a wide divergence in the time requirements of the various types of liberal arts colleges. In the present-day universities combination arrangements are freely offered whereby the M. D. and other professional degrees may be obtained at the end of a six or seven-year period, with the A.B. degree granted at the end of four years' work. Thus it is seen that in the liberal arts' department of the university the so-called straight college courses are confined to two or three years, whereas the professional college work extends over a period of four full years.

On the other hand, a number of small colleges still hold to the old curriculum of four years' undergraduate work before the award of the Bachelor's degree. The curricula of the types of colleges may vary in many ways but the general underlying courses of English, mathematics, history, foreign languages and the elementary sciences are common to them all.

In spite of the attempt of Amherst and other colleges of similar aim, to hold rigidly to the old type of a four-year course of study without the inclusion of pre-vocational or professional subjects, the great majority of young men and women are turning to the state and other universities that offer opportunities for the saving of one or more years in their preparation for their business or professional careers. When one considers the increasing demand for time at the professional end of the course for the student who desires to become a physician, lawyer, minister, engineer, teacher, one cannot help but sympathize with the combination scheme. Take, for example, a young man who is planning to practice medicine. If he completes elementary and secondary school work in the average time he will not be ready for college until he is 18. Then if he is required to spend four years for his Bachelor's degree and four years more for his Doctor's degree with an additional minimum experience as an interne in the hospital he will be 27 years old at the very least before he is through his schooling. As the public naturally wants, and should have, the best kind of specialized training on his part before risking their bodies and even their lives in his hands it is often likely that he will spend more than one year as an interne or as a hospital assistant before setting up independent practice. The question might also arise as to how long after a young man has attained his majority should he expect to remain a non-produced, and not only be somewhat of a burden to his family but be retarded

233

greatly in assuming his responsibilities as a home-maker and a citizen who should take his rightful place in all the phases of community life.

Probably a more important matter to consider is the content of the curriculum. Much has been said and written about the free elective system, about the group, or modified, elective system, and about the more or less required grouping of courses for all students. Although the elective or group systems appear predominant in most liberal arts curricula, there seems to be a swing of the pendulum in some of the eastern colleges away from too much freedom of election of studies. If, in the evolution of our educational system, the college-professional school combination should become more or less universal the liberal arts college would be in its relation to the professional school as the junior high school is getting to be to the senior high school; and the curriculum would become more or less static with few electives permitted.

The most serious problem in the present scheme of higher education is that of selecting students who are really worthy. The old method of examination in all subjects before admission to college has become almost universally succeeded by certification from accredited secondary schools. This, in turn, has been modified by the addition of intelligence tests, comprehensive examinations and personal interviews on the part of college admission officers. In spite of these attempts to choose the candidates most worthy of becoming leaders a reading of recent statistics would show that more students than ever were admitted to colleges and universities this fall. In fact, it seems unbelievable that so many hundreds are admitted into the respective freshman classes as are reported by the University of California, the University of Illinois and Columbia University. This condition is reflected in our own college for the present number of new students totals almost, if not quite as many, as the whole registration of the college at this time a year ago.

Even if the question of extent and content of the curriculum were more or less settled, there would be a tremendous waste of energy, time and money if the faculty were pouring certain mixtures of knowledge, more or less related, into the brains of unwilling or unprepared candidates. The truism still holds that knowledge is power. But knowledge cannot be precipitated into power through a negative medium. Furthermore, the knowledge referred to is that of the wise man who said: "With all thy getting, get understanding."

This additional problem of proper choice of worthy applicants for college admission is by far the most important. More than ever today is leadership needed in all phases of commercial, industrial, professional and social activities. Not only are leaders needed with clarity of vision and earnestness of purpose, but with unimpeachable character. The thickest vaults of the richest banks will avail nothing if the teacher in the school, the preacher in the pulpit, the business man at his desk, do not measure up to these standards. Doubtless most of us, if not all, are oblivious or unconcerned with the terrible situation that prevails in the former Russian empire, which is apparently an absolute break-down of an integral part of modern civilization due to the negation of the aforementioned qualities demanded for leadership. A return to the teachings of the Christ is as imperative now or more so than at any epoch in the last 2,000 years.

Further diagnosis of the college situation reveals considerable weakness in the present day teaching in colleges. An excellent criticism of this has been made in a recent book entitled "The College and New America." Dr. Hudson makes an earnest appeal for the real vitalization of the subjects taught. Too much emphasis can not be laid on making college courses vital to the students. Without doubt the greatest value a college president can be to an institution is in discovering and obtaining good teachers, rather than erecting laboratories and gymnasiums or doubling the student roll. It must be admitted that his task is unusually severe at the present because of the war re-adjustments and losses of professional men to business and industry as well as because of unattractiveness of compensation. This latter point has unfortunately been rather overstressed, for some of the recent demonstrations which included processions bearing banners with inscriptions like "Help the Professor's Family" have discouraged many worthy and interested young men from entering the profession. Whatever tends to stabilize the teacher's profession should be incouraged. Those supporting the agitation for the establishment of a federal department of education maintain that such recognition would bring about these results and more. If this phase of their argument is valid such recognition would be of incalculable benefit to the progress of the nation.

Granting, then, that we will and must have capable and consecrated teachers we shall consider again briefly the student. Whatever course he undertakes should contain certain fundamental subjects that will tend to develop him for the best possible service he can render his generation. The present age, more than any other, can really be considered the age of Socialized Service. This should, therefore, be indicated in the content of the curriculum of the college, and also in the titles of the schools to be established in the university. Just as the key words of the ancient Hebrew civilization were, "The Law and the Prophets," so the backbone of the education of the time was built upon the Mosaic law. Likewise, the curricula of the schools of ancient Greece and Rome were determined by the predominating features of their respective civilizations. The Greek scholars aimed to excel in rhetoric, oratory, painting and the graphic and plastic arts. The Romans in their day were trained to be the rulers and the law-givers of the rest of the world.

The great inventions of recent times, like those in steam and electric locomotion and the ease of communication through

236

the telephone and the telegraph, have bound nations together and made them inevitably more interrelated than in any preceding civilization. These inventions, being continually improved, have brought about many various problems that require a changed ideal of civilization. As indicated above, this may be considered Socialized Service.

The motto of a great international organization is "Service Above Self." This motto epitomizes the aims of other national and international organizations, which in some quarters seem to be more effective for good than the church. If this is even approximately true, it is immediately imperative that most serious consideration be given by all concerned to the aim rather than to the curriculum of our early colleges if our leadership of the present and the future is to be properly trained.

To be more concrete, it seems to us that the most intimate relationship possible to their communities should be held by the colleges and the universities, whether they are state, church, or independent. If any of these types of colleges is located in or near a large city, it's administration should establish schools to offer courses that would be of the greatest benefit to the citizens of the community. For example, it should so arrange its schedule that courses of importance for teachers could be given in late afternoon hours and Saturday morning hours for those desiring to make progress in their profession. Likewise, courses in accounting and business administration should be offered for those desiring advancement in the business world. A number of institutions, which are really city universities, have made great progress in this respect, but there is no reason why all educational institutions similarly situated should not offer the same advantages to their respective communities.

Lest the speaker be considered grossly vocational in his aims and to have lost sight of the value of fundamental cultural courses, he will state that he considers it of the utmost importance to have in every college of whatever type not only fundamental courses in English, history, foreign languages, science, etc., but also required courses in music and art. By this is meant that in music there should be a professor who would not only attempt to awaken an appreciation of music in every student by requiring all to participate in an occasional group "sing," but who would also arrange for concerts, recitals and other means of acquainting the students with the best there is in music.

In art the fundamental of drawing obtained in the present up-to-date public school would be the foundation stone for development of interest in outline, form, color, etc. The interest in this subject could be stimulated by a professor who could vitalize art and give a course with appropriate illustrations for study by the students. President Hughes, of Miami University, has taken the lead in putting into execution this general idea. He maintains that every wide-awake college or university should have on its staff one well-known artist, poet or dramatist who may, or may not, give any lectures during the year. He has had on his faculty the dramatist, Percy Mackaye, whose mere presence, doubtless, gives a great stimulus to the work of the student-body and who is given all the leisure he desires for the continuation of his productive work.

A plea for educating for service cannot be concluded without mention of physical education. No one who is not in good health can really render most effectual service, however well trained he may be in spirit and in mind. The old shibboleth, "mens sana in corpore sano," so familiar to the teacher and administrator, seems to be considered yet in most secondary schools and colleges to be best attained by allowing the overwhelming majority of the students to yell and sing while nine or eleven of their comrades really get the exercise in competition with a similar number from a rival institution. Much more emphasis should be placed on intramural contests than on games with outside colleges. Indeed, with a large series of group teams, in which every student would be given an opportunity to develop his body, a fairer method would be obtained for selecting frequently more promising men than those who arrive with a preparatory school reputation more or less deserved.

May we conclude, then, with a slight paraphrase of the poet's prophetic musings at his imaginary Locksley Hall. "Forward, forward let us range, the heirs of all the ages, in the foremost files of time, ever reaping something new,"—that which has been done but earnest of the things that we shall do.

Inaugural Address

by

JAMES MONROE TAYLOR

President of Vassar College

June, 1886

JAMES MONROE TAYLOR (*August 5, 1848—December 19, 1916*) *was a clergyman and the son of a clergyman. He brought to Vassar administrative ability and an abundance of energy. He was an effective public speaker and an incessant traveller. His dynamic personality was a great asset in raising over a million dollars for Vassar College. He set a high academic standard for the college, abolished the preparatory division for students and unified the faculty. He was highly successful in selecting a strong group of teachers who frequently held different views on education but retained their friendship and loyalty to him.*

It is with great pleasure that I accept these duties given me by one who for the year past has been so successful, and who has discharged the great responsibilities so acceptably. I shall enter into other men's labors. This institution has a history and traditions, and established methods of education. And these all should have the strongest influence upon its future. That they have proved successful is shown by the trained womanhood that looks back to Vassar as its Alma Mater. Whatever there is of good in the domestic life, the standards and methods of the institution, it will be my aim to preserve and strengthen. But we should be false to the trust reposed in us if we should look merely backward. The opportunities for woman's education have greatly expanded since Vassar led the way. Other institutions similarly equipped have been established. Colleges for men are opening their doors to women. The demands upon us therefore are greater than ever before. It is not enough that our standard should be high. It must be even higher. Vassar College must aim to satisfy all just claims of society upon her.

There are two great problems which call for attention now. The first grows out of the extent of the realm of knowledge, which is acknowledged by all true educators as an obstacle in the way of thorough mental training. How to select those branches that shall give the best culture is a problem that agitates the educational world, and the last word concerning it will probably not be said for a long time yet. But we think Vassar must range herself with the conservative side, making her curriculum as broad as possible, yet placing emphasis on training the mind, not merely filling it. We must educate the intellectual powers; not send out merely well informed men and women, but those who will be efficient in every department of the world's activities. The second is regarding the need of a sound religious basis for all broad and valid culture. In order to gain the confidence of the public today any institution of learning must recognize the demands of man's spiritual nature. The position of Vassar is fixed in this respect by the will of its founder. It is a Christian college. Disregarding sectarian claims, and turning away from everything like cant, its spirit should be, and we trust will be, the spirit of our Lord Jesus Christ. Without prejudice, and without consenting to be tied to any sect, it must stand in spirit and aim as a distinctively Christian college, and without this it would fail in giving a good education. The college will aim in the future as in the past to give to women facilities for attaining intellectual independence and efficiency in the work of the world, with a reverent and God-centered faith. We must never forget that the best can be better. Vassar should do the utmost with what she has, and the utmost to increase what she has.

I acknowledge the kind words spoken on behalf of the alumnae and shall rest on the loyal support of this body of women who have met and are solving the problems of the time. As heartily do I thank the students for their welcome. Yours after all must be every increase in the advantages and opportunities of the institution. I hope the spirit of your training here will exemplify the meaning of Plato's figure — that you will carry the light of truth here gained to those in darkness and ignorance whom you meet in life.

To the trustees, thanking them for their expressions of confidence, I will simply say that I will try to administer the trust faithfully. Relying upon the support of the trustees also for strength, yet in all things I shall rely most upon the help of Almighty God.

Inaugural Address

by

ANDREW DICKSON WHITE

President of Cornell University

October 7, 1868

ANDREW DICKSON WHITE (November 7, 1832——November 4, 1918) was born in Homer, New York, of English parentage. As a boy White had a thirst for knowledge which was only partially satisfied at Geneva College (now Hobart) and Yale. It was his vision and statesmanship which he demonstrated as Chairman of the New York State Senate's Committee on Education, that attracted the attention of Ezra Cornell. The vigorous fight led by White in preserving the vast land endowment of the Federal Government to the states for education was responsible for an intimate friendship which developed between Dr. White and Ezra Cornell. The result of this friendship gave dignity to vocational education on a college level for the first time in America.

Six years ago, in the most bitter hour of the Republic, in her last hour as many thought, amid most desperate measures of war, the councils of the United States gave thought and work to a far-reaching measure of peace. They made provision for a new system of advanced education; they cut this system loose from some old ideas under which education had been groaning; they grafted into it some new ideas for which education had been longing; they so arranged it that every State might enjoy it; they imposed but few general conditions, and these grounded in right reason; they fettered it with no unworthy special conditions; they planned it broadly; they endowed it munificently.

This is one of the great things in American history—nay, one of the great things in world-history. In all the annals of republics, there is no more significant utterance of confidence in national destiny out from the midst of national calamity.

Four years ago, war still raging, a citizen of this State, an artisan who had wrought his way to wealth, but who in wealth forgot not the labors and longings of poverty, offered to supplement this public gift with a private gift not less munificent. He alloyed it with no whimseys, he fettered it with no crochets, he simply asked that his bounty might carry out a plan large and fair.

Three years ago the State of New York, after some groping, accepted these gifts, refused to scatter and waste them, concentrated them in a single effort for higher education and fixed on a system of competitive examinations to bring under the direct advantages of this education the most worthy students in every corner of her domain. Six months afterwards the authorities to whom the new effort was entrusted met in this pleasant village. Among them were the highest officers of the State. He who had offered the private endowment appeared before them. He not only redeemed his promise—he did more—he added to it princely gifts which he had not prom-

247

ised; more than that, his earnest manner showed that he was about to give something more precious by far—his whole life. So was founded the Cornell University.

Months followed and this same man did for the State what she could not do for herself; he applied all his shrewdness and energy to placing the endowment from the United States on a better footing. Other States had sold the script with which they were endowed at rates ruinously low; the Founder of this University aided the State to make such an investment that its endowment developed in far larger measure than the most sanguine ever dared hope.

Such, gentlemen of the Board of Trustees and fellow citizens, are the simple landmarks in the progress of this institution hitherto-not to weary you with a long detail of minor labors and trials—such is the history in the chronological order, the order of facts; let me now briefly present it in logical order, in the order of ideas. And, first of all, I would present certain:

FOUNDATION IDEAS

On these is the structure based—these attach it firmly to the age and people for which we hope to rear it.

Foremost of these stands that corner stone embedded in the foundations by the original Charter from Congress—the close union of liberal and practical education.

Hitherto, with hardly an exception, the higher education had been either liberal or practical; by that instrument, provision was made for education both liberal and practical.

The two great sources of national wealth, agriculture and the mechanic arts, were especially named as leading objects to be kept in view. At the same time narrowness was prevented by clauses providing that other objects of study, necessary to broad and high education, should be attended to. No charter more timely in its special aims, more broad in its general aims could have been granted.

In entire harmony with the spirit and letter of this original Charter was the next foundation idea.

It was put forth by the Founder of the University himself, and in language the simplest and plainest. It gave a complete theory of university instruction. Said Ezra Cornell: "I would found an institution where any person can find instruction in any study."

Devoted to practical pursuits, he recognized the fact that there must be a union of the scientific and the aesthetic with the practical in order to produce results worthy of such an enterprise. The idea then of those who planned for the institution in the national halls at Washington, and the ideas of this man who had thought over this problem in farm and workshop on the shores of Cayuga Lake, were in unison.

Into these foundation principles was now wrought another at which every earnest man should rejoice, the principle of unsectarian education.

Perhaps no one thing has done more to dwarf the system of higher education in this land than the sectarian principle. As the result of much observation and thought I declare my firm belief that, but for our enslavement to this unfortunate principle we would long since have had great free universities, liberal and practical, the largest, the most ample in equipment, most earnest in effort, the most vigorous in thought the world has yet seen. I believe they would have had a vastly stronger hold upon the people, and an infinitely more valuable result on national education in science, literature, art and practical pursuits.

I do not say that the sectarian principle has given no good results. It has done good and great good. It built colleges which otherwise would not have been built; it stimulated men who otherwise would have remained inactive; it incited labor and sacrifice which otherwise would have been wanting; but the time has come when we want more than they have given us.

I do not deny the earnestness of the founders and promoters of these colleges. I do not deny the great attainments and self-sacrifice of multitudes of their professors. I do not deny that they are doing good work today. But I do deny that all the work necessary can be done by such means, I deny that any university worthy of that great name can ever be founded upon the platform of one sect or combination of sects. Do you ask why? I point you to the simplest facts in educational history. I will not trouble you with the argument in the abstract; look at it in the concrete. One of the most honored college presidents of New York was excluded from teaching natural philosophy in a New England faculty because he was an Episcopalian. One of the most honored college presidents of New England was excluded from teaching Greek in a New York faculty because he was an Unitarian. One of the most renowned of college presidents in the Western States was rejected from a collegiate position in this State because he was a Presbyterian. One of the main college presidencies of New England remained a long time within these latter years vacant. Why? There were scholars, jurists, statesmen in that commonwealth, who would have felt honored by the position. Why were they not called? Simply because the statutes of that University required the presiding officer to be a clergyman of a particular sect, and no one of them happened to be found willing or able to undertake the duties. One of the largest colleges in this State rejected one of the best of modern chemists because he was not of a certain sect. A noted college in a neighboring State rejected one of our most noted mathematicians and astronomers for the same reason. Nor are these extreme cases. There are those within the sound of my voice who have seen a college long suffering for want of a professor in a certain department difficult to fill. A man of the required sect was at last found admirably fitted, but this man was rejected. Why? Solely because he was not of a certain peculiar party of that particular sect.

All this is the evil growth from an evil germ. From the days when Henry Dunster, the first president of the first college in America, a devoted scholar, a thorough builder, an earnest man, was driven from his seat with ignominy and with cruelty because Cotton Mather declared him "fallen into the briars of anti-paedobaptism," the sectarian spirit has been the worst foe of enlarged university education.

Place the strongest men under a spirit like this and they are robbed of half their strength. Under such a system are wanting the very foundations of an University, because the only such foundations are foundations of liberty.

The fundamental idea of the institution which we hope to found is different. It accepts fully the principle of religious freedom in higher education as we all receive it in general education. Its Founder had quietly and characteristically announced this when he made to this town his splendid gift of a public library, and selected as trustees a body of sound-hearted, sound-minded citizens, regardless of creed or party, adding to the board the clergyman of every church in the town, Catholic and Protestant, orthodox and unorthodox.

This idea of Legislature of this State fixed firmly in our Charter. They fixed it and clenched it; for there are two clauses. The first clause is: "and a majority of the Trustees shall never be of any one religious sect or of no religious sect." The second is: "and no professor, officer or student shall ever be accepted or rejected on account of any religious or political views which he may or may not hold." On that ground we stand. The faculty now assembled is in the best sense a Christian faculty, yet it is of no one dogma: Almost every religious body is represented.

But it may be said that the system is unchristian. What then is your whole system of common schools? It is founded on the same basis. What then is your whole system of government? It is carried on in the same manner.

251

Do you trust to sectarian teaching alone to save Christianity? The great deists of the last century and the great rationalists of this century were almost without exception educated in schools where sectarian tests were rigid. Voltaire, and Gibbon, and Diderot, and Renan, and Colenso were so educated.

But, it is said that an institution for advanced education must be sectarian to be successful. Here, again, we will turn from theory to practice. I point you to the State University of Michigan; it is young, it is insufficiently endowed; it has had trials; it is one of the smaller and less wealthy States, and worse than that, in an unappreciative State. Yet it is today confessedly the greatest of educational successes in our country. It is unsectarian, but it is one of the best bulwarks of noble and enlightened Christianity in that commonwealth.

On the same basis we take our stand. We appeal from sectarians to Christians; we appeal from the sectarian in every man to the Christian in every man. Nor shall we discard the idea of worship. This has never been dreamed of in our plans. The first plan of buildings and the last embraced a University chapel. We might indeed find little encouragement in college chapel services as they are often conducted; prayers dogmatic or ceremonial; praise with doggerel hymns, thin music and feeble choir; the great body of students utterly listless or worse.

From yonder chapel shall daily ascend praise and prayer. Day after day it shall recognize in man not only mental and moral but religious want. We will labor to make this a Christian institution—a sectarian institution may it never be. We take this stand in perfect good will to all colleges and universities based upon the opposite idea. There is more than work enough in this nation for all. The books of this institution opened but a few days since show this. We have entered the largest single class ever known in the United States, and that too after rejecting over fifty candidates as ill-prepared; and yet the other colleges and universities of this and neighboring States, almost without exception, have increased their number of students.

Yet another of these foundation ideas was that of a living union between this University and the whole school system of the State.

It cannot fail to strike any thinking man with surprise that while the numbers in the public schools of this commonwealth are so great, the numbers at the colleges are so small. What is the cause of this? Is it that the people of this State do not wish any advanced education? Every other sign shows that they do wish it. Is it that they have not the means? The means were never more abundant than now. It is believed by many of us that it is because there is a want of vital connection between the higher institutions and this great system of popular instruction. We believe that the only hope for such an institution as we long to see is in pushing its roots deep down into this great rich school system.

This idea also took shape in our Charter. Under the direction of the Superintendent of Public Instruction the statute was so framed as to provide for competitive examinations in each Assembly District, and to give the scholar passing the best examination, in studies pursued in the best common schools, admission free of all charge for tuition.

Yet another of those fundamental ideas was that which, against prejudices of locality and of sect, has triumphed during these latter years in every great public body of this State, whether Legislature or Convention—the idea of concentration of revenues for advanced education.

In these days it takes large sums indeed to man and equip institutions prepared to do work of the highest and best. There must be large and varied libraries, delicate apparatus, models, the most intricate collections, cabinets, laboratories, observatories, shops, engines, instruments, tools. There must be buildings and farms, and there must be men,—men worth having. All this demands great means.

Formerly the policy of the State had been to fritter away such resources. Great funds had been scattered among a large number of institutions. Each of these had noble professors—all had done good work—but as a rule not one had the means to carry on the best work.

Smaller States east and west of us had by concentration produced far greater results. Every year saw a long line of our most earnest young men going forth to the universities of other States which had pursued a policy of concentration.

It has indeed been claimed that by scattering small colleges over the State, facilities for advanced education were increased. This may have been so before railroads practically reduced States to a tenth of their old limits. Certainly it is not so now. Concentration of means is proven to draw out a far greater number of students than the opposite policy. Again I turn from theory to fact; again I cite our neighbor, the State of Michigan, with only about an eighth of our population and with the smallest fraction of our wealth, and she has more students today in her one University, under her policy of concentrating resources, than the State of New York has in all her colleges under her policy of scattering them. The class which entered that institution a fortnight since outnumbers all the entering classes of all our colleges.

Facts like these show that you can only attract students by meeting their wants; that it is not nearness and cheapness merely, but thoroughness and fullness which attract students. Divide the University of Michigan into four parts, and scatter them over the State, and, at the very highest, you would not draw more than a hundred to each. Concentrate them, and today fifteen hundred students enter its halls.

Facts like these have had their weight. They have carried the day in legislatures and conventions against local interests, sectarian influence and the attachment of graduates to their alma mater, until concentration for advanced education may be regarded as the settled policy of the State.

Such are some of the main foundation ideas of our plan. I come now to another class.

FORMATIVE IDEAS

First of these I name the idea of equality between different courses of study.

It is determined to give special courses like those in agriculture, mechanc arts, engineering and the like, equality in honor with other special courses. To this we are pledged. It has been the custom, almost universally, to establish colleges for agriculture or the mechanic arts separate from all others, with small endowments. These have been generally placed in remote and unattractive parts of States, and, as a rule, thus treated, they have been regarded as the inferior college of an inferior caste, and have languished and died.

From that practice this State has departed. A citizen having provided mainly the endowment for a University, it unites with it or rather incorporates into its departments of agriculture and the mechanic arts, to be leading departments in full standing, at least equal to any other, equal in privilege, equal in rank of students perhaps more than equal in care.

It does not send the student in agriculture or mechanic arts to some place remote from general instruction. It gives the farmer's son the same standing that it gives the son of any other citizen. It makes him a part of a University, broad and liberal; it makes his study the equal of any study; it makes him the peer of any student.

In obedience to your wishes, gentlemen of the Board of Trustees, I have within the past two years visited a number of the leading schools of agriculture and the mechanic arts, both in the old world and in the new. I have found the better opinion unanimously in favor of the system which the State has now adopted, that of giving to these great practical arts of life equal and honored departments in an University rather than to scatter them to schools feeble and remote.

A similar principle is to govern us in the formation of courses of study in the departments of science, literature and the arts in general. It is an old custom, derived from the mother country, to force all students into one single, simple course of study. No matter what the tastes of the young student, no matter what his aims, through this one course he must go, and through none other. For generations this has been the leading policy in higher education. Noble men have been produced under this system, partly by it, partly in spite of it; but its general results have been unfortunate in the extreme. Presenting to large classes of young men no studies to attract them or stimulate them, these have conceived a dislike for higher education. Still worse, it has injured their mental quality by dragging them through one branch after another for which they cared not, droning rather than studying, a half-way mental labor more injurious than no mental labor.

The Cornell University attempts a different plan. It presents to students, coming to its halls, several courses, separate and distinct, suited to different minds, looking toward different pursuits. Acting up to the University ideas of its Founder and its Charter from State and nation, does a student desire the old, time-honored course, enriched by classical study, it gives it; does he wish more attention to modern science, to history, to the great languages and literatures of the modern world, to science as bearing on practice, it gives either of these.

But it may be said that other colleges have done this. This is partially true. A few have manfully attempted it, and they deserve all credit. As a general rule, these more recent courses have been held inferior, and the students taking them have been held inferior. Both courses and students have generally been studiously kept apart from those esteemed more ancient and honorable. Thus has risen a spirit of caste fatal to the full development of these newer courses.

The Cornell University holds these courses, if of equal duration, equal. Four years of good study in one direction are held equal to four years of good study in another. No fictitious supremacy is ascribed to either.

Another part of our plan is to combine labor and study.

The attempt is to have this a voluntary matter. It is not believed that forced labor can be made profitable either to the institution or to the student. Voluntary labor corps will be formed and the work paid for at its real value—no more, no less.

The question is constantly asked, Can young men support themselves by labor and at the same time carry on their studies? The answer as I conceive it is this. Any students, well prepared in his studies, vigorous in constitution and skilled in some available branch of industry, can, after a little time, do much toward his own support, and in some cases support himself entirely. At present the young carpenter or mason can earn enough on the University buildings during half a day to carry him through the other half, and it is hoped that, as our enterprise develops, young men of energy and mechanical ability can do much toward their own support in the shops to be constructed, and upon the University farm under direction of the professors in the College of Agriculture. In the latter especially there is hope for the most speedy solution of the problem, and it is believed that young men skillful and energetic in farm labor may, by work during the vacations and in some of the hours spared from study during the remainder of the year, accomplish their own support.

257

Still I would avow my belief that the part of this experiment likely to produce the most satisfactory results is that in which the labor itself is made to have an educational value. In the careful designing and construction of models and apparatus under competent professors, the artisan who has already learned the use of tools can acquire skill in machine drawing, knowledge of adjustment of parts, dexterity in fitting them, beside supporting himself at least in part and supplying models to the University cabinets at a moderate rate. Master mechanics thus educated are among the greatest material necessities of this country. The amount annually wasted in the stumblings and blunderings of unscientific mechanicians and engineers would endow splendid universities in every State. One of the noblest aims of this institution is to thus take good substantial mechanics and farmers from the various shops and farms of the State and give them back fitted to improve old methods, invent new, and generally to be worthy leaders in the army of industry.

With unskilled labor the problem is more difficult. Students, unskilled in labor, agricultural or mechanical, may do much toward their own support, in cases where there is quickness in learning and great physical vigor. Still the number of such cases will be found, I think, comparatively small. The chances in this direction for young men city-bred, delicately reared, or of a constitution not robust, are, I think, few.

I know well, gentlemen of the Board of Trustees, that you will do all that can be done to solve this problem; and, gentlemen of the Faculty, I know that you will earnestly second this effort. No class of students shall be regarded by us all with more favor than those who work with their hands that they may work with their brains.

Closely connected with this comes physical education. From the first this has held an important place in our plan, and I think that every person interested in our enterprise will be glad to know that the Faculty have already in this respect seconded the intentions of the Trustees. The idea of Herbert Spencer regarding man's study of himself as preliminary to other study has been carried out in our university programme. In the schedule of studies already arranged, every student in every fixed course, must pursue the study of human anatomy, physiology and hygiene, and it is hoped that by adding to this work gymnastic exercises we may do something toward preventing our scholars becoming a "feeble folk," and may bring up physical development not less than mental. I fully believe that today in the United States physical education and development is a more pressing necessity even than mental development, and we shall act upon that belief.

Still another idea which has shaped our plans for instruction is that of making much of scientific study.

The wonderful progress in natural science has aroused an interest we shall endeavor to satisfy; but, more than this, we would endeavor to inculcate scientific methods for their own sake. We would lead the student not less into inductive processes than into deductive. To carry out this idea the Faculty have arranged to commence the study of natural science at the beginning of the course, and not, as has usually been the case, to throw it into the latter part, when the student has his eye fixed on active life. We shall try this experiment. It is urged by some of the best thinkers of modern times. We hope for it not only something in the interest of science, but we believe that it will make the student stronger for studies in language and literature. But while we would give precision and strength to the mind in these ways we would give ample opportunity for those classes of studies which give breadth to the mind, and which directly fit the student for dealing with state problems and world problems. In this view historical studies and studies in social and political science will hold an honored place. But these studies will not be pursued in the interest of any party. On points where honest and earnest men differ,

259

I trust we may have courses of lectures presenting both sides. I would have both the great schools in political economy represented here by their ablest lecturers.

You have seen, fellow citizens, that nearly all these formative ideas may be included in one, and that is the adaptation of this University to the American people, to American needs, and to our own times. Not to English life and English needs, not to French or German life and needs; not to the times of Erasmus, or Bacon, or the Mathers, or Dr. Dwight, but to this land and this time. Happy was I a week since to be strengthened in these ideas by a voice from across the waters, which every American honors and which will be heard ringing nobly here as it has done in academic halls of the old world—the voice of Goldwin Smith.

I will read from a recent letter. After expressing a most earnest sympathy and promising speedy cooperation in our work here, Professor Smith thus writes:

"You say you wish I could be with you. So do I, because the occasion will be one of the deepest interest. But you would not persuade me to give you any advice. I know too well the difference between the old and the new world. At least the only advice I should give you would be: Without ignoring the educational experience of Europe to act quite independently of it, and to remain uninfluenced, either in the way of imitation or of antagonism, by our educational institution or ideas. The question of academical education on this side of the water is mixed up with historical accidents and with political struggles to which on your side there are happily no counterparts. What I would say is: Adapt your practical education, which must be the basis of the whole, to the practical needs of American life, and for the general culture take those subjects which are most important and interesting to the citizen and the man. Whatever part may be assigned to my subject in the course of general culture, I will do what I can to meet the wishes of the authorities of the University, without exaggerating the value of the subject or unduly extending its sphere."

The Faculty have been found true to this spirit. They have already voted to memorialize the Trustees that, at an early day, provision be made for some of those studies which the ordinary needs of the country call for—those studies which have so much value in a commercial country. For example, I hope to see the time and that speedily when every student in this institution shall have the opportunity to obtain the elements of mercantile law and the practice of accounts; the latter especially, not only for its practical utility, but as conducive to systematic habits of noting, comparing and preserving results, not less valuable to the man of science than the man of business.

Such are some of the main formative ideas. Let me now call your attention to some of another class.

GOVERNMENTAL IDEAS

First of these is the regular and frequent infusions of new life into the government board. The Trustees themselves proposed this; the State Legislature provided it in our Charter. The provision is two-fold. First, it makes the term of office of the Trustees five years, instead of the usual life tenure, and requires that all elections be by ballot. Next, it requires that so soon as our graduates number fifty they may elect one Trustee each year, thus giving them one third of the whole number elected. Thus it is hoped to prevent stagnation, to make a more living connection between the institution and its graduates, and to constantly pour into its councils new and earnest life.

Another of this class of ideas refers to the government of students by themselves.

The government of large bodies of young men assembled in colleges and universities presents some of the knottiest problems in education. It will be the aim of the authorities to pro-

261

mote more and more the residence of students in private families, and thus to bring the young men under family influence, and under the feeling that they are members of the community, subject to the same laws and customs which bind other members.

But our plans require that a large number reside in the University buildings. That students thus congregated are difficult to govern all know. How shall they be controlled? The usual method has been to place among them the members of the faculty of instruction, to make these a police, detective and repressive. Order under this system has generally been bad; the relations between student and instructor have been worse. In several cases so bad a spirit has arisen that members of a faculty have been assaulted with intent to kill. As to the relations thus formed, it is evident that a pedagogue policeman must be the least fascinating of instructors and the least vigorous of rulers.

It has therefore been determined to bring to bear here to some extent the combined principles of self-government and strict accountability. Students will be admitted to reside in the building only on condition that they subject themselves to a simple military organization, sufficient to enforce the University by-laws and to secure order and sanitary supervision. This organization will be conducted by officers selected from their own numbers, and will be under the superintendence of the Professor of Military Science, who is made for this purpose Commandant of the University Buildings.

We hope good results from this. It has succeeded well at military colleges, and the principle at its center formed the nucleus of Dr. Arnold's monitorial system at Rugby. The success of that experiment is a matter of history.

But, while we thus act in the spirit of our Congressional Charter, we hope to take from the military organization all its harshness.

We have faith in manly, open, social intercourse between Faculty and students. A large social hall has been provided. In this it is intended to bring students and Faculty together from time to time, to have them talk to each other, to have them know each other, and thus to transmute the traditional and most unfortunate relations which too often exist between instructors and instructed, into a relation not of a college boy to a pedagogue, but into a relation simply of man to man. But there must be no namby-pambyism, no playing with young men who would disgrace us, no sacrifice of the earnest many to the unearnest few.

We wish it distinctly understood that this is no "Reform School." It is established to give advanced education to earnest, hard-working young men, not to give a respectable resting place to unearnest and idle young men. The function of its Faculty is educating sound scholars, not reclaiming vicious boys. We have no right to give our strength or effort to reform, or drag, or push any man into an education; we have no time for that. One laggard will take more life out of a professor than a dozen vigorous scholars—one debauchee will take more time from a Faculty than a score of trusty scholars. For minor shortcomings and faults there will be some forbearance; for confirmed idleness and vice there will be none.

But I should not be frank here were I to be silent regarding a question in which great numbers of earnest citizens take a deep interest, and which has been lately pressed upon us by a most cogent and careful memorial from the public school teachers of the State of New York—the question of admitting students regardless of race or sex.

I believe myself justified in stating that the authorities of the University would hold that under the organic law of the institution we have no right to reject any man on account of race.

As to the question of sex, I have little doubt that within

a very few years the experiment desired will be tried in some of our largest universities. It has succeeded not only in the common schools, but—what is much more to the point—in the normal schools, high schools, and academies of this State. It has succeeded so far in some of the leading lecture rooms of our leading colleges that it is very difficult to see why it should not succeed in all their lecture rooms, and, if the experiment succeeds as regards lectures, it is very difficult to see why it should not succeed as regards recitations. Speaking entirely for myself, I would say that I am perfectly willing to undertake the experiment as soon as it shall be possible to do so. But no fair-minded man or woman can ask us to undertake it now. It is with the utmost difficulty that we are ready to receive young men. It has cost years of hard thought and labor to get ready to carry out the first intentions of the national and State authorities which had reference to young men. I trust the time may soon come when we can do more.

And finally, there are certain general ideas which must enter into our work in all of its parts:

PERMEATING OR CROWNING IDEAS

They are two. First, the need of labor and sacrifice in developing the individual man, in all his nature, in all his powers, as a being intellectual, moral and religious.

In the carrying out of the first of these no good means are to be rejected. Training in history and literature comes in with training in science and the arts. There need be no cant against classical studies or for them. Their great worth for many minds cannot be denied. The most perfect languages the world has ever known will always have students. The simple principle will be that of universal liberty of choice among studies. Those who feel that they can build themselves up by classical studies will be encouraged. We shall not injure such studies by tying those who love them to those who loathe them. And let me urge here that we work toward some great sciences and arts which have been sadly neglected, which nevertheless are among the most powerful in developing the whole man.

It seems to me a great perversion that while so much pains are taken in the great universities of the world to study the second rate things of literature—conventional poetry and superseded philosophy—there should be no interpretation of the great conceptions of such men as Fra Angelico, and Michael Angelo, and Raphael, and Millais; it seems wonderful that there should be so much time given to rhetoric-makers and so little to the drama of Shakespeare or to the sonnets of Milton; it seems monstrous that there should be so much effort to drill immortals in petty prosody and so little effort to bring them within reach of those colossal symphonies of Beethoven and Handel. The men of the "dark ages" who placed the most powerful of the arts second in the Quadrivium were certainly more in the light here than we.

The second of these permeating ideas is that of bringing the powers of man, thus developed, to bear upon society.

In a republic like this the way in which this is most generally done is by the speech. Its abuses are manifest. A palaver has brought many troubles. Gab has brought some curses. Educated men have often shrunk from these. Nothing could be more unfortunate. The educated men of a republic should keep control of the forum. Universities suited to this land and time should fit them to do it. Some of the steps in this preparation may seem almost absurd, but they should be taken. Almost every educated man can make himself an effective speaker—I do not say orator, but effective speaker—and every educated man should do it. In no place better than in the university can a man learn to think while on his feet; that done, the rest is easy. I would not have too much stress laid on mere oratory, but the power of summoning thought quickly and using it forcibly I would have cultivated with special care.

A second mode of bringing thought to bear upon society is by the press. Its power is well known; still its legitimate power among us might be made greater, and its illegitimate power less. I think that more and more the universities should have the wants of the great "fourth estate" in view. We should, to meet their wants, provide ample instruction in history, in political science, in social science, in the modern literatures. With all the strength of our newspaper press its best men declare the great majority of their recruits lamentably deficient in this knowledge and that power essential to their work. Here too a duty devolves upon the institutions of learning. Chosen men should be given power to work with this mighty engine. Their minds should be trained and stocked to that end.

But any sketch of the idea which this institution has aimed to embody would be imperfect without a brief supplement showing those we have endeavored to throw out. Call them

ELIMINATED IDEAS

These may be cast mainly into two groups: first, the ideas of the pedants; secondly, the ideas of the Philistines.

Of the first are they who gnaw forever at the dry husks and bitter rinds of learning and never get at the real, precious kernel! These are they who in so many primary schools teach boys to spell mechanically aloud—a thing which they are hardly called upon to do twice in a lifetime and to be utterly unable to spell correctly on paper—a thing which they are called upon to do every day of their lives.

These are they who in so many public schools teach boys geography by stupid parrotings upon leaden text-books, and leave them to come before the examiners of this University to be rejected, as more than fifty have been rejected during the last three days for statements that London is in the west of England, Havre in the south of France, Portugal the capital of Spain, Borneo the capital of Prussia, India a part of Africa,

266

Egypt a province of Russia, and the like.

These are they who in so many high schools teach young men by text-book to parse, and by their teachers' example to speak ungrammatically.

These are they who in so many colleges teach your young men endless metaphysics of the Latin subjunctive, and gerund-grindings, and second-hand dilutions of doubtful philology, with not an idea of the massiveness of statesmanship in Cicero, or the vigor of patriotism in Tacitus.

These are they who afflict young men with wearisome synopsizing of the Greek verb, with accents and quantities, until there is no time for the great thought of Plato or Thucydides.

Out upon the whole race of these owls: Let us have done with them.

Then the Philistines——men who in the world at large see no need of any education beyond that which enables a man to live by his wits and to prey upon his neighbors; men who care nothing for bringing young men within range of the great thoughts of great thinkers; men to whom "Greed is God and Gunnybags his prophet."

Of the Philistines, too, are they who, in institutions of learning, see only the hard things, the dry things, and never the beautiful things; who substitute dates for history, and criticisms for literature, and formulas for science, who give all attention to the stalk of learning and none to the bloom.

May this not be so among us. We may not be able to do all we could wish to realize our ideal, but let us work towards it. Mingle these influences with the education of our agriculturists; bring them to bear upon the rural homes of this land, and you shall see a happy change. You shall no longer be pained at that desertion of country for city which far-seeing men now so earnestly deplore.

267

Gentlemen of the Faculty: After this imperfect suggestion of the ideas underlying, forming, permeating our work, I appeal to you. The task before us is difficult. It demands hard thought, hard work. You will be called upon to exercise skill, energy and forbearance. The Faculty of this institution is the last place in the world for a man of mere dignity or of elegant ease.

But if the toil be great the reward also is great. It is the reward which the successful professor so prizes—the sight of men made strong for the true, the beautiful and the good through your help. The petty vanity of official station too often corrodes what is best in man; the pride of wealth is poverty indeed for heart, or soul, or mind; but the honest pride of the university instructor, seeing his treasures in noble scholars within the University and noble men outside its wall, is something far more worthy.

Said St. Fillippo Neri as he, day after day, came to the door of the College at Rome at the time when the English scholars passed out, young men who were to be persecuted and put to death under the cruel laws of Elizabeth of England, "I am come to feast my eyes on those martyrs yonder."

So may each of us feast our eyes on scholars, writers, revealers of nature, leaders in art, statesmen, who shall go in and out of yonder halls.

Let us labor in this spirit. The work of every one of us, even of those who deal with material forces, is a moral work. Henry Thomas Buckle was doubtless wrong in the small weight he ascribed to moral forces, but he was doubtless right in his high estimate of the moral value of material forces. He found but half the truth; let us recognize the whole truth; let it be full orbed. Every professor, who works to increase material welfare, acts to increase moral welfare.

I ask your aid as advisers, as friends. Let us hold ourselves in firm phalanx for truth and against error.

To you also, who appear in the first classes of students of Cornell University: You have had the faith and courage to cast in your lot with a new institution; you have preferred its roughness to the smoothness of more venerable organizations; you have not feared to aid in an experiment, knowing that there must be some groping and some stumbling. I will not ask you to be true to us. I will ask you to be true to yourselves. In Heaven's name be men. Is it not time that some poor student traditions be supplanted by better? You are not here to be made; you are here to make yourselves. You are not here to hang upon an University; you are here to help build an University. This is no place for children's tricks and toys, for exploits which only excite the wonderment of boarding-school misses. You are here to begin a man's work in the greatest time and land the world has yet known. I bid you take hold, take hold with the national Congress, with the State authorities, with Ezra Cornell, with the Trustees, with the Faculty, to build here by manly conduct and by study an University which shall be your pride. You are part of it. From your midst are to come its Trustees, Professors. Look to it that you be ready for your responsibilities.

Gentlemen of the Trustees: In accepting today formally the trust which for two years I have discharged really, I desire to thank you for your steady cooperation and support in the past and ask for its continuance.

You well know the trust was not sought by me. You well know with what misgivings it was accepted. In the utmost sincerity I say that it will be the greatest happiness of my life to be able, at some day not remote, to honorably resign it into hands worthier and stronger than my own.

Not a shadow of discord has ever disturbed our relations. Permit me to ask for my brothers in the Faculty the same cordiality which you have extended to me.

You have been pleased to express satisfaction with my

administration thus far; I trust that with this aid the work may be better.

And, in conclusion, to you, our honored Founder: I may not intrude here my own private gratitude for kindnesses innumerable. Sturdily and steadily you have pressed on this enterprise, often against discouragement, sometimes against obloquy. But the people of this great commonwealth have stood by you. Evidences of it are seen in a thousand forms, but at this moment most of all in the number of their sons who have come to enjoy your bounty.

You were once publicly charged with a high crime. It was declared that you "sought to erect a great monument" for yourself.

Sir, would to Heaven that more of our citizens might seek to rear monuments such as this of yours. They are indeed lasting. The names chiseled in granite in the days of Elihu Yale and John Harvard have been effaced, but Yale and Harvard bear aloft forever the names of their founders. The ordinary great men of days gone by, the holders of high office, the leaders of rank—who remembers their names now? Who does not remember the names of founders or benefactors of our universities? Harvard and Yale, Dartmouth and Bowdoin, Brown and Amherst, all answer this question.

The names of Packer, Vassar, Cooper, Wells, Cornell, they are solidly rooted in what shall stand longest in this nation. They shall see a vast expanse of mushroom names go down, but theirs shall remain forever. Their benefactions lift them into the view of all men.

But, Sir, I would bear testimony here that your name was never thrust forward by yourself. You care little, indeed, what any man thinks of you or of your actions, but I feel it a duty to state that you were preparing to deal munificently with the institution under a different name when another insisted that your own name be given it.

270

It has happened to me to see your persistence, your energy and your sincerity tested. We have been too much together for me to flatter you now, but I will say to your fellows citizens that no man ever showed greater energy in piling up a fortune for himself than you have shown to heap up this benefaction for your countrymen. You have given yourself to it.

Therefore, in the name of this commonwealth and this nation, I thank you. I know that I am really empowered to do so in their behalf as if I held their most formal credentials. I thank you for those present, for those to come. May you be long spared to us. May this be a monument which shall make earnest men more earnest and despondent men take heart. May there ever rest upon it the approval of good men. Above all, may it have the blessing of God.

Inaugural Address

by

WILLIAM ALLAN NEILSON

President of Smith College

June 13, 1918

WILLIAM ALLAN NEILSON (1869—) *was born in the village of Doune, Perth-shire, Scotland, where his father was a school-master. He graduated with honors from Edin-burgh University. Mr. Neilson received the doctorate at Harvard University, after which he taught at Bryn Mawr, Columbia Univer-sity, Barnard College, Harvard, and Radcliffe. He resigned the presidency of Smith College in June, 1939.*

Dr. Neilson is one of America's outstand-ing Shakespearian scholars and collaborated with President Eliot in editing the Harvard Classics.

Your Excellency, President Eliot, President Seelye, Members of the Board of Trustees and of the Faculty, Alumnae, Students, and Friends of the College:

An occasion such as the present calls for some statement of purpose and policy. However modestly the president of an educational institution may regard his function, however profoundly he may be convinced that it is the teachers and the taught who make the college, and not the administrative officers, he cannot shirk the responsibilities of forming definite ideas as to the general aim, and of framing methods by which this aim may best be accomplished.

In the present instance such a statement might seem to be of less than usual importance in view of the distinguished success of my predecessors. The soundness of the principles laid down by President Seelye, the extraordinary degree to which he succeeded in giving form and application to these principles, the brilliant achievement of President Burton in carrying on their development, and of the appreciation by the country of the value of the educational opportunities created by these two men—all these might be taken as justifying their successor in conceiving his duty as one of tending a well-running machine and in general of keeping his hands off.

But the two leaders whom I have the honor to follow would be the last to contemplate with satisfaction the lapsing of Smith College into a state of unprogressive complacency. The college that regards itself as having reached the limit of improvement is in a dangerous way. The growth in numbers, the advance in general educational ideas and methods, the changes in the position of women in the community, all call for a perpetual reconsideration and readjustment of our organization and procedures. And at the present time, the revolutionary changes, social, industrial, economic, even ethical and religious, which may be expected from the cataclysm which is even now shaking the world, promise to make demands from

275

those responsible for the education of the next generation for a power of adaptability and a breadth of vision such as have perhaps never been exacted in modern times.

In the midst of war, Great Britain has taken up the problem of remaking its educational system, and in the remarkable bill introduced in the House of Commons this spring there occurs an interesting passage. The desire of those drawing up the measure is stated to be to develop a stronger nation with broader human sympathies, "by offering to every child the opportunity of enjoying that form of education most adapted to fashion its qualities to the highest use." The principle which underlies this ideal is one to which most people would give immediate assent, but which is yet lost sight of in much of the controversy on educational aims. The idea of democracy does not require the application of the same educational processes to all. Rather it recognizes the variety of human beings and demands that a variety of educations be contrived to make available for each the means of enabling him to reach the limit of his possibilities. The type of education offered by such an institution as ours is a costly one that can never be enjoyed by more than a small minority, and it is and will be necessary to devote energy and ingenuity to devising means of selecting those students whose abilities entitle them to this particular opportunity. Birth and wealth, pious aspirations and social ambitions have no claim to special consideration,—this career should be open to talent and character, and to talent and character alone. It is a betrayal of our trust and a cheating of those who have a right to be here to allow our classrooms to be cluttered by the unfit, to tolerate in the academic community those whose presence lowers the moral tone or reduces the intellectual life to mediocrity.

The old Scottish communion service used to be preceded by a preliminary exercise called "the fencing of the tables," in which the unworthy were warned not to approach. These introductory remarks on the selection of the guests at our academic board may be regarded as a kind of fencing of the tables. But what is the nature of the feast to which the worthy are invited? How are we to conceive the educational opportunity which such a college as this should offer?

A generation ago the leading thinkers on such matters were roughly to be classified as belonging to two camps: the scientific and the classical. The progress of scientific investigation throughout the nineteenth century had been so rapid, and its results, both practical and theoretical, had been so dazzling, that its exponents were asserting more and more boldly their demands for a larger share in the time and resources devoted to the education of youth. The utilitarian character of the age and the weakness of opponents debilitated by a long period of scholastic privilege combined to insure a large measure of success to these champions of modernism; yet the defenders of the older culture held many points of vantage, and the war ended for a time in a compromise. But it was a truce, not a permanent peace. Every few years the quarrel is reopened, with changes in the terms and in the precise form of the issue, but at bottom with the same old antagonists. It is at least as old as Aristophanes; it is the war of the ancients and moderns which rent the France of Boileau and Perrault; it is the battle of the books of Swift; it rages to-day in the pages of the Atlantic Monthly where the rival hosts are led by Mr. Abraham Flexner and Professor Paul Shorey. It will probably never disappear, since it is based upon a conflict of temperaments; and as long as human nature remains as we have known it, its variety will provide a succession of irreconcilable opponents.

But educational institutions cannot rest with such a deadlock as this, nor ought they be satisfied with an arrangement in which the curriculum is determined by an accomodation based on the relative voting power of the rival parties. What is needed is not a debate where each seeks to score on his opponent by the brilliance of his dialectic, but an examination by each of the strength rather than the weakness of the contrary position, with a view to reaching a synthesis which will combine the contributions of either school and provide a new and richer discipline.

The educational value of science is quite different from its economic value. It is to be studied in institutions like this which aim at contributing to the perfecting of the individual, not because it makes men richer or life more comfortable, but because it helps to explain the world we live in, to make nature more intelligible, and to teach the student to grasp one kind of truth. "It also," to quote a great English scholar, "gives man an escape from the noisy present into a region of facts which are as they are and not as foolish human beings want them to be; an escape from the commonness of daily happenings into the remote world of high and severely trained imagination; an escape from mortality in the service of a growing and durable purpose, the progressive discovery of truth." The handling of the measuring glass and the dissecting knife is not merely a cultivation of the hand and eye, it is a training in the indispensable quality of precision and begets a moral disgust at slovenly inaccuracy. These are things which even the classical scholar cannot afford to despise unless he wishes to undermine his own foundations.

The educational value of the humanistic discipline on the other hand, lies fundamentally in its power to open to us the past, to make available for our life to-day the results of the efforts of generations of men to solve the problem of living together and to see life as a whole. Thus it includes not merely not even primarily as is often assumed, the learning of Latin and Greek, but the history of earlier civilizations and what is meant by philosophy in the broadest sense. In it, as thus understood, there is no antagonism to science. The science of past ages is within its scope; the sciences of to-day is only the latest chapter.

The method, of course, is different. Modern science deals with natural phenomena, and with the apparatus of observation and experiment employed to find the nature and laws of these phenomena. Humane studies are for the most part book studies: the medium is the written and printed word. Facts are involved here, also, as thought and imagination are involved in scientific investigation; but the main theme is men, not things, and the way men have conceived the relation of things.

From this statement it appears that for the balanced development of the individual both sets of values are indispensable, and the quarrel persists partly because each has at times been untrue to itself, partly because each has misrepresented the other. The scientist sometimes forgets the honor of his calling and dogmatizes when he ought to teach the method of ascertaining facts, sometimes degenerates into the mere collector and forgets to ask those questions the hope of answering which is the justification of his task. And he has sometimes sought to discredit his opponent by fixing attention upon his failure to attain his aims when truth required the honest investigation of these aims themselves.

To the blame attaching to the classical party I propose to devote more detailed attention——first, because they have come nearer wrecking their own cause than the scientists, and, second, because as the humanist by training and tradition I feel more bound to try to contribute, however humbly, to the solution of a problem which is approaching a critical stage. For there is no use disguising the fact that the study of the classics, which has claimed to be the central citadel of humanism, is in perilous plight. Despite academic privileges and bonuses, the students of to-day who continue to study Latin and Greek beyond the point of compulsion are becoming fewer and fewer; and the majority of the faithful few may be discovered on inquiry to be prompted by the desire for a livelihood rather than a larger life.

The foundation of the revolt against the classics is a wide-spread indignation at being cheated. Hundreds of thousands of students have spent the major part of their studying time for years upon two languages with the implicit understanding that they would finally have access to two great civilizations through reading the records in the original tongues. They paid the price in time and energy and at the end did not get what they had paid for. They could not read Latin or Greek, or could not read either with such a degree of ease or pleasure as to induce two per cent to keep it up. They were indignant, I say, and the inevitable revolt came. When the fight was on they did what all belligerents are tempted to do, they annexed many additional grievances and laid hold on all the weapons within their reach; but the fact remains that they revolted because they had been cheated.

Everyone must admit that for the professional scholar of language or of the antique civilizations the mastering of the tongues is essential to thoroughness and to self-respect. Let us continue by all means to insist on this so that the prospective scholar may begin his laborious task in time. But let us be clear that within the select group of the college-trained this is the necessary equipment of a still more select group; and do not let us pretend that a man cannot be cultivated without an accomplishment that most cultivated men will confess they do not possess.

Having been, I hope, quite clear on this matter of the linguistic mastery of Latin and Greek, let me hasten to add that I am a profound believer in the classics. I am prepaid to maintain that a knowledge of Greek and Roman literature and civilization should be a part of any broad scheme of cultural education; that such a knowledge is, with one possible exception, the most necessary part. That exception is Hebrew literature and civilization. But the teachers of this subject have never forbidden us to read the Bible or study the history of the Israelites until we had mastered their language. The barrier which has shut off generations of students from a knowledge of classical civilization has been the classical teacher's infatuation for the subjunctive. The deadly enemy of the classics is not science, or mathematics, or modern literature, or vocational utilitarianism; it is linguistic fanaticism, the insistence that no one shall enter these fair domains save through the one door of language.

For there are other doors. In the time spent in the usual attempt to master Latin and Greek a student could read in translation most of the literary masterpieces of antiquity, could acquire a fair knowledge of the history and politics of the Greeks and Romans and of their mode of life, could be introduced to the sculpture and architecture of Athens, to the great achievements of Rome in law, in colonization, in public works; and could learn enough of their religion and mythology to appreciate the allusions in modern literature better than the student of the languages who has plodded through only some dozen books. I am perfectly aware of the inferiority of translations or originals——if the originals are read by one who has really mastered them. My claim is that if the classical contribution is to be saved for modern culture, it is to be done by candidly facing the failure of the present method for the general student, by availing ourselves freely of those means of access to the past that do not require a command of the languages, and by recognizing that the enjoyment which is derived from reading the masterpieces of antiquity in the original tongue so as to savor the subtler qualities of style is bound to be the privilege of a very few even among college men and women.

I cannot take time here to discuss the difficulties to be

281

overcome before this more rational method of making ancient culture accessible can be generally adopted. The chief obstacle, if I may say it without offense, is the scarcity—the scarcity, not the absence—among classical teachers of men and women with an interest in ideas and a power of teaching literature as literature and not as grammar. It is not that teachers of Latin and Greek are less able than other; the difficulty of the studies they have mastered disproves that. It is rather that tradition has so long led to their preoccupation with syntax that they have seldom developed their capacity for handling ideas in a large way or of perceiving and revealiing beauty. It will need several academic generations before we can equip our schools and colleges with teachers who will make classical studies again deserve the name of the humanities. Yet, lest I be misunderstood, let me explicitly declare that the line of great teachers of these subjects has never died out.

In the new English Education Bill which I have already quoted there is an interesting piece of evidence that the synthesis of the new and old cultures has already made progress. In it the humanities are defined as those studies which shall acquaint the student "with the capacities and ideals of mankind, as expressed in literature and are, with its achievements and ambitions as recorded in history, and with the nature and laws of the world as interpreted by science, philosophy, and religion." Such a definition summarizes with admirable conciseness and comprehensiveness the aim of education regarded as a storing of the mind with the things a cultivated person ought to know. It seems to me an adequate definition of the academic opportunity we set out to discuss from the point of view of knowledge.

There are, however, other points of view. The insistence upon what knowledges are to be taught is apt to result in one of the main defects of our education to-day the too exclusive cultivation of the receptive attitude. It is now without significance that the non-academic occupations of our undergraduates are commonly spoken of as "student activities," as if the classrooms were the scene merely of student passivities. The training of the present generation of college teachers has been such that we are not likely to have too little emphasis on the need for a solid basis of fact in our scholarship. More necessary is it to dwell on the importance of eliciting the idea behind the facts, of teaching the significance as well as the dates of events. There is some ground for the criticism that the American scholar of to-day is more distinguished for what he knows than for what he thinks. In a women's college especially it is necessary to guard against excessive docility; to avoid *ex cathedra* pronouncements; to seek to rouse doubt, objection, resistance, that the student may become accustomed to do her own thinking and be trained rigorously to accuracy in that thinking. From the earliest stages of education, the effort should be made to call for active curiosity as to the meaning and relation of every fact that is taught.

Such a discipline is highly contributory to that full and free development of personality which in one aspect is the aim of all education. It is of the highest importance both to society and the individual that each person should acquire such power of self-expression as to count for what she is worth in the community. We may well ask, therefore, what other elements in college training can be used for this end.

The answer is to be found, I believe, in the arts. One of these, the art of writing, is already admitted to all curricula. Its universal acceptance, however, is due rather to the fact that it is an indispensable tool for other subjects than because it is itself an art, and so a means of self-expression. For the purpose under discussion, however, the art of writing is to be treated not merely as a formal exercise in correctness and elegance, or as the means by which other people's opinions are reproduced, but as a channel through which the reactions of the student, emotional as well as intellectual, to all her other studies and to her experiences in life may find utterance. The teaching of this subject may be so developed as to become the focus of the student's whole intellectual life, the point where she interrogates herself as to what all she is doing and learning amounts to, what is its significance to her personally.

The recognition of music and the fine arts, especially on the side of practice, as legitimate parts of the academic curriculum has been slow and reluctant in modern times, though familiar enough to the Greeks. The reluctance has been due in part to the tendency already mentioned to emphasize the passive view of education as something done to the student and not by her, partly to the defect of scholarship, in many of the teachers of these subjects, partly to low scholastic standards. It is true that it is harder to examine rigorously the results of an attempt to inculcate good taste in letters or music or art than to test a knowledge of Latin paradigms or mathematical demonstrations. But examinations are a means and not an end, and their applicability is no final test of the educational value of a study. If the results of a good course cannot be gauged by examination, so much the worse for the examination. Apart from the value of the practice of music and art as modes of expression, it may be parenthetically remarked, the appreciation of them and a knowledge of their history is a matter of special importance in the curriculum of a woman's college. Foreign visitors to America seldom fail to observe the great preponderance of women in our concerts and galleries. More and more they are going to be not only the audience and spectators but also the controllers of these things. It is clear that it is of enormous public importance that our educated women should have discriminating taste and sound scholarship in the whole field of the arts. It is one of the enviable distinctions of Smith College that in these matters it has long held an advanced position, and it would be folly not to take pains that this position should be maintained and deserved.

The agencies for the development of the free expression of personality are not all to be found in the course of study.

284

The manifold organizations of student life are of immense value in preparing women for what I have spoken of as "counting for what they are worth in the community." In the revelation of the practical capacity of the college-trained women which has been made by the war, it may be argued that the power which has been displayed is due as much to these extra-curricular activities as to the purely academic courses. Such activities need control and regulation; but since nothing encourages development so much as responsibility, I hope that this regulation may be entrusted more and more to the discretion of the students, individually and corporately. The same principle applies to the whole matter of conduct. We have to look forward to the granting of more rather than less liberty to the undergraduate, and make it clear that this is no place for those who cannot be trusted with liberty. President Seelye interpreted our founder's intention as the education of gentle-women, not the establishing of a misses' finishing school, and we will not now reverse his policy.

So far I have been discussing aims and methods on the assumption that the purpose of such a college as this is agreed to be purely cultural. But it is useless to ignore the fact that there has been for a number of years a powerful movement to bend our educational institutions, from the high school up, to utilitarian purposes, to the preparation for earning money in trades and professions. The movement has so far had more effect on the men's colleges, and has in some cases resulted in the telescoping of the course of liberal arts with professional courses, in others in the infiltration of so-called vocational studies the methods among the cultural studies. The pressure on the women's colleges was for a time retarded by the establishment of such admirable institutions as Simmons College; and one cannot too strongly approve the principle of the setting up of colleges of a variety of types, each good in its kind, instead of attempting all kinds of training in each institution. But the war has added to the force of the demand that the college graduate should be ready for immediate technical service, and it is more than likely that when peace comes we shall all have to reconsider our positions on this question and defend our conclusions.

We should recognize at once that in one respect we have been long vocational; we have prepared large numbers for the vocation of teaching. We have a few courses explicitly announced as for teachers; but the vocational element has pervaded our curriculum and determined the choice of studies far more than is indicated by these special courses. The newer question, however, concerns other vocations, many of such a nature that the preparation for them cannot be justified on cultural grounds. It is perhaps rash to commit oneself on a matter that is sure to be affected by circumstances after the war which no one can clearly foresee. But some principles may be tentatively laid down.

Where a subject can be taught so that it will gain a professional value without lessening its effect in stimulating and training thinking and in broadening the intellectual outlook, I see no reason why it should not be so taught. This is done in some departments now, and a large part of our success in meeting the new situation will depend on our skill in devising courses and methods that will serve adequately the double purpose. But in general the college of the type to which Smith belongs will continue to be properly engaged in developing personality and in providing the background and the intellectual aptitude rather than the technical equipment of the expert. There are many vocational subjects of which all the underlying principles and the fundamental knowledge can be fully provided in a cultural course, and the professional application added in a comparatively short time. But to introduce a considerable element of purely professional studies and students would almost certainly entail a reduction of that element of disinterested curiosity in things and ideas which it is one of the main purposes of the college to cultivate.

There is, however, an extension of our present activities which I may be permitted to suggest here. The vocation which we of the cultural colleges are oftenest reproached with not preparing for is the domestic. Personally I should deplore the introduction among our winter studies of a department of what is called Domestic Science. But in our courses in hygiene, zoology, botany, chemistry, and fine arts we already provide a large part both of the training and the knowledge involved in such a department. I believe it would be possible to draw these things to a focus and give them a practical application in a comparatively short course following graduation—a course very much shorter than is required in vocational schools because it would be administered to students already to a large extent trained and informed. Such a course might well be conducted here each summer for the students who had just graduated—not an exhaustive course for teachers of the science, but a concentrated one adequate for the prospective practitioners of the art.

I have used the greater part of my time in discussing the undergraduate and the curriculum because the college is for the student. But even in so superficial a survey as this, a glance is due at the other bodies which constitute the institution.

First, the faculty. Thanks to the increase of endowment under the administration of President Burton, the college now approximates the average of one teacher to ten students which is regarded as adequate. As a further increase in the number of students is neither to be expected nor desired, and as more rigorous selection of entrants may reduce the freshman classes considerably, it is to be hoped that this proportion may be maintained.

There is room in the American college faculty for a variety of talent. Sound scholarship and teaching ability are of course desirable in all, and it would be fatal to the intellectual temper of the college if we failed to maintain and recruit the group of distinguished productive scholars on whom our standing in the learned world depends. To do this against the allurements of richer and better equipped rivals is not always easy; but something can be done by making the hours of teaching reasonable and the burden of administration light.

But the great teacher is almost as rare as the great scholar, and for the undergraduate student is of even greater immediate importance. Smith has had on its faculty a succession of personalities whose influence in the classroom and out of it is perhaps the most gratefully remembered of all the benefits to which the alumnae look back. Good scholars can usually be found by searching; great teachers are the gift of heaven. All we can do is to cherish those we have and hope for more.

The life of the college is indebted also to those members of the faculty who serve it in the details of administration, and who bring their experience and sagacity to bear on the thousand and one petty problems on whose solution depends so largely the smooth running of the machine. It is the duty of the administration to watch lest such occupations absorb too much of the time and ability that are due first to teaching and study.

The faculties of American colleges have of late years been asserting their right to be regarded as one of the governing bodies of their institutions, not merely as aggregations of men and women engaged to perform particular services. The full and free recognition of this right will surely be all to the advantage of the colleges, giving them the benefit of much expert knowledge and increasing the dignity and *esprit de corps* of the faculties themselves. It may further be expected that it will encourage broader thinking on the problems of education as against thinking in terms of the individual teacher or department.

Next, the alumnae. The discovery of the graduate as a pillar of the college is one of the achievements of the American system. Nowhere else in the world, I believe, is the loyalty of the alumni so important a factor in the growth and influence of academic institutions. Already their services are recognized by the granting to them of a voice in the government of the college; and it appears probable that the graduate which at present manifests itself in sporadic gifts may ultimately become organized, and that the body of graduates will see it to be their duty to undertake the systematic increase of resources which is demanded by every flourishing institution. There are evidences also of a tendency on the part of the alumnae of the various colleges to associate themselves in good works for the community apart from the college, and certainly there could be no greater testimony to the value of the education given by an institution than the activity of its graduates in the elevation of our common life. Here again the war has operated, and there is no more distinguished instance of the tendency I am speaking of than that afforded by the heroic achievements of the Smith College Relief Unit in France.

Of the Board of Trustees, the remaining element constituting the college, I refrain from speaking. I have been so short a time within range close enough for the observation of that august body, that I do not feel myself justified in discussing either its accomplishments or its possibilities, farther than to hint that as its range of vision has been widened and its vitality increased by the appointment of nominees of, but not from, the faculty. The point of view of the teacher, supposed to be represented by the president, is apt to be lost sight of as his days of active teaching recede into the distance; yet it is obvious that no single point of view is more important in determining the general policy of an institution of learning.

In this attempt to indicate the main lines of policy which it seems to me advisable to follow in Smith College, I am painfully conscious of the doubtfulness of some of the ideas, of the hopeless triteness of others, of my own inexperience and inadequateness in dealing with all. I have felt these last months that a man's inaugural address should be written by his predecessor. "Let not him that girdeth on his armour boast himself as he that putteth it off." So, despairing of expressing in my own words those essential things, those "durable satisfactions of life," to use the phrase of our honored guest, for which this college has stood and, as far as I can compass it, will continue to stand, I close with the words of the great scholar I have already quoted. "All these things are good," he says, after enumerating the worthy desires of many men's hearts, "all these things are good, and those who pursue them may well be soldiers in one army or pilgrims on the same eternal quest. If we fret and argue and fight one another now, it is mainly because we are so much under the power of enemy. . . . The enemy has no definite name, though it is certain we all know him; he who puts always the body before the spirit, the dead before the living; who makes things only to sell them; who has forgotten that there is such a thing as truth, and measures the world by advertisement or by money; who daily defiles the beauty that surrounds him and makes vulgar the tragedy; whose innermost religion is the worship of the lie in his soul. The Philistine, the vulgarian, the great sophist, the passer of base coin for true, he is all about us, and, worse, he has his outposts inside us, persecuting our peace, spoiling our sight, confusing our values, making a man's self seem greater than the race and the present thing more important than the eternal. From him and his influence we find our escape by means of old books into that calm world of theirs, where stridency and clamor are forgotten in the ancient stillness, where the strong iron is long since rusted, and the rocks of granite broken into dust, but the great things of the human spirit still shine like stars pointing man's way onward to the great triumph or the great tragedy, and even the little things, the beloved and tender and funny and familiar things, beckon across gulfs of death and change with a magic poignancy, the

290

old things that our dead leaders and forefathers loved, *viva adhuc et desiderio pulcriora,* living still and more beautiful because of our desire."

Inaugural Address

by

DANIEL COIT GILMAN

President of Johns Hopkins University

February 22, 1876

*DANIEL COIT GILMAN (July 6, 1831
—October 13, 1908) was born in Norwich,
Connecticut. He entered Yale College in 1848
when Dr. Woolsey was president; Dwight
Dana and James Hadley were professors. He
was responsible for the plan of the Sheffield
Scientific School at Yale where he taught for
seventeen years. Upon a second call of the
University of California, in 1872, he accepted
the presidency.*

*Gilman accepted the presidency of Johns
Hopkins University, January 30, 1875. It was
as the first president of Johns Hopkins that
we get the true dimensions of his ability and
leadership. His emphasis upon "personality
plus science" at once marked Johns Hopkins
University as the oustanding institution of
higher learning of this country. Upon his retirement from Johns Hopkins, he accepted the
presidency of the Carnegie Institute, of Washington.*

If this assembly, with one voice, could utter the thought now uppermost, there would be a deep, quick, hearty acknowledgment of the bounty of Johns Hopkins.

His beneficence, so free, so great, so wise, promoting at once the physical, intellectual and moral welfare of his fellowmen, awakens universal surprise and admiration, and calls for our perpetual thanks.

In respect to the giver, I can say but little to you, the citizens of Baltimore, who knew him so well; who remember his industry, sagacity and intellectual force; who have tested his integrity, and found that his word was as good as his bond; who recall his fore-sight, his enterprise, and his belief in the future of this city and state; who recollect that more than once in financial crises he hazarded his own fortune for the protection of others; who heard, it may be from his own lips, the motives and hopes which promoted these royal gifts; who believe that great acquisitions involve great responsibilities, but who know how hard it was for one long accustomed to power to yield that power to others; to you, his fellow-citizens, who saw the steps by which this benefactor toiled upward to the temple of Fortune, and there unsatisfied, went higher, by more arduous steps, to the temple of Charity, where he bestowed his gifts.

While I leave to others the commemoration of our founder, you must let me refer to the tributes of admiration which his generosity has called out on the remotest shores of our own land, and in the most venerable shrines of European learning. The Berkeley laurel and the Oxford ivy may well be carved upon his brow when the sculptor shapes his likeness; for by wise men in the east and by rich men in the west, his gifts are praised as among the most timely, the most generous, and the most noble ever bestowed by one, for all.

The genesis of American munificence is a bright chapter of our history. From the days of the Puritan minister, who gave his name to our oldest University, and the days of the London merchant, who endowed the second college in New England, each generation has surpassed its predecessors. It is a striking coincidence that among the very earliest names on this heraldic roll, is that which our foundation bears. The schools which Edward Hopkins, a colonial governor, established in 1660, by his will, and his gifts to Harvard, still keep alive his name and influence. So may the name of our founder live for more than two hundred years to come, and his gifts be immortal. Johns Hopkins might have used the very words of Edward Hopkins, who desired to bestow "some encouragement for the breeding up of hopeful youths, for the public service of the country in future times."

We may conjecture a spiritual if not a physical descent in the line of Hopkins. In 1676, the name is written on the door of an endowed grammar school at New Haven, older than Yale, and second only to Harvard; in 1776, the name is signed to the Declaration of Independence; in 1876, it distinguishes a University foundation. To our contemporary, we may apply the words with which the deeds of the colonial governor are recounted. After saying that his last will is an interesting monument of private friendship and public spirit, that friends and domestics were not forgotten, that his public gifts were "for the promotion of religion, science and charity," the historian adds this eulogy:*"Thus did this lofty and intellectual spirit devise and distribute blessings in his own age, and by his wisdom, prepare and make them perpetual for succeeding times."*

THE ENDOWMENT

The total amount of the public gifts of Johns Hopkins is more than seven million dollars. The sum of $3,500,000 is appropriated to a university; a like sum to a hospital; and the rest to local institutions of education and charity. Let us compare these benefactions with some others. Thirty years ago, when the gift of Abbott Lawrence to Harvard College was made

296

known it was said to be "the largest amount ever given at one time during the life time of the donor to any public institution in this country,"—the amount was $50,000; the gift of Smithson, so well administered in Washington, amounted to over half a million; the foundation of Stephen Girard surpassed two million dollars.

You may see from these figures what great munificence has brought us together. So far as I can learn, the Hopkins foundation, coming from a single giver, is without a parallel in terms or in amount in this or any land. But beware of exaggeration. These gifts are often spoken of as if the whole, instead of the half, was intended for the university, and then as if an equal amount was given to the hospital; and so it happens that dreams of monumental structures and splendid piles and munificent salaries flit through the mind which can never become real. Do not forget how much wealth accumulated by older colleges—in repute, experience and influence, and also in material things. The property of Harvard College is more than five million dollars; that of Yale must equal our endowment. The land investments of a university in the Northwest are said to exceed these values; and Ezra Cornell, while he lived, expected that the endowments at Ithaca would approach, if not surpass, the funds of Harvard. The income yielding funds of Harvard in 1875 were over three millions; those of Yale near a million and a half. Even these figures look small compared with the accumulations of Oxford and Cambridge.

Now turn our capital into income. Our university fund yields a revenue of nearly $200,000. Let us compare this amount with the resources of our two richest colleges. Harvard, in 1874-5, (in all departments), received from tuition $168,541.72; from property, $218,715.30; a total of $387,257.02. The college alone, not including the library, the general administration, or any of the special departments, cost $187,713.-20, which is nearly our whole income. Yale College reports its academic expenses (i.e., exclusive of those in the scientific, theological, law, medical and art departments), in 1874-5, as $126,073.56.

But all our revenue is not at once available; for, as the capital cannot be spent for buildings, some income must be reserved for this. Of course, the buildings will be good and costly. If now we deduct from our income, as a building fund, one hundred thousand dollars annually, it will take several years to accumulate the requisite amount. Of that which remains a large sum will be absorbed by taxation, administration and the purchase of books, instruments and collections. Thus it is evident that the educational income at present is not large. Its expenditure requires great discretion and prudence. The trustees are men of liberal views in respect to professional salaries, but they see as clearly as a schoolboy sees through a problem in short division that, the larger the divisor, the less the quotient; the more salary, the less chairs; the more eminent and costly the teachers, the fewer can be secured. I wish that every one who sees the need of a great university, and who knows the range of human science, would take a pencil and distribute our income in the departments which he would like to see promoted. If his experience is like mine, he will find that before his pencil has half gone down the column of the sciences, the income has been twice expended.

I fear that these remarks are a little ungracious, and I would gladly repress them; but the private and public utterances of thoughtful men have been so vague as to what it is possible for the trustees of this university to accomplish at once, and our friends are so very generous in their expectations that I feel compelled, at the very outset, to utter a word of caution. If our physicists could bring us "Aladdin's Lamp," or our chemists produce "the philosopher's stone," or our merchants give us "the widow's curse," our aspirations should not be checked by our restricted means; but, till the original benefaction is supplemented by other gifts, or the growth

298

of Baltimore increases the value of our present investments, we must be contented with good work in a limited field.

ITS FIVE-FOLD ADVANTAGES

To many the magnitude of our founder's bounty seems its principle value; that is, in fact, but half its glory. With a self-renunciation which is rare and noble, he attached to the gift no burdensome condition or personal whim. The almoners of his bounty are restrained by no shackles bequeathed by a departed benefactor, as they enter upon their course bearing in the one hand the ointment of charity and in the other the lamp of science. His trustees are free—free to determine principles, to decide upon methods, to distribute income, to select professors, to summon students, and even to alter, from time to time, their own plans—as the enlightenment of the world bestows its radiance upon their undertaking.

In selecting trustees the choice of our founder fell upon those of his friends and acquaintances whom he believed would be free from a desire to promote, in their official action, the special tenets of any denomination or the platform of any political party. In a land where almost every strong institution of learning is either "a child of the church" or "a child of the state," and is thus liable to political or ecclesiastical control, he has planted the germ of a university which will doubtless serve both church and state the better because it is free from the guardianship of either. It was his wish—it is our wish— that here should be a seat of learning so attractive that at its threshold students would gladly cease to discuss sectarian animosities and political prejudices, in their eagerness for the acquisition of Knowledge and their search for Eternal Truth. As in olden time the courtier's and the peasant's sons laid aside their distinctive costumes when they donned the academic dress, let us hope that here the only badges will be those which mark the scholar.

Another advantage attends our foundation. It is established in a large town, in an old state, near to the financial and the political Capitals of the Republic; and at the junction of national highways which connect the North and the South, the East and the West. This is in fact a metropolis or middle city. Such geographical considerations will surely affect our future. Baltimore, moreover, is prepared for this foundation. Professional schools of law, medicine and theology already attract large numbers of students. Technical instruction in the useful arts is to some extent provided in the Maryland Institute. The votaries of the natural sciences are associated in an Academy, which only needs an endowment to enable it to take rank with kindred societies elsewhere. The city, with a liberality which is praised at home and abroad, maintains two excellent high schools for young ladies, and for young men a City College, so well organized, so well taught and so well supported, that it relieves our foundation of doing much which is called "collegiate" in distinction from "university" work. There are good private schools. There are excellent collections of paintings and rare opportunities for the study of music, both as a science and an art. More than all this the foundation of George Peabody, in which a capital of a million and a quarter of dollars is forever set apart for the promotion of culture, has now, with increasing strength, survived the perils of infancy, and gained a place among the very best establishments to be found in any part of our land. Its library is extraordinary for our country; not because of its size, (some 60,000 volumes) but because it has been selected with an experienced eye, among the most modern and most useful of the publications of the world.

The advantage which will come to the new University in its medical department from the establishment of a hospital, on a separate but allied foundation, is most obvious. Obvious though it is, the most enlightened can not over-estimate its value. If so large a sum as the hospital fund ($3,500,000) were consecrated under any circumstances to the relief of suffering, the promotion of health, and the preservation of life——humanity would rejoice; but when such a foundation is connected with a university, so that on the one hand it commands all the resources of human learning, and on the other makes known through accomplished teachers the results of its experience, we may confidently expect that its influence for good will be more than doubled; that its immediate work in the case of the sick and wounded will be better done than would otherwise be possible; and that its remedial and preventive agencies will extend to thousands who may never come within its walls, but whose ills will be relieved by those taught here.

The timeliness of our foundation is the last of the advantages which I shall name. We begin our work after discussions lasting for a generation respecting the aims, methods, deficiencies, and possibilities of higher education in this country; after numerous experiments, some with oil in the lamps and some without; after costly ventures of which we reap the lessons, while others bear the loss; after Jefferson, Nott, Wayland, Quincy, Agassiz, Tappan, Mark Hopkins, Woolsey, have completed their official services and have given us their supreme decisions; while the strong successors of these strong men, Eliot, Porter, Barnard, White, Angell and McCosh, are still upon the controversial platform; we begin after the national bounty has for fourteen years, under the far-reaching bill of Senator Morrill of Vermont, promoted scientific education; and after scores of wealthy men have bestowed many million dollars for the foundation of new institutions of the highest sort.

DISCUSSIONS ELSEWHERE

Educational discussions and movements are not restricted to our new country. In old England, questions like these are constantly rife, (in addition to many of purely local interest): How may professorships in the old universities be restored to the dignity or influence, of which they have been in part deprived by the excessive preponderance of collegiate instruction; how may the university influences be extended to all the large towns; how may science gain a more generous recognition in the ancient seats of learning; how may endowments for research be established without leading to sinecure fellowships; how may ecclesiastical fetters be removed from academic institutions; how may the universities, by their systems of local examinations, best promote the welfare of the preparatory schools or the training of young persons who are not likely to enter the university; how may the university better provide for the innumerable modern callings, which lie outside of the old "professions" but require an equal culture.

In France, there has not been since the Revolution, I presume, such interest in the promotion of universities as now. I pronounce no opinions, but I call attention to the remarkable law which was passed last year, relinquishing the exclusiveness of a State foundation, and declaring university instruction to be free. Those who have hitherto been oppressed, as they have thought, by a hard law, now seize with alacrity the opportunity to found new institutions, and the offerings of the faithful are freely poured out to restore to the Church those intellectual agencies from which she has been cut off.

At a distance, Germany seems the one country where educational problems are determined; not so, on a nearer look. The thoroughness of the German mind, its desire for perfection in every detail, and its philosophical aptitudes are well illustrated by the controversies now in vogue in the land of universities. In following, as we are prone to do in educational matters, the example of Germany, we must beware lest we accept what is there cast off; lest we introduce faults as well as virtues, defects with excellence. Some of the ablest men in the new empire are now questioning whether "the Real School" system, after a trial of so many years, is justified of its works —and whether "'the gymnasium," somewhat modified, should not be the training place of all who seek a higher culture.

Others are questioning whether it is not a mistake to maintain polytechnic schools, and special schools of agriculture, forestry, mining, etc., apart from the universities; and whether it would not be better to combine the higher educational foundations under one direction and in one centre. Some of the best scientific men declare their belief that the university instruction in science, following the gymnastic discipline, is better far as a preparation for what are called the modern pursuits, than the training which is given by the REAL school and the Polytechnic, and so they assert that an exaggerated value has been attached to technical training.

I only allude to these discussions in passing. It would take many hours to unfold them. But it is well to bear in mind that the most enlightened institutions in our country, and the most enlightened countries in Europe, are those in which educational discussions are now most lively; and it behooves us, as we engage in a new undertaking, to listen, ponder, and observe; and above all to be modest in the announcement of our plans. It should make the authorities cautious in offering, and the public cautious in demanding a completed scheme for the establishment of a university in Baltimore.

Our caution is none the less needed when we remember that at the present moment Americans are engaged in promoting the institutions of higher education in Tokio, Peking and Beirut, in Egypt and the Hawaiian Isles. The oldest and the remotest nations are looking here for light.

What is the significance of all this activity? It is a reaching out for a better state of society than now exists; it is a dim but an indelible impression of the value of learning; it is a craving for intellectual and moral growth; it is a longing to interpret the laws of creation; it means a wish for less misery among the poor, less ignorance in schools, less bigotry in the temple, less suffering in the hospital, less fraud in business, less folly in politics; it means more study of nature, more love

303

of art, more lessons from history, more security in property, more health in cities, more virtue in the country, more wisdom in legislation, more intelligence, more happiness, more religion.

THE HIGHER EDUCATION

The institutions which are founded in modern society for the promotion of superior education may be grouped in five classes: 1, Universities; 2, Learned Societies; 3, Colleges; 4, Technical Schools; and 5, Museums (including literary and scientific collections). It is important that the fundamental ideas of these various institutions should be borne in mind.

The University is a place for the advanced special education of youth who have been prepared for its freedom by the discipline of a lower school. Its form varies in different countries. Oxford and Cambridge universities, are quite unlike the Scotch, and still more unlike the Queen's University in Ireland; the University of France has no counterpart in Germany; the typical German universities differ much from one another. But while forms and methods vary, the freedom to investigate, the obligation to teach, and the careful bestowal of academic honors are always understood to be among the university functions. The pupils are supposed to be wise enough to select, and mature enough to follow the courses they pursue.

The Academy, or Learned Society, of which the Institute of France, with its five academies, and the Royal Society of London, are typical examples—is an association of learned men, selected for their real or reputed merits, who assemble for mutual instruction and attrition, and who publish from time to time the papers they have received and the proceedings in which they have engaged. The University is also an association of learned men, but the bond which holds them together differs essentially from that of the academy. In the universities teaching is essential, research important; in academies of science research is indispensable, tuition rarely thought of.

The College implies, as a general rule, restriction rather than freedom; tutorial rather than professorial guidance; residence within appointed bounds; the chapel, the dining halls, and the daily inspection. The college theoretically stands *in loco parentis*; it does not afford a very wide scope; it gives a liberal and substantial foundation on which the university instruction may be wisely built.

The Technical Schools present the idea of preparation for a specific calling, rather than the notion of a liberal culture. They have in view the imparting of knowledge which will be useful in the practice of a profession, and often set forward as a motive, an assured introduction to the openings which are ready for those who have received their training.

Museums, Galleries, and Libraries (of which the British Museum is the grandest type), are indeed connected with the other agencies we have named, but they often have an independent existence. They fulfill a two-fold purpose. They preserve and store away the treasures of art, literature and science; and they distribute widely among the people those seeds of culture which are developed by artistic, historic and scientific acquisitions.

Thus we say that the Academy of Sciences promotes the intellectual attrition of the most learned men; the University favors the liberal and special culture of advanced students; the College trains aspiring youth for the future intellectual freedom; the Technical School affords a good preparation for a specific vocation; and the Museum provides materials for study, adapted like the world itself, to interest the most profound and the most superficial.

Now it is clear that we might have a University without the four adjuncts I have named; and we might have the four accessories without the University, but practically wherever a strong University is maintained, these four-fold agencies revolve around it. It is the sun and they are the planets. In Baltimore you have hitherto had a College, an Academy of Sciences, Professional Schools and a Scholars' Library, but you have not had such an endowed University as that which is now inaugurated.

Indeed this new foundation might almost adopt the preamble which John Calvin prefixed to the statutes of the Academy of Geneva: "Verily hath God heretofore endowed our commonwealth with many notable adornments, yet hath it to this day had to seek abroad for instruction in good arts and disciplines for its youth, with many lets and hindrances."

But soon I hope we may add what Eramus said at Oxford: "It is wonderful what a harvest of old volumes is flourishing here on every side; there is so much of erudition, not common and trivial, but recondite, accurate and ancient, both Greek and Latin, that I should not wish to visit Italy, except for the gratification of traveling."

The earliest foundations in our country were colleges, not universities. Scholars were often graduated early in this century at the age when now they enter. Earnest efforts are now being made to establish universities. Harvard, with a boldness which is remarkable, has essentially given up its collegiate restrictions and introduced the benefits of university freedom; Yale preserves its college course intact, but has added a school of science and developed a strong graduate department; the University of Michigan and Cornell University quite early adopted the discipline of universities, and already equal or surpass not a few of their elder sisters; the University of Virginia from its foundation has upheld the university in distinction from the college idea. The cry all over the land is for university advantages, not as superseding but as supplementing collegiate discipline.

As we, my friends, are called upon to develop a university, it becomes important not only to distinguish its essential idea from that of any other institution, but also to form a clear conception of its special province; of various plans which have governed its organization; of the good which it promotes; of the questions which are settled; of the questions which are not settled; and especially of the bearing of all these points on our land, our times, our foundation. Thus only shall we make a contribution to the intellectual agencies of this country, and add a positive gain to American learning and education in the second century of the Republic.

The tenor of my remarks has implied perhaps more diversity of opinion than really exists in respect to universities. The truth is, most institutions are not free to build anew; they can only readjust. It has been playfully said that "traditions and conditions" impede their progress. But whatever may be the concrete difficulties, on many abstract principles there is little need of controversy. Our effort will be to accept that which is determined,—to avoid that which is obsolescent, to study that which is doubtful,—"slowly making haste."

TWELVE POINTS DETERMINED

Is, then, anything settled in respect to university education? Much, very much. Can we draw a statement of what is agreed upon? At any rate we can try.

The schedule will include twelve points on which there seems to be a general agreement.

1. All sciences are worthy of promotion; or in other words, it is useless to dispute whether literature or science should receive most attention, or whether there is any essential difference between the old and the new education.

2. Religion has nothing to fear from science, and science need not be afraid of religion. Religion claims to interpret the word of God, and science to reveal the laws of God. The interpreters may blunder, but truths are immutable, eternal and never in conflict.

307

3. Remote utility is quite as worthy to be thought of as immediate advantage. Those ventures are not always most sagacious that expect a return on the morrow. It sometimes pays to send our argosies across the seas; to make investments with an eye to slow but sure returns. So is it always in the promotion of science.

4. As it is impossible for any university to encourage with equal freedom all branches of learning, a selection must be made by enlightened governors, and that selection must depend on the requirements and deficiencies of a given people, in a given period. There is no absolute standard of preference What is more important at one time or in one place may be less needed elsewhere and otherwise.

5. Individual students cannot pursue all branches of learning, and must be allowed to select, under the guidance of those who are appointed to counsel them. Nor can able professors be governed by routine. Teachers and pupils must be allowed great freedom in their method of work. Recitations, lectures, examinations, laboratories, libraries, field exercises, travels, are all legitimate means of culture.

6. The best scholars will almost invariably be those who make special attainments on the foundation of a broad and liberal culture.

7. The best teachers are usually those who are free, competent and willing to make original researches in the library and the laboratory.

8. The best investigators are usually those who have also the responsibilities of instruction, gaining thus the incitement of colleagues, the encouragement of pupils, the observation of the public.

9. Universities should bestow their honors with a sparing hand; their benefits most freely.

10. A university cannot be created in a day; it is a slow growth. The University of Berlin has been quoted as a proof of

the contrary. That was indeed a quick success, but in an old, compact country, crowded with learned men eager to assemble at the Prussian court. It was a change of base rather than a sudden development.

11. The object of the university is to develop character—to make men. It misses its aim if it produces learned pedants, or simple artisans, or cunning sophists, or pretentious practitioners. Its purport is not so much to impart knowledge to the pupils, as to whet the appetite, exhibit methods, develop powers, strengthen judgment, and invigorate the intellectual and moral forces. It should prepare for the service of society a class of students who will be wise, thoughtful, progressive guides in whatever department of work or thought they may be engaged.

12. Universities easily fall into ruts. Almost every epoch requires a fresh start.

If these twelve points are conceded, our task is simplified, though it is still difficult. It is to apply these principles to Baltimore in 1876.

We are trying to do this with no controversy as to the relative importance of letters and science, the conflicts of religion and science, or the relation of abstractions and utilities; our simple aim is to make scholars, strong, bright, useful and true.

This brings me to the question which has brought you here.

The Johns Hopkins University: *What will be its scope?* The Trustees have decided to begin with those things which are fundamental and move gradually forward to those which are accessory.

They will institute at first those chairs of language, mathematics, ethics, history and science which are commonly grouped under the name of the Department of Philosophy.

The Medical Faculty will not long be delayed; that of

309

Jurisprudence will come in time; that of Theology is not now proposed.

I have lately met with an ancient saying in respect to the development of youth. "At five," the precept read, "he was to study the Scriptures; at ten, the Mishna; at thirteen, the Talmud; at eighteen, to marry; at twenty, to attain riches; at thirty, strength; at forty, prudence, and so on to the end." So we begin with the essential, proceed to the important, expect enlarged endowments, and look for strength, prudence and the other virtues as we grow in years.

In organizing a faculty, the first chairs to be filled are those which everywhere, always and by all people in the modern Republic of Letters, are regarded as needful. We must provide for the study of languages, ancient and modern; mathematics, pure and applied; science, natural and physical. All this is assumed as granted. But if we should do all this well and do nothing more, we should not add much to the intellectual resources of the country. We must ask ourselves other questions: What special departments of learning are now neglected in the higher institutions of this country? What can we provide for? In what order shall we proceed?

These problems require profound consideration; their answers must depend on manifold conditions; their solution will doubtless be the result of many counsels. Partly to elicit the suggestions of other teachers, and partly to exhibit what seem to me the inevitable demands of this place, I shall suggest some of the departments of higher education which seem to require attention from us. I cannot now tell all I think and hope.

As a fundamental proposition, bear in mind that we shall aim to choose the fittest teachers, and shall then expect them to do their very best work. None but a college officer will appreciate all that this brief sentence carries with it.

THE MEDICAL SCIENCES AND BIOLOGY

When we turn to the existing provisions for medical instruction in this land and compare them with those of European universities; when we see what inadequate endowments have been provided for our medical schools, and to what abuses the system of fees for tuition has led; when we see that in some of our very best colleges the degree of Doctor of Medicine can be won in half the time required to win the degree of Bachelor of Arts; when we see a disposition to treat diplomas as blank paper by the civilians at home and the profession abroad; when we read the reports of the medical faculty in their own professional journals; when we see the difficulties which have been encountered at Harvard, Yale, and elsewhere, in late attempts to reorganize the medical schools; when we see the prevalence of quackery vaunting its diplomas, it is clear that something should be done. Then, turning to the other side of the picture, when we see what admirable teachers have given instruction among us in medicine and surgery; what noble hospitals have been created; what marvelous discoveries in surgery have been made by our countrymen; what ingenious instruments they have contrived; what humane and skillful appliances they have provided on the battlefield; what admirable measures are in progress for the advancement of hygiene and the promotion of public health; when we see what success has attended recent efforts to reform the system of medical instruction; when we observe all this, we need not fear that the day is distant—we may rather rejoice that the morning has dawned which will see endowments for medical science as munificent as those now provided for any branch of learning, and schools as good as those which are now provided in any other land.

It will doubtless be long, after the opening of the University, before the opening of the Hospital, for this interval may be spent in forming plans for the department of Medicine.

But in the meantime we have an excellent opportunity to provide instruction antecedent to the professional study of medicine. At the present moment medical students avoid the ordinary colleges. A glance at the catalogues is enough to show

311

that the usual classical or academic course is unattractive to such scholars. The reasons need not be given here. But who can doubt that a course may be maintained, like that already begun in the Sheffield School at New Haven, which shall train the eye, the hand and the brain, for the later study of medicine? Such a course should include abundant practice in the laboratories of chemistry, zoology and physics; the study of the anatomy, physiology, and pathology of the lower forms of life; an investigation of the elements of physics and mechanics, and of climatic and meteorological laws; the geographical distribution of disease; the remedial agencies of nature and art; and, besides these scientific studies, the student should acquire enough of French and German to follow with ease European science, and enough of Latin for his professional needs. In other words, in our scheme of a university, great prominence should be given to the studies which bear upon Life,—the group now called Biological Sciences.

Such facilities as are now afforded under Huxley in London, and Rolleston at Oxford, and Foster at Cambridge, and in the best German universities, should here be introduced. They would serve us in the training of naturalists, but they would serve us still more in the training of physicians. By the time we are ready to open a school of medicine, we might hope to have a superior, if not a numerous, body of aspirants for one of the noblest callings to which the heart and head can be devoted.

When the medical department is organized, it should be independent of the income derived from student fees, so that there may not be the slightest temptation to bestow the diploma on an unworthy candidate; or rather let us say, so that the Johns Hopkins diploma will not be a greenback, but will be worth its face in the currency of the world.

THE MODERN HUMANITIES

Next to the study of Man, in his relations to Nature, comes the study of Man in his relations to Society. By this I mean his history, as exemplified in the monuments of literature and art, in language, laws and institutions, in manners, morals and religion. More particularly still I refer to the principles of good government, including jurisprudence on the one hand, and political economy on the other. Legislation, taxation, finance, crime, pauperism, municipal government, morality in public and private affairs, are among the special topics. The civil law, international law, the early history of institutions, in short, the history of civilization and the requirements of a modern State come under this department. If we may judge from what is said by some of the best publicists, the United States, at this moment, is suffering from the neglect of these studies. There is a call for men who have been trained by other agencies than the caucus for the discussion of public affairs; men who know what the experience of the world has been in the development of institutions, and prepared by intellectual and moral discipline to advance the public interests, irrespective of party, indifferent to the attainment of official stations. To this end our plans converge.

NATIONAL SURVEYS

It is generally conceded by our most influential men of science and of affairs, that before many years have passed, an accurate survey of the area of the United States, corresponding with the ordnance and geographical surveys of Great Britain, France, Switzerland and Germany, must be undertaken. Under what auspices and upon what plan remains to be determined. At present the heads of all the governmental surveys acknowledge the difficulty of finding men enough, qualified enough, to carry forward efficiently such work in all its manifold departments, astronomical, geodetical, topographical, meteorological, geological, zoological, botanical, economical. If our University can provide instructions in these departments of physical research, looking forward to the future development, not only of Maryland and the Atlantic Seaboard, but also of the entire land, it will do a good service.

313

There is a department of engineering which may also receive special attention here. The needs of cities or large towns are such in our day that every centre of population, where fifteen or twenty thousand persons are assembled, should have the services of a competent scientific engineer. He must of course have a general mathematical training; but he should also know how to use these fundamental principles in municipal affairs, in the preparation of exact maps, in the determination of the supplies of water, and the methods of drainage, in the construction of roads, boulevards, pleasure grounds and parks, the building of wharfs and docks, the supervision of gas works and fire engines, the erection of public buildings, monuments and places of assembly. There should be a recognized preparation for this work of civic or municipal engineering—in distinction from civil engineering, which is a more vague and general term, including perhaps the subordinate branches to which I have referred.

Architecture is closely connected with this department. So far as I am aware there are now, in this new country where so much building is in progress, but two schools for the professional study of this, the first of arts.

I can hardly doubt that such arrangements as we are maturing will cause this institution to be a place for the training of professors and teachers for the highest academic posts; and I hope in time to see arrangements made for the unfolding of the philosophy, principles and methods of education in a way which will be of service to those who mean to devote their lives to the highest departments of instruction.

But in forming all these plans we must beware lest we are led away from our foundations; lest we make our schools technical instead of liberal; and impart a knowledge of methods rather than principles. If we make this mistake, we may have an excellent Polytechnicum but not a University.

THE FACULTY AND STUDENTS

Who shall our teachers be?

This question the public has answered for us; for I believe there is scarcely a preeminent man of science or letters, at home or abroad, who has not received a popular nomination for the vacant professorships. Some of these candidates we shall certainly secure, and their names will be one by one made known. But I must tell you, in domestic confidence, that it is not an easy task to transplant a tree which is deeply rooted. It is especially hard to do so in our soil and climate. Though a migratory people, our college professors are fixtures. Such local college attachments are not known in Germany; and the promotions which are frequent in Germany are less thought of here. When we think of calling foreign teachers, we encounter other difficulties. Many are reluctant to cross the sea; and others are, by reason of their lack of acquaintance with our language and ways, unavailable. Besides we may as well admit that London, Paris, Leipsic, Berlin and Vienna, afford facilities for literary and scientific growth and influence, far beyond what our country affords. Hence, it is probable that among our own countrymen, our faculty will be chiefly found.

I wrote, not long ago, to an eminent physicist, presenting this problem in social mechanics, for which I asked his solution. "We cannot have a great university without great professors; we cannot have great professors till we have a great university: Help us from the dilemma." Let me tell his answer: "Your difficulty," he says, "applies only to old men who are great; these you can rarely move; but the young men of genius, talent, learning and promise, you can draw. They should be your strength."

The young Americans of talent and promise—there is our strength, and a noble company they are: We do not ask from what college, or what state, or what church they come; but what do they know, and what can they do, and what do they want to find out.

315

In the biographies of eminent scholars, it is curious to observe how many indicated in youth preeminent ability. Isaac Casaubon, whose name in the sixteenth century shed lustre on the learned circles of Geneva, Montpellier, Paris, London and Oxford, began as professor of Greek, at the age of twenty-two; and Heinsius, his Leyden contemporary, at eighteen. It was at the age of twenty-eight, that Linnaeus first published his *Systema Naturae*. Cuvier was appointed professor in Paris at twenty-six, and, a few months later, a member of the Institute. James Kent, the great commentator on American law, began his lectures in Columbia College at the age of thirty-one. Henry was not far from thirty years of age when he made his world-renowned researches in electro-magnetism; and Dana's great work on mineralogy was first published before he was twenty-five years old, and about four years after he graduated at New Haven. Look at the Harvard lists:—Everett was appointed Professor of Greek at twenty-one; Benjamin Peirce of Mathematics at twenty-four; and Agassiz was not yet forty when he came to this country. For fifty years Yale College rested on three men selected in their youth by Dr. Dwight, and almost simultaneously set at work; Day was twenty-eight, Silliman, twenty-three, and Kingsley, twenty-seven, when they began their professorial lives. The University of Virginia, early in its history, attracted foreign teachers, who were all young men.

We shall hope to secure a strong staff of young men, appointing them because they have twenty years before them; selecting them on evidence of their ability; increasing constantly their emoluments, and promoting them because of their merit to successive posts, as scholars, fellows, assistants, adjuncts, professors and university professors. This plan will give us an opportunity to introduce some of the features of the English fellowship and the German system of privat-docents; or in other words, to furnish positions where young men desirous of a university career may have a chance to begin, sure at least of a support while waiting for promotion.

Our plans begin but do not end here. As men of distinction, who have won the highest rank in their callings, are known to be free, we shall invite them to come among us.

For a time, at least, we shall also look to the faculties of other colleges for occasional help. Many years ago, among the plans for establishing a university, in distinction from a college, at Cambridge, Professor Peirce proposed that various colleges should send up for a portion of the year, and for a term of years, their best professors, who should receive a generous acknowledgment for this service, and good opportunities for work, but should not renounce their college homes. Without having heard of his plan, which I think had been made public, the Trustees of the Johns Hopkins University have worked out a kindred scheme. They propose to ask distinguished professors from other colleges to come to us during a term of years, each to reside here for an appointed time, and be accessible, *publice et privatim*, both in the lecture room and the study.

Where do we look for students?

At first, at home, in Baltimore and Maryland; then, in the States adjacent; then, in the regions of our country where, by the desolations of war, educational foundations have been impaired; and presently, according to the renown of the faculty, which we are able to bring here, and the completeness of the establishment, we hope that our influence will be national.

Of what grade will they be? Mature enough to be profited by university education. The exact standard is not yet fixed. It must depend on the colleges and schools around us; there must be no gap in the system, and we must keep ahead, but the discussions now in progress, respecting the City College, Agricultural College and St. John's College, must delay our announcements. Our standard will doubtless be as high as the community requires.

What will the buildings be?

At first, temporary, but commodious; in the heart of the

317

city, accessible to all; and fitted for lectures, laboratories, library and collections. At length, permanent, on the site at Clifton; not a mediaeval pile, I hope, but a series of modern institutions; not a monumental, but a serviceable group of structures. The middle ages have not built any cloisters for us; why should we build for the middle ages? In these days laboratories are demanded on a scale and in a variety hitherto unknown, for chemistry, physics, geology and mineralogy, comparative anatomy, physiology, pathology. Oxford with its New Museum; Cambridge with its Cavendish laboratory; Owens College with its excellent work-rooms; South Kensington with the new apartments of Huxley and Frankland; Leipsic, Vienna, Berlin, all afford illustrations of the kind of structures we shall need. Already measures have been initiated for the improvement of Clifton as a university site. Although it will take time to develop the plans, I hope that we shall all live to see the day when the simplicity, the timeliness, and the strength which characterized our founder's gift, will be also apparent in the structures which his trustees erect; and when that site, beautiful in itself and already well planted, may be, in fact, an academic grove, with temples of learning, so appropriate, so true, and so well built that no other ornament will be essential for beauty, and yet that in their neighborhood no work of art will be out of place.

Our affiliations deserve mention. Already harmonious relations have been established between this University and the Peabody Institute, the Academy of Sciences, and the City College, and the departments of State and City Education. I may also add that the authorities of the scientific institutions in Washington have evinced in many ways good will toward their new ally in Baltimore. As this University grows, we may anticipate perpetual advantages from its proximity to the national capital, where the Smithsonian Institution, the Engineer Corps, the Naval Observatory, the Coast Survey, the Signal Service, the Botanical Gardens, the Congressional Library, the National Museum, the Territorial Surveys, the Army Medical and Surgical Collections, and the Corcoran Art Gallery are such powerful instruments for the advancement of science, literature and art.

The relation of this University to the *higher education of women* has not been as yet discussed by the Trustees, and doubtless their future conclusions will depend very much upon the way in which the subject is brought forward. I am not at liberty to speak for them, but personally have no hesitation in saying that the plans pursued in the University of Cambridge (England), especially in the encouragement of Girton College, seem likely to afford a good solution of a problem which is not without difficulty, however it is approached. Of this I am certain, that they are not among the wise, who depreciate the intellectual capacity of women, and they are not among the prudent, who would deny to women the best opportunities for education and culture.

I trust the day is near when some one, following the succession of Peabody and Hopkins, will institute here a "Girton College," which may avail itself of the advantages of the Peabody and Hopkins foundations, without obliging the pupils to give up the advantages of a home, or exposing them to the rougher influences which I am sorry to confess are still to be found in colleges and universities where young men resort. For the establishment in Baltimore of such a hall as Girton I shall confidently look.

THE UNIVERSITY FREEDOM

If we would maintain a university, great freedom must be allowed both to teachers and scholars. This involves freedom of methods to be employed by the instructors on the one hand, and on the other, freedom of the courses to be selected by the students.

But this freedom is based on laws,—two of which cannot be too distinctly or too often enunciated. A law which should govern the admission of pupils is this, that before they win this privilege they must have been matured by the long, preparatory discipline of superior teachers, and by the systematic, laborious, and persistent pursuit of fundamental knowledge; and a second law, which should govern the work of professors, is this, that with unselfish devotion to the discovery and advancement of truth and righteousness, they renounce all other preferment, so that, like the greatest of all teachers, they may promote the good of mankind.

I see no advantages in our attempting to maintain the traditional four-year class-system of the American Colleges. It has never existed in the University of Virginia; it is modified, though not nominally given up at Harvard; it is not an important characteristic of Michigan and Cornell; it is not known in the English, French or German universities. It is a collegiate rather than a university method. If parents or students desire us to mark our prescribed courses, either classical or scientific, lasting four years, it will be easy to do so. But I apprehend that many students will come to us excellent in some branches of a liberal education and deficient in others—good perhaps in Greek, Latin and mathematics; deficient in chemistry, physics, zoology, history, political economy, and other progressive sciences. I would give to such candidates on examination, credit for their attainments, and assign them in each study the place for which they are fitted. A proficient in Plato may be a tyro in Euclid. Moreover, I would make attainments rather than time the condition of promotion; and I would encourage every scholar to go forward rapidly or go forward slowly, according to the fleetness of his foot and his freedom from impediment. In other words, I would have our University seek the good of individuals rather than of classes.

The sphere of a university is sometimes restricted by its walls, or is limited to those who are enrolled on its lists. There are three particulars in which we shall aim at extra-mural influence: first, as an examining body, ready to examine and confer degrees or other academic honors on those who are trained elsewhere; next, as a teaching body, by opening to educated persons (whether enrolled as students or not) such lectures as they may wish to attend, under certain restrictions — on the plan of the lectures in the high seminaries of Paris; and, finally, as in some degree at least a publishing body, by encouraging professors and lecturers to give to the world in print the results of their researches.

CONCLUSION

Let us now, as we draw near the close of this allotted hour, turn from details and recur to general principles.

What are we aiming at?

An enduring foundation; a slow development; first local, then regional, then national influence; the most liberal promotion of all useful knowledge; the special provision of such departments as are elsewhere neglected in the country; a generous affiliation with all other institutions, avoiding interferences, and engaging in no rivalry; the encouragement of research; the promotion of young men; and the advancement of individual scholars, who by their excellence will advance the sciences they pursue, and the society where they dwell.

No words could indicate our aim more fitly than those by which John Henry Newman expresses his "Idea of the University," in a page burning with enthusiasm, to which I delight to revert.

What will be our agencies?

A large staff of teachers; abundance of instruments, apparatus, diagrams, books, and other means of research and instruction; good laboratories, with all the requisite facilities; accessory influences coming both from Baltimore and Washington; funds so unrestricted, charter so free, schemes so elastic, that as the world goes forward, our plans will be adjusted to its new requirements.

321

What will be our methods?

Liberal advanced instruction for those who want it; distinctive honors for those who win them; appointed courses for those who need them; special courses for those who can take no other; a combination of lectures, recitations, laboratory practice, field work and private instruction; the largest discretion allowed to the Faculty consistent with the purposes in view; and, finally, an appeal to the community to increase our means, to strengthen our hands, to supplement our deficiencies, and especially to surround our scholars with those social, domestic and religious influences which a corporation can at best imperfectly provide, but which may be abundantly enjoyed in the homes, the churches and the private associations of an enlightened Christian city.

Citizens of Baltimore and Maryland—This great undertaking does not rest upon the Trustees alone; the whole community has a share in it. However strong our purposes, they will be modified, inevitably, by the opinions of enlightened men; so let parents and teachers incite the youth of this commonwealth to high aspirations; let wise and judicious counsellors continue their helpful suggestions, sure of being heard with grateful consideration; let skillful writers, avoiding captiousness on the one hand and compliment on the other, uphold or refute or amend the tenets here announced; let the guardians of the press diffuse widely a knowledge of the benefits which are here provided; let men of means largely increase the usefulness of this work by their timely gifts.

At the moment there is nothing which seems to me so important, in this region, and indeed in the entire land, as the promotion of good secondary schools, preparatory to the universities. There are old foundations in Maryland which require to be made strong, and there is room for newer enterprises, of various forms. Every large town should have an efficient academy or high school; and men of wealth can do no greater service to the public than by liberally encouraging, in

322

their various places of abode, the advanced instructions of the young. None can estimate too highly the good which came to England from the endowment of Lawrence Sheriff at Rugby, and of Queen Elizabeth's school at Westminister, or the value to New England of the Phillips foundations in Exeter and Andover.

Every contribution made by others to this new University will enable the Trustees to administer with greater liberality their present funds. Special foundations may be affiliated with our trust, for the encouragement of particular branches of knowledge, for the reward of merit, for the construction of buildings; and each gift, like the new recruits of an army, will be the more efficient because of the place it takes in an organized and efficient company. It is a great satisfaction in this world of changes and pecuniary loss to remember what safe investments have been made at Harvard and Yale, and other old colleges, where dollar for dollar is still shown for every gift.

The atmosphere of Maryland seems favorable to such deeds of piety, hospitality, and "good-will to men." George Calvert, the first Lord Baltimore, comes here, returns to England and draws up a charter which becomes memorable in the annals of civil and religious liberty, for which, "he deserves to be ranked," (as Bancroft says), "among the most wise and benevolent lawgivers of all ages;" among the liberals of 1776 none was bolder than Charles Carroll of Carrollton; John Eager Howard, the hero of Cowpens, is almost equally worthy of gratitude for the liberality of his public gifts; John McDonogh, of Baltimore birth, bestows his fortune upon two cities for the instruction of their youth; George Peabody, resident here in early life, comes back in old age to endow an Athenaeum, and begins that outpouring of munificence which gives him a noble rank among modern philanthropists; Moses Sheppard bequeaths more that half a million for the relief of mental disease; Rinehart, the teamster boy, attains distinction as a sculptor, and bestows his well-won acquisitions for the encouragement of art in the city of his residence; and a Baltimorean still living, provides for the foundation of an astronomical observatory in Yale College; while Johns Hopkins lays a foundation for learning and charity, which we celebrate today.

Let me enlist attention from the youth of Baltimore. For you, my young friends, these great advantages are provided. What will be your response? Is there not among you some book-binder's boy, like Michael Faraday, who will be left by our Royal Institution to a line of research for which the world will be better; is there not here some private teacher, like Cuvier, or some minister's son, like Agassiz, burning with a desire to pursue the study of natural history; is there not some sophomore in college, like Alexander Hamilton, ready to discuss the questions of public finance, eager to be trained by a master economist; is there not in Baltimore a genius in mathematics, like Gauss, who at three years old corrected his father's arithmetic, at eighteen entered the University of Gottingen where he made a discovery which puzzled geometers "from the days of Euclid," and who died at seventy-seven, among the most eminent of his time? If so, I say it is for you, bright youths, that these doors are opened. Enter the armory and equip yourselves.

GENTLEMEN OF THE BOARD OF TRUSTEES:—
The duty you assigned me of unfolding your plans is now imperfectly discharged. I hope that I have not struck too low a key in speaking of the opportunities, and on the contrary, that I have not said anything in rivalry or boast. If I have seemed cautious, you are sanguine, invigorated by the force of a lofty purpose, and the comforting consciousness of ample means. If I have seemed sanguine, you are cautious, aware that there are other institutions, older, richer, and more experienced than this, whose example we must study, and whose help we must seek.

Before concluding, I repeat in public the assent which I have privately made to your official overtures. In speaking of your freedom from sectarian and political control, you express-ed to me a hope that this foundation should be pervaded by the spirit of an enlightened Christianity; while you proposed to train young men for the service of the State and the responsi-bilities of public life, you hoped the University would never engage in sectional, partisan and provincial animosities. In both these propositions I now as then express my cordial and entire concurrence.

Our work now begins. This place is felicitous, midway between the extremes of North and South, and redolent of memories and of men and women whose names the world will never forget. This day is suggestive, reminding us of one whose wise moderation wrought great achievements. This year is auspicious, inviting us to sink political animosities in sentiments of fraternal good will, and of patriotic regard for a re-united republic. This company is inspiring; the city, the state, and the older seats of learning, far and near, here express their good will. Most welcome among their utterances are the words with which the oldest college in the land extends its fellowship to the youngest of the band.

So, friends and colleagues, we launch our bark upon the Patapsco, and send it forth to unknown seas. May its course be guided by looking to the heavens and the voyage promote the glory of God and the good of Mankind.

Permit one word of a personal character before I take my seat. My life thus far has been spent in two universities, one full of honors, the other of hopes; one led by experience, the other by expectations. May the lessons of both, the old and the new, be wisely blended here. There is not a place in all the land which I should be so glad to fill as that in which I have been placed by your favorable consideration; but the bur-dens will be heavy unless your kind indulgence is continued. Standing almost within sight of the monument which has given a name to this city, do not deem it presumptious if I adopt the words which Washington addressed to the citizens of Baltimore in 1789, and say on his memorial day, as he said then:

"I know the delicate nature of the duties incident to the part I am called to perform, and I feel my incompetence without the singular assistance of Providence to discharge them in a satisfactory manner; but having undertaken the task from a sense of duty, no fear of encountering difficulties, and no dread of losing popularity shall ever deter me from pursuing what I take to be the true interests of my country."

Inaugural Address

by

JAMES H. KIRKLAND

Chancellor of Vanderbilt University

September 25, 1893

JAMES HAMPTON KIRKLAND (September 9, 1859—August 5, 1939) was born in Spartenburg, South Carolina. He graduated from Wofford College, in 1877 and received the doctorate from the University of Leipzig, 1885. He was the recipient of six honorary degrees. Kirkland taught Greek and Latin at Wofford College before accepting the chancellorship of Vanderbilt University in 1893, the position which he held for forty-five years. His long and distinguished career as Chancellor of Vanderbilt had a profound influence upon higher education throughout the South. He was the founder of the Association of Colleges and Secondary Schools of Southern States and was chairman of the Board of Trustees of the Carnegie Foundation for Advancement of Teaching, in 1922-23.

The story of the development of higher institutions of learning in the United States forms one of the most interesting chapters in the general educational history of our country. Not simply in building up a system of public schools have we displayed our national wisdom, but quite as much in providing nobler homes of learning and means of higher culture. It has been long observed that educational influences, like the cool air of the mountain tops, move from higher regions to lower levels, and our fathers of two centuries ago were not ignorant of this fact. Hence, coincident with their efforts in organizing lower schools, they began to make preparations for the more advanced culture of their children. In 1636, sixteen years after the landing of the "Mayflower," the General Court of Massachusetts Bay agreed to give 400 pounds towards the founding of a school or college. This was the institution which, receiving two years later half the property of the Reverend John Harvard, changed its name to Harvard College. Even before that time, in 1619, the Virginia Company in England voted ten thousand acres of land in the colony for the establishment of a seminary of learning, and a site and a name were actually selected in 1624. But it was not till 1693 that a grant and charter were obtained for William and Mary College. During the next century twenty-two names were added to the roll of American colleges, and some of these remain to this day among our most flourishing institutions. The story of the early days of these institutions, of their struggles for existence and growth, of the faith and labors of their officers, excites to-day our admiration and sympathy. The nineteenth century shows a marked improvement. Each single decade surpasses almost the whole preceding century, and the work of one year is forgotten in the larger tasks and greater success of the succeeding one. This development has continued up to this very time, and never has so much been done for the cause of higher education as is being done just now. Never has so much money been put into colleges and universities, or plans projected on so large a scale. Now we almost dream of being able to equal the magnificent institutions of the Old World. But let no one think that we have reached a point where we may rest satisfied or stop in our advancement. The work of higher education is really just beginning to be properly taken hold of by the American people. Oxford and Cambridge still have incomes that surpass the whole capital of most American universities. Our brightest and most advanced students still go abroad not simply to secure that culture that comes by foreign travel, or a more perfect knowledge of the European tongues, but to secure more thorough drill in fundamental studies, to get the advantage of more scientific training; in a word, to get access to better workshops and better workmen than we can provide. No, our work has just begun. Our young men still go into the pulpit deficient in general and special training, trusting that inspiration may prove an antidote for ignorance and laziness; our lawyers know little law and our doctors less medicine when they begin their dangerous careers; our teachers do not regard their work as a profession at all, and enter the schoolroom with a rashness and incompetency that is enough to make angels weep. Our nation, our body politic, still cries aloud for a larger proportion of cultured and educated men that may serve to leaven and sweeten and save the whole mass of our population. Our work is not done; only a fair beginning has been made.

When we observe the growth of colleges in America we see that they owe their existence to three factors; that three lines of influence and effort, acting sometimes separately, sometimes unitedly, have produced them. These three organizing forces have been the Church, the State, and private benefactions. To-day the Church and State are drifting apart in their educational efforts. One influence prevails in one commonwealth, in another the other. Jealousies and bickerings have arisen, and the advocates of one policy are led to the attacking of promoters of the other. The Church accuses the state of irreligion; the State rejoins with the charge of narrowness, sectarianism, and bigotry. In the early days of our country's history this was less so than at present, and State and Church united their efforts to promote and found institutions of learning. Theocratic influences were very powerful in the early constitution of the New England colonies, and the movement which resulted in the founding of Harvard was largely due to the desire of providing means of training for ministers of the gospel. This same influence was back of the efforts that produced William and Mary. In those early days weakness secured unity. Church and State, alike moved by love of learning, and feeling keenly the necessity of building up the civilization of this new country on culture and character, and not merely on material resources, joined hands in the task they had set before them. I do not care to discuss the question whether education should be carried on by the Church or State; in fact, I have little sympathy with that discussion in the abstract. Theoretically both sides can make out a satisfactory case. The fundamental principles of both sides are right, and from their respective standpoints both Church and State have a right to devote themselves to this work. The truth is that education is an interest so vast and so vital that it justifies every honest and unselfish effort for its advancement. Society in general, the cause of civilization itself, is in close alliance with the cause of colleges and universities. Neither State nor Church can exist to-day in their highest development without such institutions, and it is of each sometimes the privilege. sometimes the duty to foster and promote them. The question is not so much one of principle as of policy and a wise investment of resources. The State should not be led by any outburst of national enthusiasm to provide in duplicate what is already sufficiently provided for. It can better afford to pay the tuition fees of its sons at an institution already well established and thoroughly equipped than to provide a complete university plant of its own. Nor should denominational zeal lead to the establishment of an oversupply of poorly equipped colleges, which drag out a meager existence, gather patronage together only by the application of the Church whip, and serve at the same time to starve the bodies of their professors and the minds of their pupils. In educational institutions what we need now above all things is not quantity, but quality.

But there is a third factor that has been largely prominent in advancing the interests of higher education, and that is private beneficence. Before the college of the Massachusetts colony had begun operations John Harvard turned into its coffers the half of his property, amounting to something like 800 pounds, and his library of 320 volumes. This gift was pronounced by President Quincy, more than a hundred years afterward, "the noblest and purest tribute to religion and science that the Western world has yet witnessed." Following this example, Americans have ever been noted for their liberality, in building up institutions of learning, indeed towards all enterprises that have the good of mankind for their object. The adoption of the name of the benefactor has in many cases marked the gratitude of the recipients and perpetuated the memory of the generous donors. Thus have been derived the names of Harvard, Yale, Brown, Cornell, and in more recent times, Johns Hopkins, Vanderbilt, Clark, Tulane, and Leland Stanford, Jr. But not every generous act can be rewarded with an honor so great as the naming of a university. Thousands of benefactors have contributed their little to the cause of education, and been content with the blessing of an approving conscience and the knowledge that they were contributing to the highest life and noblest development of the people. This fact is a most peculiar one in the history of American institutions. No other country in the world can show such a record. From private gifts have sprung not only those institutions that stand outside of Church and State, but all of those that are fostered by the Church. The American people have grasped the idea that the foundations of character must be laid in colleges as well as in Churches, and that in contributing to their colleges and universities they are serving both God and their country. This is the foundation on which nearly all of our institutions rest. This explains their history; this is their past, this the ground of faith for the future. Their capital is not solely or chiefly in the invested bonds of the endowment fund, but in the loyal hearts of their constituency, in the love that these bear their children and their country.

In the history of Vanderbilt University two of the educational factors above mentioned have united their forces—namely, religious zeal and private beneficence. To both of these full acknowledgement is due. The one made known our wants; the other supplied them. The one showed a people struggling for the light of knowledge, anxious to provide the best things in an educational way for the South; the other proved the generous nature of a noble man, striving to leave the world better than he found it. The one was only the dream of enthusiasts; only the other made that dream a reality. Listen to a word of history.

The felt want of some means of higher education throughout the bounds of the Methodist Episcopal Church, South, led in 1871 to the appointment of delegates to a Convention to "consider the subject of a university such as would meet the wants of the Church and country." This convention met in Memphis, January 24, 1872, and was composed of delegates from Tennessee, Alabama, Mississippi, Louisiana, and Arkansas. A general plan for a university was adopted, a Board of Trust nominated, and shortly afterwards a charter of incorporation secured, under the title of "The Central University of the Methodist Episcopal Church, South." It was determined that $1,000,000 was necessary for the success of the enterprise, and no steps were to be taken toward the selection of a site or the opening of any department of the University until a subscription of $500,000 should have been raised. How long it would have taken to raise this amount happily we need not now stop to inquire. The South in those days had not recovered from the exhaustion of the war; trade was disorganized, and wealth but slowly accumulating. The very efforts

to realize what had been determined on showed that the enterprise was doomed to failure, and would simply add one more
to the long roll of worthy, but abandoned plans. It was at this
time, in the hour of defeat and failure, that Commodore Vanderbilt came to the rescue with an offer, made through Bishop
McTyeire, of $500,000. The offer was gladly accepted, the
few conditions that accompanied it were complied with, and
in gratitude to the founder the name was changed from Central to Vanderbilt University. Rightly do we speak of Commodore Vanderbilt as our founder. Central University existed
only on paper; Vanderbilt is built in brick and stone. We point
with pride to the portrait of Commodore Vanderbilt that
adorns this chapel wall, but this University will perpetuate
his memory long after the colors have faded from the canvas.
Some of the citizens of Nashville are even now privately planning to erect a statue in his honor to be located near these
grounds. This is a worthy and delicate token of appreciation,
and the University wishes them success in their plan; but better even than bronze or marble is the monument that is erected
to his memory in these buildings. To these we point with ever
increasing thankfulness, and say: *Si monumentum requiris,*
circumspice. Commodore Vanderbilt afterwards increased his
donation to $1,000,000, and when he died, after $400,000 had
been spent on grounds and buildings, there was still left
$600,000 for permanent endowment. Mr. William H. Vander-
bilt increased this fund to $900,000, and added buildings to the
value of $160,000. The last addition to the buildings of the
campus was made possible through the generosity of Mr. Corn-
elius Vanderbilt, the present head of the Vanderbilt family,
who in 1888 contributed $30,000 toward the erection and
equipment of the Mechanical Engineering Hall, and for the
purchase of books for the library. Aside from the help given
by our founder, and continued by his descendants for two
generations, but little has been done for Vanderbilt University. In the beginning of our history the citizens of Nashville
made a donation of about $28,000 for grounds and buildings.

From time to time since then a few friends have added scholarships and prizes, some of them endowed, and some of them supported by yearly contributions. For these we are grateful, since by these means we are enabled to extend some slight help to a few students, but every year the demands on us in this direction far exceed our ability to relieve. More has been done along this line in the Biblical Department, and a Sustentation Fund has been created, the income of which is every year loaned to needy and worthy young men who are preparing for the ministry. This fund was gotten together partly through small contributions, partly in some of larger amount. The most notable of the latter was the bequest of Mrs. Sarah E. Atkinson of Memphis, which amounted to more than $40,000. But this fund is small when measured by the service to which it is put, and the friends of ministerial education are urgently requested to add to it liberally. This short paragraph completes the record of our benefactions.

Let us now see what has been done by Vanderbilt University for the cause of education. When Vanderbilt opened her doors in the fall of 1875, 307 young men presented themselves; the last year's catalogue shows 733 names on our roll. Our departments of instruction in the beginning were four; now they are seven. Let it be understood, too, that this increase in numbers has been made not by adhering to a low standard, for all the while we have been engaged in raising our standard to such a plane as would put us on a par with the best institutions of the land. Our engineering courses require five years for completion. Our School of Pharmacy is one of the few in the whole country that requires two full years of nine months each for the completion of the course, and provides also a third year for those who desire more advanced instruction. Our Law Department allows no student to graduate without two years of professional study. Our Dental Department has recently changed its requirements from two to three full courses of lectures, and in spite of this fact has hardly suffered any material diminution of attendance. Just this year the Medical Department puts the same law into operation, and demands three courses for graduation. The Biblical Department has been made more thorough with almost every year of its history. No student can receive instruction in this department who has not passed through the Sophomore class in college, and no one can receive a degree who has not already taken the degree of A.B. from some reputable institution of learning.

To the development of the Academic Department we point with feelings of peculiar pride and satisfaction, for it is on this department that the largest part of our resources must necessarily be spent, and it is to this department that we look for the largest returns. This department must be a feeder to the Biblical, Law, Dental, and Medical Departments; it must also provide courses of liberal culture for those who do not intend to enter any of the learned professions; and it must train all who desire to devote themselves to the work of teaching. When the first session was opened in 1875, 115 students were enrolled in the Academic Department; but it was found that not half of this number were properly prepared for college work, and the authorities of the University had to authorize the formation of preparatory classes. In his first annual report the Chancellor said: "If we had stood firmly by our rules, we should have rejected fully two-thirds of those that presented themselves for matriculation." So low has been the general standard of collegiate education throughout the South, and so small the number of good preparatory schools, that this incubus had to be retained and carried until five years ago. Then we cut off all preparatory classes, and instituted a rigid system of entrance examinations. Our numbers fell, of course; only 115 students matriculated the first year under the new system; but experience has proved the wisdom of our action. The whole tone of the student body has been elevated. Our numbers have increased in four years from 115 to 194, while at the same time we have been enforcing more rigidly our requirements for entrance.

Schools are springing up all over our patronizing territory that have the express purpose of preparing boys for Vanderbilt. Parents are recognizing the fact that if they wish their sons to be educated here they must begin to prepare them for us some three years in advance. The Louisville Conference has set a most worthy example in establishing an endowed training school at Elkton, Kentucky, whose special purpose is to prepare young men for Vanderbilt. The citizens of Elkton have contributed liberally to this enterprise, and the school has just been domiciled in one of the most practical and elegant school buildings in the South. We recommend this form of investment to other progressive towns, and declare ourselves ready to promote in every possible way the furtherance of such enterprises. In the manner above mentioned we have established a standard of admission, and are maintaining a grade of scholarship that makes us worthy of being placed by the side of the very best institutions of any portion of our land. But further. A very great advance in educational work has recently been made in the establishment of a proper distinction between college and university work. These terms, so long used indiscriminately, are beginning to have a definite and distinct meaning. The college is the institution that prepares a young man for his professional school, or gives him that ordinary amount of culture that every one who can afford it ought to have. It culminates in the Bachelor degrees. The university takes up the work where it is left off by the college. Its courses are intended for those who desire a more advanced and specialized training in science or literature, particulary for those who intend to make teaching their profession. It adds from three to five years of study to the Bachelor courses, and gives as the reward for this work the Master and Doctor degrees. The development of true university work is transforming the whole system of American education. It is sending into our schools men that have some adequate preparation for the tasks they are undertaking. It is equipping others for general literary or scientific work, and professional men are finding it to their advantage to take these higher courses. Vanderbilt University has been quite successful in her efforts to build up this part of her work. For the past three years we have had an average of 35 university students per year, representing almost as many institutions, and these located not merely in the South, but scattered all over the country. Among the institutions represented we might mention the University of Virginia; Randolph-Macon, Virginia; Emory and Henry, Virginia; Trinity, North Carolina; University of South Carolina; University of Georgia, Emory, Georgia; University of Alabama; University of Tennessee; Tulane University, Louisiana; Central College, Missouri; Hardin College, Missouri; Hendrix College, Arkansas; Southwestern University, Texas; Center College, Kentucky; Ogden College, Kentucky; Miami College, Ohio; Wooster University, Ohio; Iowa State Agricultural College; Ursinus College, Pennsylvania; Swarthmore College, Pennsylvania; University of the City of New York; Williams College, Massachusetts; Yale University, Brown University, Rhode Island; and the University of the Cape of Good Hope.

For the students that we have equipped with this higher training service has been found in the best schools and colleges of the South. So great has been the demand for them that we have had difficulty in keeping them until they could complete their courses. More than once have we had to relinquish men who were profiting most largely by their opportunities here to allow them to go serve other institutions. We have supplied three men for the Faculty of the University of Mississippi; three for Wofford College, South Carolina; two for Emory and Henry, Virginia; and two for Millsaps, Mississippi. These are but a few of the many instances that I could name.

Such is the record of Vanderbilt University; such the story of the past eighteen years. The success that has been met with is the surest testimony to the wisdom of its founders and projectors. Grateful we are to the kind friends of the North who put the University here; grateful, too, that this trust was committed to one so wise, so prudent, so far-seeing as the first President of the Board. The impress of his grand character will long rest on all the University organization, and his memory will remain fresh in the hearts of all the officers whose privilege it was to be associated with him. After a work so gloriously done, under the shade of magnolias that his own hand planted, he sleepeth well. To my predecessor, too, in the office of Chancellor, is due no small part of the credit for the wise organization and equipment of this institution. His presence on this occasion forbids that I should speak as I would like to do of his services. May you still abide with us for many years, and see the work that your hands have helped to start prospering and enlarging!

Serus in caelum redeas diuque
Laetus intersis populo.

With the opening of the present session a new chapter begins in the history of Vanderbilt University. When I reflect on the character of the men who have hitherto had the direction of affairs you will not wonder that I tremble under the weight of responsibility that is placed on me. Indeed, I should be unwilling to undertake the task at all were I not sure of the cordial support of the Trustees, the Faculty, the alumni, and the students. Fellow-teachers, fellow-students, friends of the University in every station, we have a great work to do. Let us not for one moment falter or despair. We have already gone too far to turn backward; we have mounted too high to look downward.

Vanderbilt University stands committed to several lines of policy from which we do not intend to recede. It stands committed to the elevation of the standard of professional training, and we shall try in the future to make still further advances along this line. Especially does it stand committed to the thorough training, in literary as well as theological studies, of all the young men who are to enter the pulpit of the Southern Methodist Church. Further, Vanderbilt University stands committed to a college department, elevated in its standard, broad in its scope, liberal in its spirit, and Christian in its character. This I regard as the most important part of the work that we have yet accomplished. There are some of our friends who have argued that Vanderbilt should abandon its college work entirely, and devote itself exclusively to university or postgraduate work. Let me say here that I regard this as entirely pre-mature, and we have no thought of doing so for many a long year to come. The best contribution that we have made to the educational interests of the South is the development of a college of high grade and broad scope of instruction, under whose protected shadow academies and training schools could spring up, and which should stimulate by a generous rivalry other colleges to better work and a more advanced standard. There are two types of the college in our country. I omit entirely that large class of institutions bearing the name of college which really are nothing more than schools, and often schools of a low order. I speak only of the better class of colleges—those that are trying to do honest and faithful work. These as I have said, we may divide into two classes. The one class includes those that, by reason of small endowment, are compelled to limit their course of instruction to a few fundamental studies. They have a small Faculty, little or no scientific apparatus, and not much variety of courses. They give in their way a good intellectual training, though it is not one adapted to every student, and one that is sadly out of keeping with this progressive age in which we live. The other type of college is that which tries to make the college the representative educationally of the present condition of civilization. This is the type to which Vanderbilt is committed. This demands a recognition of the fact that the road to knowledge does not lead solely along the windings of mathematical curves or through the intricacies of the Latin subjunctive. Life is larger than any one study. In the past few decades our horizon has been immensely widened. New fields of research have been opened, new sciences developed. This immense enrichment and enlargement of our civilization calls for corresponding enlargement of the college course. Provision must be made for new branches of study, and for utilizing new facilities in the prosecution of old ones. The world is demanding larger tasks, and we must prepare our young men for them. Railroads are waiting to be built, mines must be opened, rivers be deepened, new sources of wealth developed; new worlds must be discovered in the drop of water on the grass and in the star dust of the sky. A generation ago a few weeks sufficed for all that a class was expected to learn about electricity, and fifty dollars was perhaps enough to pay for the apparatus necessary for illustration. A few days ago I saw the notice that one of our sister institutions was erecting an electrical laboratory at a cost of $200,000. Such is the age in which we live, and colleges must conform to it. They, too, say:

> " 'Tis life whereof our nerves are scant,
>   O life, not death, for which we pant;
> More life, and fuller, that we want.' "

Vanderbilt is further committed to the idea of a genuine university above and beyond the college course. This is that part of our work by which we can leave our most permanent impress on Southern education. In a vast stretch of territory we stand best prepared to do this work, and the responsibility for its continuance falls upon us. It is in such a school that we are to train the leaders of our progress, those who shall give character to the age in which they live and lift civilization to higher levels. The measure of success we have already met with shows the seasonableness of our attempt to develop this kind of work in the South. But no part of educational work is so costly, none demands such immense outlays in providing instruction and means of research, none brings in less return in fees. But, on the other hand, no part of our work is so useful or so necessary, none adds so much to our reputation as a university. We cannot give up this part of our work; rather,

341

must we enlarge our facilities and increase our efforts in this direction.

But here we are met by a great difficulty, and I beg, you will allow me to speak candidly about it. If Vanderbilt University has been so successful in the past, it is because her resources have been devoted unstintedly to the cause of education, and she has been allowed to grow as rapidly as the surroundings demanded. The food that universities thrive on is gold. Without that, nothing can be achieved; with this, all things are possible. The sustenance that this University has had in the past has produced wonders, but it is not sufficient for the future. If the future that I have depicted for Vanderbilt is to be realized, we must increase our endowment and enlarge our income. Already we are cramped for funds, and it is a serious question every year how we can carry on the work so auspiciously begun. The management of the funds of the University has been marked by the wisest economy. Not a cent has been lost by defalcation of agents or unfortunate investments. The only wonder in the history of this institution is that so much has been done with so meager an endowment. Let me take the public into my confidence and state a few facts and figures. We have no secrets, nothing that we desire to hide from the knowledge of our friends. Ours is a trust, a commission from the donors to be discharged for the best interest of the general public and the cause of education. There are no private interests to be subserved, and we are glad to take this opportunity of indicating to the world the manner in which our obligations are being discharged. Our endowment, is as you all know, something more than $900,000. This is invested so as to bring us in an unusually large interest; in fact, nearly seven per cent, the sum actually realized being something more than $60,000. Out of this yearly income four of our departments must be supported. These four departments have a teaching force of thirty-eight, including fourteen professors, six adjunct professors, nine instructors, nine assistants. This

342

force is smaller than it ought to be, smaller than our needs require, but as large as our income will allow. Our teaching force cost slightly more than $50,000 per year. The rest of our income is consumed in supplies for our laboratories, repairs and additions to our scientific apparatus, care of grounds and buildings including insurance, provision for heat, light, and water, and a number of other items, small separately, but considerable in the aggregate. Of course our income is increased somewhat by fees from students, but this is smaller than would be supposed from the number of the students, because of two reasons: First, students in the Biblical Department pay no tuition; secondly, free tuition is also given in the Academic Department to all sons of ministers engaged in the active work of the ministry. Beside this, quite a number of poor students, who are not able to raise the necessary amount for their expenses, are allowed to give their note for tuition. Never has Vanderbilt University seen the day when a poor but worthy student had to leave her halls because he could not pay for the instruction he received. From this it will be seen that our resources are taxed to the utmost to maintain the work of the University at the high standard we have set for it, and there is but little chance for further development without increase of endowment. This we must have, this we shall have. Were we content to stop short in our advancement, to arrest our progress, to stand idly by hardening into a fossil state, waiting for some other institution to arise and do our work, we should be false to our trust, false to the generous founder who put us here, false to the people whom we are to serve, false to ourselves, and false to our God. Our embarrassments are the greater because of our splendid opportunities and the magnitude of the work on which we have already entered. We feel the painfulness of our limitations because of the vital force within us. We are growing, and therefore we fret at the shackles that bind us. The opinion prevails largely that Vanderbilt University is rich and in need of nothing. I wish indeed that this were so, but candor compels me to undeceive you. We are poor, and in need of many things. The income from our productive fund is, as I have stated, about $60,000. This would have been sufficient a century ago, but to-day is only a beginning. Harvard and Columbia have each a yearly income as large as our whole endowment, and there are some five or six institutions that have not far from half a million each. It is absolutely impossible for a university to hold its position to-day without an income of several hundred thousand dollars.

Let me indicate some of our most pressing needs. We need above all things an increase in our force of instruction. We need a number of new Chairs at once. Several that we now have ought to be divided, for many of our professors are virtually filling two Chairs at once. This is the first place for enlargement, as it is the last place where an institution can afford to economize. It is the corps of professors that makes an institution great. These must give it name and reputation; these must be the attraction which draws students to our halls. I feel profoundly grateful that my associates are men of such noble mold; men whose characters are as pure as their scholarship is profound, whose wisdom in council is a ground of confidence for the future, whose presence is an uplifting force in the lives of the young men with whom they mingle, and whose memory will be an inspiration to them through life. Let me keep them all, but give me more like them. The work is waiting for them to do. Again, we need better equipment for work in science. We need a special building for our museum, with an endowment for the purpose of adding to it year by year necessary collections. Too long has it been housed in the small rooms at its disposal in Science Hall. We need special buildings for laboratories—chemical, physical, biological. The School of Chemistry occupies the basement of this building, and it has already grown to such proportions that place can hardly be found for the regular students. Year by year we have added desks, until all the available space is occupied. What shall we do next? Besides, the basement of a three-story building is by no means an ideal place for a chemical laboratory. It is poorly ventilated and badly lighted. It is not pleasant for the rest of us to be hung up over the witches' brewing pot, nor can we expect chemists themselves to concoct a magic moly in quarters so unfavorable. For the physical laboratory we lack not only a building, but a large amount of apparatus. This we are trying to supply year by year, but our progress is but slow. We need also more and better dormitories. In those that we have board is kept as low as $10 or $12 per month, but we are able to accommodate only a small part of the applicants for these rooms. Our gymnasium is fast getting too small. We must have a new one close by the athletic field; and then, with the generosity characteristic of men, we shall give the old one to the girls, and require calisthenics of them. But above all things, next to the enlargement of the endowment, we need a library and a regular income for the same to keep it supplied with books. The library is the very heart of the university. Books are our life. Special laboratories, important and necessary as they are, are only for special students; the library is the workshop of every student and every professor. University work, in the proper sense, is an absolute impossibility without ample library facilities. To carry on research, to prosecute investigation in any line of knowledge, requires first of all an acquaintance with what has already been done along that line in the past ages. This can only be gotten from books. This is one of the points in which the very best of our American institutions are far behind those in Europe. Every year we see American professors going abroad solely for the purpose of working in European libraries. It is pathetic to see our professors trying to supplement the needs of the library by putting their own books at the service of the graduate students, and to see our librarian carefully dividing and apportioning the small pittance that comes into his hands for the purchase of books. We want a sum of from $200,000 to $400,000 for an endowment for a library; then we want half of that amount for a library building. Surely we shall not have long to wait for a blessing so sadly needed.

And now you have listened patiently to the story of the past, to the statement of our present condition and of our hopes for the future. Suffer me in conclusion to appeal to the friends of education everywhere to give us their encouragement and support. I appeal to the alumni, whose large attendance on this occasion I note with peculiar satisfaction. You stand in a most intimate relationship to the University. You owe it a peculiar debt. Whatever you attain in an intellectual way, whatever success you meet with in life, you owe in a large measure to the training you have received here. Vanderbilt must lean more heavily on its alumni for support. The time will come when a large part of the control and government of the University will be in your hands. Get ready for that time by keeping in constant touch with the needs of the University. Let not your love for her grow cold, nor your efforts in her behalf grow feeble. As our alumni become able, we shall expect them to give liberally to supply the wants of the University. Soon we hope you may be able to endow a Chair to be called by your name and to testify to your love. In the meantime we call upon you to lend your assistance to the movement recently set on foot to raise yearly contributions for the help of needy students. There are many young men who are looking with longing eyes toward these grounds and buildings, and beyond them are dreaming of a life of scholarship and culture, but between them and these an impassable gulf is fixed that can only be bridged by the expenditure of a few hundred dollars. Alumni, you have tasted the benefits of education; have you no offering for those to whom circumstances have been less favorable? About twenty of your number have responded and pledged something like $200 for the next year. I call upon you at once for two hundred contributors, and $2,000 per year for this purpose.

I appeal to the members of the Southern Methodist

Church from the Atlantic to the Pacific to come to the help of this great University. There are many who are able to endow individual Chairs by contributing $50,000 for that purpose. No nobler monument could anyone rear to himself than this, to perpetuate his name and to promote the welfare of his country. Other institutions have found friends ready to do this. The University of Virginia has five endowed professorships; Washington and Lee, seven; Amherst, eight; Princeton, ten; Dartmouth, eleven; Harvard, thirteen; and Williams, seventeen. These are but a few of many such cases. Will not some friend of Vanderbilt University step forward and be the first to set so noble an example? This institution was committed by its founder to the care of the Southern Methodist Church. This was done, I make bold to assert, not to pander to our denominational pride, but to make it perfectly sure that this institution would forever maintain a distinctly Christian character. Are there no obligations on the part of the Church growing out of that relationship? Are all the obligations on our side? Ye who were so anxious, twenty years ago, to raise a million dollars for the founding of a great university, come now and lay your offerings on this altar, and by that act increase threefold the efficiency of the institution of whose labors you have all this time been reaping the benefit. But not to the members of the Methodist Church alone do we appeal. We appeal to the whole South, and we have a right to do so. We are working for the cause of education in its broadest sense, and so for the good of the whole country. No spirit of narrowness or prejudice controls us here. While our Biblical Department must necessarily be kept in close relation to the Church whose doctrines it undertakes to expound, the other departments stand simply for the broad work of Christian education. We have no peculiar tests for professors or students. We demand first of all that our professors shall be Christian men and competent scholars, but further than that we have no questions to ask and no instructions to give. The ministers of every denomination have

347

the same privilege of sending their sons to us for instruction in the Academic Department free of charge. The Faculty cares a great deal for the Christian character and upright life of their students, but we give ourselves no concern about their denominational preferences. This we believe to be the spirit in which our founder meant us to do the work; this we believe to be the true spirit for labors such as ours. Standing on this broad basis, we appeal to all the friends of education everywhere to lend us their sympathy and encouragement, and to help us by the contribution of their means to give to this section of our common country, advantages as great as those enjoyed even by the most favored.

And, last of all, I appeal to the residents of this beautiful city, who sit under the shade of our trees and listen to the music of our college bell. The University belongs to you in a peculiar sense. The benefits that accrue to our whole section from the existence of this University are yours in an enhanced degree. Your sons need not leave the protection of the paternal roof to secure the fullest education, whether general, technical, or professional. The presence of the University creates an atmosphere of culture, stimulates intellectual life, and elevates the whole tone of society. The schools of Plato and Aristotle have done more to make Athens immortal than the silver mines of Laurium, and your institutions of learning are crown jewels of this fair city. Make this your University; think of it as such; speak of it as such; love it as such.

And now, invoking the sympathy and support of all who love Vanderbilt University and desire her prosperity, I turn to the tasks that await me. Reverently do I lay my hands to this great work. Though conscious of my own insufficiency, I am sustained by my faith in the greatness of the undertaking, and I look to the future with confidence that our fondest dreams for Vanderbilt will be more than realized.

"In this faith
I shall not count the chances——sure that all
A prudent foresight asks we shall not want,
And all that bold and patient hearts can do
We shall not leave undone. The rest is God's."

Inaugural Address

by

DAVID STARR JORDAN
President of Stanford University

October 1, 1891

DAVID STARR JORDAN (January 19, 1851—*September* 19, 1931) *was born on a farm near Gamesville, New York, of English parentage. As a boy Jordan attended the local ungraded school. His favorite sport, during his spare time on the farm, was to list species of plants which he found and to study their structural deficiencies and resemblances.*

In January, 1885, he was elected to the presidency of Indiana University where he remained until, in 1891, he was called as first president of Stanford. There, one of his first tasks was to select a faculty of unusual talent, a task at which he was most successful.

We come together to-day for the first time as teachers and students. With this relation the life of the Leland Stanford Junior University begins. It is such personal contact of young men and young women with scholars and investigators which constitutes the life of the University. It is for us as teachers and students in the University's first year to lay the foundations of a school which may last as long as human civilization. Ours is the youngest of the Universities, but it is heir to the wisdom of all the ages, and with this inheritance it has the promise of a rapid and sturdy growth.

Our University has no history to fall back upon; no memories of great teachers haunt its corridors; in none of its rooms appear the traces which show where a great man has ever lived or worked. No tender associations cling, ivy-like, to its fresh new walls. It is hallowed by no traditions; it is hampered by none. Its finger-posts still point forward. Traditions and associations it is ours to make. From our work the future of the University will grow as a splendid lily from a modest bulb.

But the future with its glories and its responsibilities will be in other hands. It is ours at the beginning to give the University its form, its tendencies, its customs. The power of precedent will cause to be repeated over and over again everything that we do—our errors as well as our wisdom. It becomes us then to begin the work modestly, as under the eye of the coming ages. We must lay the foundations broad and firm, so as to give full support to whatever edifice the future may build. Ours is the humbler task, but not the least in importance, and our work will not be in vain if all that we do is done with sincerity. As sound as the rocks from which these walls are hewn should be the work of every teacher who comes within them. To the extent that this is true will the University be successful. Unless its work be thus "wrought in a sad sincerity," nothing can redeem it from failure. In this feeling, and realizing, too, that only the help we give to the men and women whose lives we reach can justify our presence here, we are ready to begin our work.

We hope to give to our students the priceless legacy of the educated man, the power of knowing what really is. The higher education should bring men into direct contact with truth. It should help to free them from the dead hands of old traditions and to enable them to form opinions worthy of the new evidence each new day brings before them. An educated man should not be the slave of the past, not a copy of men who have gone before him. He must be in some degree the founder of a new intellectual dynasty, for each new thinker is a new type of man. Whatever is true, is the truest thing in the universe, and mental and moral strength come alike from our contact with it.

Every influence which goes out from these halls should emphasize the value of truth. The essence of scholarship is to know something which is absolutely true; to have, in the words of Huxley, "some knowledge to the certainty of which no authority could add or take away, and to which the tradition of a thousand years is but as the hearsay of yesterday." The scholar, as was once said of our great chemist, Benjamin Silliman, must have "faith in truth as truth, faith that there is a power in the universe good enough to make truth-telling safe, and strong enough to make truth-telling effective." The personal influence of genuineness, as embodied in the life of a teacher, is one of the strongest moral forces which the school can bring to its aid, for moral training comes not mainly by precept but by practice. We may teach the value of truth to our students by showing that we value it ourselves.

In like manner the value of right living can be taught by right examples. In the words of a wise teacher, "Science knows no source of life but life. The teacher is one of the accredited delegates of civilization. In Heine's phrase, he is a Knight of the Holy Ghost. If virtue and integrity are to be propagated, they must be propagated by the people who possess them. If this child-world about us that we know and love is to grow up into righteous manhood and womanhood, it must have a chance to see how righteousness looks when it is lived. That this may be so, what task have we but to garrison our State with men and women? If we can do that, if we can have in every square mile in our country a man or woman whose total influence is a civilizing power, we shall get from our education system all it can give and all that we can desire." So we may hope that this new school will do its part in the work of civilization, side by side with her elder sister, the University of the State, and in perfect harmony with every agency which makes for right thinking and right living. The harvest is bounteous, but tools and workmen are still all too few; for a generous education should be the birthright of every man and woman in America.

I shall not try to-day to give you our ideal of what a university should be. If our word is successful, our ideals will appear in the daily life of the school. In a school, as in a fortress, it is not the form of the building but the strength of the materials which determine its effectiveness. With a garrison of hearts of oak, it may not matter even whether there be a fortress. Whatever its form, or its organization, or its pretensions, the character of the university is fixed by the men who teach. "Have a university in shanties, nay in tents," Cardinal Newman has said, "but have great teachers in it." The university spirit flows out from these teachers, and its organization serves mainly to bring them together. "The university," to use Emerson's words, "should bring every ray of light to its hospitable halls, that their combined influence may set the heart of youth in flame." Strong men make universities strong. A great man never fails to leave a great mark on every youth with whom he comes in contact. Too much emphasis cannot be laid on this, that the real purpose of the university organization is to produce a university atmosphere, such an atmosphere as gathered itself around Arnold at Rugby, around Dollinger at Munich, around Linnaeus at Upsala, around Werner at Freiberg, around Agassiz at Cambridge, around Mark Hopkins at Williamstown, around Andrew D. White at Ithaca, around all great teachers everywhere.

A professor to whom original investigation is unknown should have no place in a university. Men of commonplace or second hand scholarship are of necessity men of low ideals, however much the fact may be disguised. A man of high ideals must be an investigator. He must know and think for himself. Only such as do this can be really great as teachers. Some day our universities will recognize that their most important professors may be men who teach no classes, devoting their time and strength wholly to advanced research. Their presence and example will be, perhaps, worth more to the student body a hundred-fold than the precepts and drill of the others. They set high standards of thought. They help to create the university spirit, without which any college is but a grammar school of little higher pretensions.

And above and beyond all learning is the influence of character, the impulse to virtue and piety which comes from men whose lives show that virtue and piety really exist. For the life of the most exalted, as well as the humblest of men, there can be no nobler motto than that inscribed by the great scholar of the last century over his home at Hammarby: *"Innocue vivito; numen adest."* Live blameless; God is near. "This," said Linnaeus, "is the wisdom of my life." Every advance which we make toward the realization of the truth of the permanence and immanence of law, brings us nearer to Him who is the great first cause of all law and all phenomena.

But while the work of the teachers must make the kernel of the university, we must rejoice that here at Palo Alto even the husks are beautiful. Beauty and fitness are great forces in education. Every object with which the young mind comes in contact leaves on it its trace. "Nothing is unimportant in the life of man," and the least feature of our surroundings has its influence, greater or less. "There was a child went forth every day," Walt Whitman tells us, "and the first object that it looked upon, that object it became." It may be for a moment or an hour, or "for changing cycles of years." The essence of civilization is exposure to refining and humanizing influences. "A dollar in a university," Emerson tells us, "is worth more than a dollar in a jail," and every dollar spent in making a university beautiful will be repaid with interest in the enriching of the students' lives.

It has been a reproach of America that for the best of her sons and daughters she has done the least. She has built palaces for lunatics, idiots, crippled, and blind, nay, even for criminals and paupers. But the college students, "the young men of sound mind and earnest purpose, the noblest treasures of the State," to quote the words of President White, "she has housed in vile barracks." The student has no need for luxury. Plain living has ever gone with high thinking. But grace and fitness have an educative power too often forgotten in this utilitarian age. These long corridors with their stately pillars, these circles of waving palms, will have their part in the students' training as surely as the chemical laboratory or the seminary room. Each stone in the quadrangle shall teach its lesson of grace and of genuineness, and this valley of Santa Clara, the valley of holy clearness, shall occupy a warm place in every student's heart. Pictures of this fair region will cling to his memory amid the figures of the draughting-room. He will not forget the fine waves of our two mountain ranges, overarched by a soft blue Grecian sky, nor the ancient oak trees, nor the gently sloping fields, changing from vivid green to richest yellow as the seasons change. The noble pillars of the gallery of art, its rich treasures, the choicest remains of the ideals of past ages—all these and a hundred other things, which each one will find out for himself, shall fill his mind with bright pictures, never to be rubbed out in the wear of life. Thus in the character of every student shall be left some imperishable trace of the beauty of Palo Alto.

Agassiz once said, "The physical suffering of humanity, the wants of the poor, the craving of the hungry and naked, appeal to the sympathies of every one who has a human heart. But there are necessities which only the destitute student knows. There is a hunger and thirst which only the highest charity can understand and relieve, and on this solemn occasion let me say that every dollar given for higher education in whatever department of knowledge, is likely to have a greater influence on the future character of our nation than even the thousands, hundred thousands, and millions which we have spent or are spending to raise the many to material comfort."

I need not recall to you the history of the foundation of the Leland Stanford Junior University. It has its origin in the shadow of a great sorrow, and its purpose is the wish to satisfy for the coming generations the hunger and thirst after knowledge—that undying curiosity which is the best gift of God to man. The influence of the boy, to the nobility of whose short life the Leland Stanford Junior University is a tribute and a remembrance, will never be lost in our country. To him we owe the inspiration which led the founders to devote the earnings of the successful ventures of a busy life to the work of higher education.

Six years ago, in one of our California journals, these words were used with reference to the work which we begin to-day: "Greater than the achievement of lasting honor among one's fellow-men of later generations, is it to become a living power among them forever. It rarely happens to one man and woman to have both the power and the skill to thus live after death, working and shaping beneficently in the lives of many —not of tens nor of hundreds, but of thousands and of tens of thousands as the generations follow on. Herein is the wisdom of money spent in education, that each recipient of influence becomes in his time a center to transmit the same in every direction, so that it multiplies forever in geometric ratio. This power to mold unborn generations for good, to keep one's hands mightily on human affairs after the flesh has been dust for years, seems not only more than mortal but more than man. Thus does man become co-worker with God in the shaping of the world to a good outcome."

The Golden Age of California begins when its gold is used for purposes like this. From such deeds must rise the new California of the coming century, no longer the California of the gold seeker and the adventurer, but the abode of high-minded men and women, trained in the wisdom of the ages, and imbued with the love of nature, the love of man, and the love of God. And bright indeed will be the future of our State if, in the usefulness of the University, every hope and prayer of the founders shall be realized.

Inaugural Address

by

G. STANLEY HALL

President of Clark University

October 2, 1888

GRANVILLE STANLEY HALL (February 1, 1844—April 24, 1924) was born in Ashville, Massachusetts, of English parentage. G. Stanley Hall mastered the work of local schools with great ease and, in 1863, entered Williams College. While an admirer of the methods of Mark Hopkins, young Hall did not "fall under his spell," but chose a professor with a more progressive tendency in philosophy. Following his study in Europe, Hall gave a course in pedagogy at Harvard; later he was called to Johns Hopkins University where he established a psychological laboratory. Hall soon became what was considered the foremost educational critic in this country. He was selected as the first president of Clark University.

We are here to mark in a simple way, as befits its dignity, a rare event which we hope and pray may prove not only the most important in the history of this favored city, but of forever growing significance for our state and nation, for culture and humanity.

Located with great forethought in a city whose culture ensures that enlightened public sentiment so needful in maintaining the highest possible academic standards, in a city whose wealth and good will, we trust, are as fair a promise as can anywhere be given or asked of that perpetual increase of revenue now required by the rapid progress of science—in a city central among the best colleges of the East, whose work we wish not only to supplement but to stimulate, whose higher interests we hope to serve, and whose good will and active cooperation we invite; governed by trustees of eminence in the nation as well as in the state, who ask no sectarian and no political questions of their appointees, whose influence without and whose counsels within are of inestimable and well appreciated value; consecrating ourselves to the toil of science at an hour so peculiarly critical and so opportune in the university development of the country, I must believe that not only every intelligent inhabitant of Worcester, but every unbiased friend of higher education everywhere, will wish to add to our already unexpectedly large endowment of public and private good will at home and abroad, his and her hearty, ungrudging and reiterated God-speed.

Just because, instead of the easy and wasteful task of repeating what is already well done about us, we strive to take the inevitable next step and to be the first, if we can, upon the higher plane; because we must study not only to utilize all available experience wherever we can, but to be wisely bold in innovations wherever we must; because there will be indifference and misconception from friends who do not see all the importance of our work at first; because there are difficulties inherent in the very nature of that work itself as great as the work is needed, we must go slowly and surely, establishing but few departments at first, and when they are made the best possible, adding new and most related ones as fast as we can find the men and money to support them. We must prolong the formative period of foundation and must each and every one realize well that we are just entering upon years of unremitting toil, in which patience and hope will be tempered with trial. But our cause is itself an inspiration, for it is in the current of all good tendencies in higher education, and of the ultimate success of what is this day begun, there is not a shadow of doubt or fear.

Our history begins more than twenty years ago, in the plans of a reticent and sagacious man, whose leave we cannot here await to speak of, who in affluence maintains the simple and regular mode of life inbred in the plain New England home of his boyhood;—plans that have steadily grown with his fortune and that have been followed and encouraged with an eager and growing interest, which extended to even minor items by the devoted companion of his life. Besides a large fund already placed to our account, he has given his experience and unremitting daily care, worth to us large sums in economies, and resulting in well appointed building, and a solidity of materials and thoroughness of workmanship which I believe are without a parallel of their cost and kind in the country. Not only in the multifarious work of the university office, its methods of estimates, orders, book-keeping, of individual accountability for all books, apparatus, supplies and furniture, but in the larger questions of university polity without and effective administration within, in the definition of duty for each officer, the strict subordination and the concentration of authority and responsibility sure to appeal to all who have the instinct of discipline, and which are exceptionally needful where the life of science is to be so free, and the policy so independent; in the express exemption, too, of all instructors who can sustain the ardor of research from excessive teaching and examination, in the appointment of assistants in a way to keep each member of the staff at his best work, and to avoid the too common and wasteful practice in American universities of letting four thousand dollar men do four hundred dollar work, in the ample equipment of each department, that no force be lost on inferior tools—in all these and many other respects the ideal of our founder has been to make every where an independent application of the simplest and severest but also the largest principles of business economy.

As business absorbs more and more of the talent and energy of the world, its considerations more and more pervading, if not subordinating, whether for better or worse, not only the arts, the school, the press, but all departments of church and the state, making peace and war, cities or deserts, so science is slowly pervading and profoundly modifying literature, philosophy, education, religion and every domain of culture. Both at their best have dangers and are severe schools of integrity. The directness, simplicity, certainty and absorption in work so characteristic of both are setting new fashions in manners, and even in morals, and bringing man into closer contact with the world as it is. Both are binding the universe together into new unities and imposing a discipline ever severer for body and mind. When their work, purified of deceit and error, is finished, the period of history we now call modern will be rounded to completeness, culture will have abandoned much useless luggage, the chasm between instruction and education will be less disastrous, and all the highest and most sacred of human ideals will not be lost or dimmed, but will become nearer and more real.

When one who has graduated with highest honors from this rigorous school of business, after spending eight years of travel abroad studying the means by which knowledge and culture, the most precious riches of the race, are increased and transmitted, and finding no reason why our country, which so excels in business, should be content with the second best in science, devotes to its services not only his fortune at the end of his life, but also years yet full of exceptional and unabated energy, we see in such a fact not only the normal, complete, if you please, post graduate ethical maturity of an individual business life, but also a type and promise of what wealth now seems likely to do for higher education in America. It is no marvel that our foundation has already been so often so conspicuously and so favorably noted in authoritative ways and places in an European land where, if monarchy should yield to a republic, university culture could not penetrate its people as it now does. It is thus a more typical and vital product of the national life at its best than are foundations made by state or church in which to train their servants. In thus giving his fortune to a single highest end as sagaciously and actively as he has acquired it, may our founder find a new completeness of life in age, which Cicero did not know, and taste

> —"all the joy that lies
> In a full self-sacrifice."

The very word science, especially when used in its relation to business, is too often degraded by cheap graduates who are just fit to look after established industrial processes, but are useless if competition finds or needs new and better ones; who certify to analysis of commercial products that good chemists know are impossible; who, if international competition in manufactures were more free, would give place to better trained, perhaps German, experts still faster than they are doing; who, in criminal, medical and patent law suits often have the address to carry judge and jury against far better chemists, but who have no conception of the higher quality and more rigorous methods of their own science; who make chemistry, physics and geology mercenary, culinary, the servants instead of the masters of industrial progress, and the very "life-springs of all the arts of peace or war." This evil, although so great and common that even the best men in other professions too rarely see the high ideal culture power of real science, is yet only incidental and temporary.

A good illustration of the high and normal technological value of pure science is at hand in dyeing, one of the most scientific among the many increasing chemical industries. England furnishes nearly all the raw, formerly valueless, material for coal tar colors, out of which Germany made most of the seventeen and a half million dollars' worth manufactured in 1880. England bought back a large fraction of the colored goods, and Germany made the profits, because she could furnish the best training in pure chemistry. It is for this reason that she is driving other countries out of the field in other leading chemical industries. The great factories there employ from two or three to more than a score each of the good, and often the best, university trained chemists at large salaries, and the best of these spend a good part of their time in original research in the factory laboratories. The prospect of these lucrative careers has had very much to do in filling the chemical laboratories of the universities with hundreds of students, and the German government (best that of Prussia) has met the demand by erecting and equipping new and sometimes magnificent laboratories at nearly all of her universities. New artificial processes of making organic products of commerce have freed thousands of acres of land where they were formerly, grown, and have made new industries and often impaired old ones. Many professors of chemistry make large outside incomes, nearly all are sanguine; some even declare that before very long leading drugs, and even food, that will equal if not actually excel nature's products, will be made artificially. The leading professor in one of the largest chemical laboratories of Germany told me in substance that he no longer went after outside technical work, but now made it a virtue to wait for it to seek him, and it has been strongly urged that even the government should take steps to prevent the migration of German chemists to the universities of other countries, lest Germany lose her pre-eminence in chemical industries.

This remarkable contact of the marvelous new business life and energy of Germany, particularly of North Germany, (which in both suddenness and vigor equals any of the wonderful developments in this country), with staid and tranquil academic ways, has had some marked reverberations and given new direction and impetus to other studies in some other departments where it is not directly felt. It has led to the erection and equipment by the government of great technological schools, and has shown to business men and employers that no course in the sciences which under-lie technology can be too advanced, prolonged or severe to be practical. Where ought the value and significance of such a training be better appreciated than here in the land of Fulton, Morse, Bell and Edison?.

There are, however, eminent chemists in Germany, and many more in surrounding European countries, who deplore what they call the irruption of the technical spirit into the universities. They fear the proximity of the factory and the patent office to the university laboratory has narrowed the field of view and made methods of research relatively less severe. They complain that in their teaching they must hasten over inorganic chemistry, neglecting all the other elements for the carbon compounds and that there are almost no inorganic chemists in Germany; that in choosing between several substances inviting research, one of which promises great commercial value and the other none, strict scientific impartiality is lost; that in the eagerness for practical results, problems are attempted too complex for the present methods of experimenters who are trying to "eat soup with a fork," as one sadly told me, and that thus while published researches are more numerous they are less thorough and have introduced many formulae that neither prove nor agree, so that much work now accepted must be done over again and far more thoroughly; that even Liebig set a bad example in this respect, and that many new products, of which university chemists boast, are so inferior to those of nature as to be really adulteration.

What I have tried to illustrate mainly in the field of one science is more or less true under changed ways and degrees in the sphere of others. The sciences are also at the very heart of modern medical studies. Biology explores the laws of life upon which not only these studies but human health, welfare and modern conceptions of man and his place in nature so fundamentally rest. The law of the specific energy of nerves, e. g. which Helmholtz says equals in importance the Newtonian law of gravity, and more than anything else made physiology the science which has had so large a share in raising the medical profession in Germany to a position in the intellectual world such as it never had before, doing for it in some degree what chemistry has done for dyeing, and even instruments like the ophthalmoscope, which almost created a department of medical practice, or the spectroscope, now indispensible in the Bessemer process, sugar refining, in wine and color-dye tests, the detection of photographic sensibilators, in the custom house and in two important forms of medical diagnosis,—all these, to cut short a long list of both epoch-making laws and important instruments, are the direct products of whole souled devotion to unremunerative scientific research.

It is hard for medical students to realize that they can not understand hygiene, forensic medicine, pharmacology and toxicology without a rigorous drill in chemistry; that they must know physics to understand the diagnostic and therapeutic use of electricity, ophthalmology, otology, the mechanism of the bones, muscles, circulation, etc.; that zoology is needed to teach sound philosophic thought, generic facts about the laws of life, health, reproduction, and disease. These, and sometimes also sciences like mineralogy, anthropology, and psychology, are required in Europe, with much more rigor than is common with us, of every medical student. Thus doctors, like technologists, cannot know too much pure science. An eminent medical practitioner in Europe compares young physicians who slight the basal sciences of their profession and pass on to the clinical, therapeutic and practical parts, to young men who grow prematurely old and sterile. The phrase of Hippocrates, "God-like is the physician who is also a philosopher," is still more true and good in its larger, more modern and looser translation, viz., exalted is the physician who knows not only the most approved methods of practice but also the pure sciences which underlie and determine both the dignity and value of his profession.

Medical instruction on the one hand must select as its foundation those sciences and those parts of the sciences most useful in meeting man's great enemy, disease. It needs far more anatomy than physics and little mathematics, astronomy or geology. Technical instruction on the other hand is and must be so organized as to reflect the state of industry. It properly lays more stress upon chemistry with its many applications than upon biology, which has far fewer; more upon electricity than upon molecular physics; and more upon organic than inorganic chemistry. The university, which is entirely distinct from and higher than any form of technical or professional instruction can be, should represent the state of science *per se*. It should be strong in those fields where science is highly developed, and should pay less attention to other departments of knowledge which have not reached the scientific stage. It should be financially and morally able to disregard practical application as well as numbers of students. It should be a laboratory of the highest possible human development in those lines where educational values are the criterion of what is taught or not taught, and the increase of knowledge and its diffusion among the few fit should be its ideal. As another puts it, "The more and better books, apparatus, collections and teachers, and the fewer but more promising students, the better the work." In Europe, besides its duty to science the university must not fail of its practical duty to furnish to the state good teachers, preachers, doctors, advocates, engineers and technologists of various kinds. Here a university can, if it chooses, do still better and devote itself exclusively to the pure sciences. These once understood, their applications are relatively easy and quickly learned. The university must thus stand above, subordinate and fructify the practical spirit, or the latter will languish for want of science to apply.

The important facts that are both certain and exact, and the completely verified laws, or well ordered, welded cohesion of thought that approach such mental continuity as makes firm, compactly woven intellectual or cerebral tissue, are so precious in our distracted and unsettled age, that it is no marvel that impartial laymen in all walks of life are coming to regard modern science in its pure high form as not only the greatest achievement of the race thus far, but also as carrying in it the greatest, though not yet fully developed, culture power of the world, not only for knowledge but also for feeling and conduct. It is of this power that universities are the peculiar organs; to them is now committed the highest interests of man; from them and from science now comes the light and advancement of the world. They became and remained the asylums of free thought and conviction when Rome and all other privileged orders declined, and their germs were brought and piously and early planted on these shores by our fathers. This term is not only "the noblest in the vocabulary of science," but universities are the chief nurseries of talent, where is kept alive the holy fervor of investigation that in its passion for truth is fearless of consequences and has never been more truly and loftily ideal than now, when its objects of study are often most crassly material. It is their quality more than anything else that determines not only the status of the medical and all technological professions, but also whether the legal profession is formal, narrow, mercenary and unlearned as it seems now in danger of becoming in Germany, because even the German

371

universities, despite their great preeminence in all other respects, are by general consent of the most incompetent Germans themselves, relatively weak in those departments which underlie the practice of law or broadly based on history and social or economic science, informed in administrative experience, and culminating in judicial talent and statesmanship. Universities largely determine whether a land is cursed by a factious, superstitious, half-culture clergy, or blessed by ministers of divine truth, who understand and believe the doctrines they teach; who attract and enlarge the most learned, and penetrate the life of the poor and ignorant, quickening, comforting and informing in a way worthy of the Great Teacher Himself; and making their profession as it should be——the noblest of human callings.

Compared with our material progress, we are not only making no progress, but are falling behind in higher education. It has been estimated that but five per cent of the practicing physicians of this country have had a liberal education, and that sixty per cent of our medical schools require practically no preliminary training whatever for admission, while European laws require a university training for every doctor before he can practice. Again, we apply science with great skill but create or advance it very little indeed. Should the supply of European science, which now so promptly finds its way here and fertilizes and stimulates to more or less hopeful reaction our best scholars, and upon which we live as upon charity, be cut off by some great war or otherwise, the unbalanced and short sighted utilitarian tendencies now too prevalent here would tend toward the same stagnation and routine which similar tendencies unchecked long ago wrought out in China. We all most heartily believe in and respect technical and applied science and all grades of industrial education, but these are as much out of place in a truly academic university as money-changers were in the temple of the Most High.

But yet the fact that these and other evils and difficulties are now so widely seen and so deeply felt, that endowments for higher education seem now the order of the day, that the largest single endowment in this country has already so effectively begun so many reforms in scarcely more than a decade in Baltimore; that churchmen, statesmen and business men now need only to see their own interests in a way a little larger and broader, as they are now tending to do, to co-operate more actively than they ever have done in strengthening our best foundations—such considerations sustain the larger and more hopeful view that our country is already beginning to rise above the respectable and complacent mediocrity still its curse in every domain of culture and will show that democracy can produce—as it must or decline—the very highest type of men as its leaders. The university problem seems to be fairly upon us. We now need men in our chairs whose minds have got into independent motion; who are authorities and not echoes; who have the high moral qualities of plain and simple living and self-sacrificing devotion to truth, and who show to this community and the country the spectacle of men absorbed in and living only for pure science and high scholarship, and are not mere place-holders or sterile routine pedagogues, and all needed material support is sure to come.

A word so characteristic here that it might stand upon our very seal, is concentration. Of this our founder, in declining to scatter his resources among the countless calls from individuals, institutions and causes, from excellent to vicious, and refusing us as yet, in the one work he has set out to accomplish, no needed thing, sets an example. We have selected a small but closely related group of five departments, and shall at first focus all our means and care to make these five the best possible. Neither the historical origin nor the term university has anything to do with completeness of the field of knowledge. The word originally designated simply a corporation with peculiar privileges and peculiarly independent to do what it chose. We choose to assert the same privilege of election for ourselves that other institutions allow their students, and offer the latter in choosing their subjects a larger option between institutions. The continental habit of inter-university migration also on the part of students, if once adopted here, would, no doubt, stimulate institutions no less than it has stimulated competing departments in the same university. Our plan in this respect implies a specialization as imperatively needed for the advanced students, as it would, we admit, be unfortunate for students still in the disciplinary collegiate stage. If our elementary schools are inferior to the best in Europe, and if our fitting schools are behind the French Lycee, the German Gymnasium and the great English schools, it is our universities that are comparatively by far the weakest part of our national system. The best of these best know that 50 to 100 instructors cannot do the work of 350; that they cannot hope at present to rival European governments which erect single university buildings, costing nearly four million dollars each, as at Berlin and Vienna, nor equal the clinical opportunities of large European cities with poorer populations and more concentrated hospital systems. Our strongest universities are far too feeble to do justice to all the departments, old and new, which they undertake. Our institutions are also too uniform; the small and weak ones try to copy every new departure of the stronger ones as the latter copy the far stronger institutions in Europe. If the best of them would do work of real university grade, they should specialize among the fields of academic culture, doing well what they do, but not attempting to do everything, the American system might yet come to represent the highest educational needs of the country. In contrast with the present ideal of horizontal expansion and that waste of unnecessary duplication, we believe our departure will be as useful as it is new.

Again, concentration is now the master word of education. In no country has the amount of individual information been so great, the range of intelligence so wide, the number of studies attempted by young men in colleges and universities so large for the time and labor given to each, the plea for liberal and general, as distinct from special and exclusive studies, been so strong. This is well, for general knowledge is the best soil for any kind of eminence or culture to spring from, and because power, though best applied on a small surface, is best developed over a large one and not in brains educated, as it were, in spots. More than this, our utilitarian ideal of general knowledge is far more akin to that of Hippias, who would make his own clothes and shoes, cook his own food, etc., or to that of Diderot, who would learn all trades, than to the noble Greek ideal of the symmetrical all-sided development of all the powers of body and mind. The more general knowledge the better; but everything must shoot together, in the brain. In the figure of Ritcher, the sulphur, saltpeter, and charcoal must find each other or the man makes no powder. The brain must be trained to bring all that is in it to a sharp focus without dispersive fringes. The natural instinct of every ambitious youth is to excel, to do, or make or know something better than any one else, to be an authority, to surpass all others, if only in the most exacting specialty. Learning thus what true mental freedom is, he is more docile in all other directions.

If it be extravagant to say that no minds are so feeble that they cannot excel, if they concentrate all their energies upon a point sufficiently small, nothing is more true than that the greatest powers fail if too much is attempted. This is not only a wise instinct that makes for economy, but in the parliamentary committee rooms, in corporation meetings, in the court room, in business, in science, in the sick chamber, the modern world in nearly every department is now really governed by experts—by men who have attained the mastery that comes by concentration. The young man who has had the invaluable training of abandoning himself to a long experimental research upon some very special but happily chosen point was typically illustrated is a man I knew; With the dignity and sense of finality of the American senior year quick within him, his first teacher in Germany told him to study experimentally one of the score of muscles of a frog's leg. He feared loss and limitation in trying to focus all his energies upon so small and insignificant an object. The mild dissipation of too general culture, the love of freedom and frequent change, aided by a taste breezy philosophic romancing, almost diverted him from the frog's leg. But as he progressed he found that he must know in a more minute and practical way than before—in a way that made previous knowledge seem unreal—certain definite points in electricity, chemistry, mechanics, physiology, etc., and bring them to bear in fruitful relation to each other. As the experiments proceeded through the winter, the history of previous views upon the subject were studied and understood as never before and broader biological relations were gradually seen. The summer, and yet another year were passed upon this tiny muscle, for he had seen that its laws and structure are fundamentally the same in frogs and men, that just such contractile tissue has done all the work man has accomplished in the world, that muscles are the only organ of the will. Thus, as the work went on, many of the mysteries of the universe seemed to centre in his theme; in fact, in the presence and study of this minute object of nature he had passed from the attitude of Peter Bell, of whom the poet says,

"A cowslip by the river's brim,
A yellow cowslip was to him,
And it was nothing more."

up to the standpoint of the seer who "plucked a flower from the crannied wall," and realized that could he but understand what it was, "—root and all and all in all, he would know what God and man is." Even if my friend had contributed nothing in the shape of discovery to the great temple of science, he had felt the *omne tutit punctum* of nature's organic unity, he had felt the profound and religious conviction that the world is lawful to the core; he had experiences what a truly liberal education, in the the modern as distinct from the mediaeval sense, really is. We may term it non-professional specialization.

Perhaps the most thorough and comprehensive government reports ever made in any language are those of the English parliamentary commissioners on endowments. The first of these occupied nearly nineteen years and fills nearly two-score heavy folio volumes. In all, about twenty thousand foundations, new and centuries old, large and small, devoted to a vast variety of uses, good and questionable, were reported. The conclusions drawn from this field of experience, which is far richer and wider in England than elsewhere, was that of all the great popular charities, higher education has proven safest, wisest and best, and that for two chief reasons—first, because the superior integrity and ability of the guardians who consented to administer such funds, the intelligence and grateful appreciation of those aided by them, and the strong public interest and resulting publicity—all three combined to hold them perpetually truest, to the purpose and spirit of the founders; and secondly, because in improving higher education, all other good causes are most effectively aided. The church can in no other way be more fundamentally served than by providing a still better training for her ministers and missionaries. Charity for hospitals and almshouses is holy, Christ-like work, but to provide a better training for physicians and economists, teaches the world to see and shun the causes of sickness and poverty. Sympathy must always tenderly help the feeblest and even the defective classes, but to help the strongest in the struggle for existence, is to help not them alone, but all others within their influence.

Of all the many ways of supporting the higher education, individual aid to deserving and meritorious students is one of the most approved. In the University of Leipzig, e.g., four hundred and seven distinct funds can aid eight hundred and forty-nine students. Of these funds the oldest was established in

1325, and they are increasing in number, more new ones having been given between 1880 and 1885 than in any entire decade before. In size they range from thirty-five thousand to fifty dollars, in Berlin from one hundred and forty thousand to one of less than forty dollars. In cases where conditions are specified the most frequent limitation is to students from a certain locality and next to those of a certain family. By the older founders students of theology were more often preferred, but the more recent funds are for medicine, law, philology and pure science, and a fund for over two hundred thousand dollars lately given the University of Marburg is for advanced students in those sciences which underlie medicine. These funds are often given, named for, held and sometimes awarded by churches or their pastors, magistrates, heads of fitting schools, boards of education, representatives of prominent families, for students of their name, the donor himself or herself, individual professors, etc., subject of course to satisfying the university examiners. Many are tenable for one, more for three, and some for five and six years. The funds must be invested with security, and with interest commonly less than four per cent. In Cambridge and Oxford provision is made for nearly 1000 fellows and eight hundred scholars not to mention the exhibitions at Oxford. The fellowships are more lucrative and are designed for more advanced men than are provided for in the German universities, the fellows aiding the master in internal administration. In England, besides the religious and other founders, as in Germany, the great historic industrial and mercantile corporations provide many of the fellowships and scholarships, particularly those of the sixteenth and seventeenth centuries, and they are granted by bishops, curates, heads of business corporations, masters of the great schools, heads or fellows of colleges. In France, where these foundations were swept away by the revolution, stipends and bursaries are provided annually by the Government. New appropriations for the most advanced students of all was the secret of the remarkable *Ecole Pratique des Hautes Etudes,* founded in 1868, of which a recent report just printed for the Exposition says, condensing its substance, that its purpose has always been to foster scientific zeal with no shade of temporal interest, that it restored the almost obliterated idea of higher education, gave unity to scientific interests throughout France, and made her feel the scholarly desirderata of the age, made young professors not only well instructed, but trained in good methods, that although its profound researches are not manifest to the public, has given a more scientific character to all the faculties, and rendered a service to the state out of all proportion to its cost. In France individuals co-operate with the state in this work.

Has there ever been devised a form of memorial to and bearing the names of husbands, wives, children or parents, by which even the smallest funds could be bestowed in a way more lastingly expressive of the individuality, spirit and the special lines of interest of the donor, more worthy the dead and more helpful to the highest ends of life? Since the first endowment of research in the Athenian Porch and Grove, thousands and thousands of donations of this sort have borne tangible witness to the sentiment so often and vividly taught by Plato that in all the world there is no object more worthy of reverence, love and service than eugenic, eupeptic, well-bred, gifted young men, for in them is the hope of the world.

The more advanced our standards are to be, the fewer will be our students, and the more expensive their needed outfit of books and apparatus. If we divide our running expenses only by the number of students our present fellowships and scholarships allow us to receive out of our two hundred and fifty applicants, the amount we spent per student, the first year, will probably be without a parallel. Besides this, for a number of students with important researches on hand we are expending hundreds of dollars each for their individual needs, and should be glad to do so for more as good men. The best students very often graduate with empty pockets, but with their zeal and power at its best, and when an extra year or two would make a great difference in their entire career. Also, as the field of knowledge grows more complex, the economy of energy needed for concentration is impossible without the leisure secured by comfortable support.

Connected with all the protection, exemptions and privileges so dearly prized and tenaciously clung to by the mediaeval universities, there have always been dangers sometimes grave and not yet entirely obviated. The new charity is often popularly called a science as well as a virtue. Its axiom is that no man has a right to give doles to beggars without satisfying himself personally or through some agency to that end that his gift will do good and not harm to the recipient. History, and I may add personal observation, shows that the same general law holds true to some extent in universities. I believe they should not award fellowships to men fresh from college (save in the very rarest cases), unless they are able to guide and direct as well as to follow their work in every detail. A fellow should be encouraged and stimulated by a daily and familiar intercourse with the professors. His methods, reading and researches should be kept at their best and the entire resources of the institution should be a soil for his most rapid and helpful growth. Students thus served, even if their gratitude does not prompt them, as in some late instances in Germany, to study, revive and try to conform with piety to the ideal of ancient and almost forgotten donors, whose provisions they enjoyed, will not be lacking in appreciation. To appoint a man to use such funds in electing among undergraduate courses, or to take his chances among the confusing multifarious subjects offered in foreign institutions is, I believe, in most cases of small utility, and in some cases that I know, positively harmful. May the methods of exclusion we are studying be so effective that neither our precious funds nor the precious energy of our instructors be wasted upon the idle, stupid or unworthy students, now too often exposed in vain for four years to the contagion of knowledge.

"Education used to be a question for ladies and for schoolmasters," said a French statesman last spring, but it is now not only a question of state on which the support of all great institutions depends, but the great question into which all others issue if profoundly discussed or studied. So greatly do republics need the whole power of education, and so serious is their struggle for existence against ignorance and its attendant evils, that it has well been said that the problem whether this form of government be permanent is at bottom a question of education. But monarchies are no less dependent upon the education of their leaders and servants. In his famous address declaring that if Germany was ever to be free and strong, it must be by becoming the chief educational state in Europe, must realize the platonic republic in which the education of its youth was the highest care of the rulers, Fichte laid down the policy which has been one of the chief causes of the wonderful development of that country. Moreover, evolution, which shows that even life itself is but the education of protoplasm, cells and tissues, that the play-instinct in children and the love of culture in adults, not only measure the superfluous individual energy over and above that required by the processes necessary to life, but are perhaps largely the same, also makes it plain that the hunger for more and larger education of life is but the struggle of talent to the full maturity and leadership which is its right.

For myself I have no stronger wish or resolve than that in the peculiarly arduous labors I expect, I may never forget that this institution should be a means to these high purposes and not degenerate to an end in itself; and may it be as true of our graduates to remotest time, as it is of us in a unique way and degree to-day, that we could not love Clark University so much, loved we not science and education more.

381